Teacher Language Awareness

CAMBRIDGE LANGUAGE TEACHING LIBRARY

A series covering central issues in language teaching and learning, by authors who have expert knowledge in their field.

Teacher Language Awareness

Stephen Andrews
University of Hong Kong

CAMBRIDGE
UNIVERSITY PRESS

CAMBRIDGE UNIVERSITY PRESS
Cambridge, New York, Melbourne, Madrid, Cape Town, Singapore, São Paulo

Cambridge University Press
The Edinburgh Building, Cambridge CB2 8RU, UK

www.cambridge.org
Information on this title: www.cambridge.org/9780521530194

First published 2007

Printed in the United Kingdom at the University Press, Cambridge

A catalogue record for this publication is available from the British Library

Library of Congress Cataloging-in-Publication Data
Andrews, Stephen, 1948–
    Teacher language awareness / Stephen Andrews.
      p. cm. — (Cambridge language teaching library)
    Includes bibliographical references and index.
    ISBN 978-0-521-53019-4 (pbk.) — ISBN 978-0-521-82318-0 (hardback)
    1. Language and languages—Study and teaching. 2. Language awareness.
    I. Title. II. Series.
    P53.454.A53 2007
    418'.007—dc22

                                                      2007017363

ISBN 978-0-521-53019-4 paperback
ISBN 978-0-521-82318-0 hardback

Contents

Acknowledgements

Although I am solely responsible for the final version of this book (including any errors), the ideas it contains are the product of more than 30 years' professional involvement in language education and have inevitably been influenced by colleagues, as well as students, past and present. I would like to express my thanks to all those I have had the good fortune to encounter within the profession (some only via the printed page), too numerous to mention individually, whose ideas may have had an impact upon my own thinking.

At the same time, I feel that I should acknowledge the influence, contribution and support of certain specific individuals. During the time I have been involved with language teaching, I have been fortunate enough to have been taught by two of the major figures in Applied Linguistics and Language Education: Eric Hawkins, the 'father' of Language Awareness, with whom I completed my Postgraduate Certificate in Education at the University of York Language Teaching Centre in 1971–2; and Christopher Brumfit, who supervised my doctoral research at the University of Southampton in the 1990s. I encountered these scholars at very different stages of my professional life, but both were an inspiration, not just because of the depth and breadth of their expertise but also because of their humanity and their passion for language education. I owe Chris a particular debt of gratitude as my PhD supervisor. His premature death in March 2006 robbed the profession of one of its finest scholars.

I should also like to thank my friend and colleague Amy Tsui for her unstinting support during the time that I was working on this book, and conducting the research upon which much of it is based. I am especially grateful to Amy for allowing me to gather data of my own from Marina, the 'expert' teacher in her 2003 book (A. B. M. Tsui, *Understanding expertise in teaching*, Cambridge University Press), for use in Chapter 6 of this book, and for permitting me access to the data from the 'Good Practices' project (Tsui et al., 2005), as discussed in Chapter 8.

Two friends and former colleagues also deserve a particular vote of thanks: Arthur McNeill and Peter Falvey. Arthur's work on Teacher Language Awareness and lexis has influenced me greatly. He made a major contribution to the early work on this book, and a number of his

Acknowledgements

ideas (and words) have no doubt found their way into this final version. Peter's influence on my thinking about L2 teachers' language proficiency, knowledge and awareness began in the late 1980s, when we were working at the University of Cambridge Local Examinations Syndicate (UCLES, now known as Cambridge Assessment) on the Cambridge Examinations in English for Language Teachers (CEELT), and continued when we were colleagues in Hong Kong throughout the 1990s. His friendship and support helped me through a number of troughs during my doctoral studies.

I should also like to thank everyone else who has contributed in different ways to this book: the publishing team at Cambridge University Press (particularly Mickey Bonin, for his initial support for such a book, and Jane Walsh for seeing it through to publication) for all their professional help, support, patience and flexibility; Jacqueline French for her painstakingly professional editing; Song Yanan for her invaluable help with the references; Joffee Lam for his help with the statistical analyses in Chapter 8; 'Marina', and all the other teachers who allowed themselves to be tested, interviewed and observed when I was gathering data for the book; and the anonymous reviewers of earlier versions of the manuscript for their extremely constructive advice and suggestions.

This book is dedicated to my wife, Veronica, our children (Merryn, Jamie, Tom, and Tamsin) and my mother-in-law, Kathleen McCarthy.

Introduction

1 What is the book about?

This book is concerned with Teacher Language Awareness, or TLA, defined by Thornbury (1997:x) as 'the knowledge that teachers have of the underlying systems of the language that enables them to teach effectively'. The focus of the book is the language awareness of L2 teachers (i.e. teachers of a Foreign or Second Language (EFL/ESL)), and the examples are drawn from the teaching of L2 English. However, the issues raised are equally applicable to teachers of any language that is not the mother tongue of their students. In many cases, they are likely to be of relevance to teachers of the mother tongue, too.

The book concentrates on teachers' knowledge and understanding of the language systems, in the belief that these systems are at the heart of the language acquisition process and must therefore form the core of any teacher's language awareness. As the quotation above from Thornbury makes clear, TLA applies to all the language systems and assumes their interdependence, given that they are, as Carter (in Bolitho et al., 2003:253) points out, 'closely interwoven in the construction of meanings and of texts, both spoken and written'. The specific focus of the present book is on TLA as it relates to grammar. However, the discussion and the examples in the following chapters acknowledge and reflect the interrelationship between the language systems, and in particular between grammar, lexis and discourse.

The basic argument presented in the book is that the possession of an adequate level of TLA is an essential attribute of any competent L2 teacher. The assumption underlying that argument is that there is a relationship between the language awareness of the L2 teacher and the effectiveness of that teacher as indicated by the language learning achieved by his/her students. Put simply, the book assumes that TLA has a positive impact on student learning: TLA is seen as a potentially crucial variable in the language teaching / language learning enterprise, in the sense that the language-aware L2 teacher is more likely to be effective in promoting student learning than the teacher who is less language-aware.

The book discusses the findings of a number of studies conducted in a variety of locations and in a range of areas relevant to TLA. However, the snapshots of the teaching of L2 English presented and discussed in the book are all drawn from one particular context: the Hong Kong secondary school. Although the official English Language curriculum in Hong Kong has been based on communicative principles since the early 1980s, the vast majority of schools and teachers have adopted a very 'weak' version of communicative/task-based language teaching, in which the explicit teaching of grammar continues to play a significant role. The Hong Kong teachers whose performance is examined in the book are all non-native speakers (NNS) of English.

2 Who is this book for?

Although Teacher Language Awareness has received scant attention in terms of published research, it is an area of increasing concern to those involved in language teacher education, as well as those responsible for quality assurance in language teaching. Because of this, the book should be of interest to a wide range of people with an involvement or interest in language education issues: practising teachers, students on in-service teacher education programmes, language teacher educators, academics and other professionals engaged in language education.

3 What is the purpose of the book?

The book sets out to address the following fundamental questions about teachers' knowledge of the systems of language, i.e. their TLA: what form does this knowledge take, and what is its potential impact on teacher effectiveness? The aim in the following chapters is to examine these and related questions by exploring the nature of teachers' knowledge of the language systems (with particular reference to grammar), and the relationship between teachers' knowledge and their handling of language-related issues in their teaching.

The purpose of the book is to encourage teachers and others involved in language education, including teacher educators, to think more deeply about the importance of TLA, the nature of TLA and the impact of TLA upon teaching (and, potentially, upon learning). The book is intended to contribute to a greater understanding of TLA, making teachers more aware of the potential significance of their language-related interventions, and enabling teacher educators to adopt a more principled approach to the planning of those parts of their programmes associated with TLA. At the same time, I hope that the book will provoke debate and raise questions that will help to establish the beginnings of a research agenda for TLA.

4 What is the book NOT about?

This book does not set out to develop teachers' awareness of language via any direct treatment. There are no language-analysis tasks designed to stimulate teachers' reflections on the workings of different parts of the language systems. A number of books containing tasks of this type are already available, such as Bolitho and Tomlinson's *Discover English* (1980; 1995), Wright's *Investigating English* (1994) and Thornbury's *About Language* (1997). The interested reader need look no further than these three texts to find a wealth of activities intended to foster the development of TLA.

The book does not promote particular approaches to the teaching of grammar. Frequent reference is made to data from studies of teachers' language awareness as it relates to grammar. However, in the analysis of these data, there is a deliberate attempt to avoid evaluation of the methodology employed by individual teachers: instead, the discussion focuses exclusively on language-related issues.

There is also no attempt to suggest that a teacher's explicit knowledge of grammar should be based exclusively upon any single model of language. My own views of language and of grammar are the product of a number of influences, including the grammars of Leech and Svartvik (1975), Quirk et al. (1985), Biber et al. (1999) and Carter and McCarthy (2006), as well as systemic functional linguistics (see, e.g., Halliday, 1985), which emphasises the role of the language systems as a resource for making meaning, the close interrelationship of grammar and lexis (the 'lexico-grammar') and the importance of discourse grammar. Inevitably, where judgemental comment is made on an individual teacher's awareness in relation to, for example, a specific feature of grammar, such comment passes through the filter of my own perspective on language. However, as far as possible, such remarks are based upon what might reasonably be expected of that teacher within the prevailing norms of the context within which he or she works. They are *not* set within a single theoretical framework of grammar.

The aim is therefore not to specify the precise form or extent of the knowledge that teachers of language should have about grammar. In my view, the knowledge of the language-aware teacher should not be based upon any single theoretical model, but rather upon informed, principled eclecticism. Such knowledge is not static: it is constantly changing, developing, renewing itself. The developments in any teacher's language awareness over the course of a career are likely to occur idiosyncratically, as a result of a combination of factors, including exposure to theoretical developments and reflections on practical experience. The adequacy and appropriateness of an individual teacher's language awareness at any stage of his or her career need to be considered in relation to the demands posed by the context in which that teacher is working at that time.

5 How is the book organised?

The book consists of a Prologue, followed by nine chapters and an Epilogue. The Prologue introduces some of the major questions addressed in the main body of the book, with snapshots from the Hong Kong secondary school classroom. Chapter 1 provides a brief overview of the history of interest in Teacher Language Awareness, in the context of the increased attention since the late 1970s to 'Language Awareness' generally, and to the role of explicit language knowledge in language learning in particular. Chapter 2 presents a detailed analysis of the language awareness of the L2 teacher, exploring the complex nature of TLA, its significance in L2 teaching and learning, how it affects teacher behaviour and its potential impact on pedagogical practice. Chapter 3 examines some of the issues and debates concerning the value of explicit knowledge about the language systems, particularly grammar, for L2 learning and teaching, together with the implications for TLA of current understandings of these issues.

Chapters 4 and 5 revisit issues originally discussed in Chapter 2. Chapter 4 focuses on L2 teachers' knowledge, beliefs, feelings and understandings about the content of learning (i.e. the subject-matter cognitions which form the core of any teacher's language awareness). Chapter 5 explores various aspects of TLA in pedagogical practice, in particular (a) how the L2 teacher's language awareness both influences and is influenced by that teacher's engagement with the content of learning, and (b) the relationship between TLA and teaching materials. Both chapters draw extensively on data from Hong Kong secondary school teachers and classrooms.

Chapters 6 and 7 consider the TLA of teachers of L2 English at different stages of their careers and from different backgrounds. Chapter 6 examines the TLA of novice, highly proficient and expert teachers, while Chapter 7 attempts a dispassionate analysis of the TLA of native-speaker (NS) and non-native-speaker (NNS) teachers.

Chapter 8 focuses on the relationship between TLA and student learning. While acknowledging the difficulty of identifying any direct causative connection between TLA and students' learning outcomes, the chapter discusses relevant research in relation to three themes: teachers' subject-matter knowledge; teacher engagement with the content of learning; and teachers' awareness of learner difficulties.

Chapter 9 also looks at TLA and learning, but in this case focusing on teachers' own learning. The chapter examines issues relating to the development of the L2 teacher's language awareness, and principles that might be applied to the planning of TLA-related courses and activities.

The Epilogue returns to the central argument of the book – that possession of an adequate level of TLA is an essential attribute of any competent L2 teacher – and sets it within the context of the broader debate about teacher professionalism in general and L2 teacher professionalism in particular.

Prologue: The challenge of being 'language-aware'

Snapshot 1a: Clara

It's a warm afternoon in early October in a large modern co-educational secondary school in Hong Kong's New Territories. The air-conditioners are on in all the classrooms, making the ambient temperature pleasantly comfortable, but also creating a constant background whirring. A Secondary 5 class of forty Hong Kong Chinese 16-year-olds is listening with varying degrees of attention, as their English teacher, Clara, takes them through a set of exercises they were expected to have completed for homework.

Clara, like her students, is Hong Kong Chinese and shares their mother tongue, Cantonese. Clara is in her fourth year as a full-time secondary school teacher of English. She has a first degree from Canada (in Social Sciences rather than English) and is currently studying part-time for an initial qualification as a teacher of English.

Clara's students will be taking their first major public examination (the Hong Kong Certificate in Education Examination, or HKCEE) at the end of the academic year, and they are already accustomed to lessons in most subjects dominated by practice tests and past papers. Although most of the students do not have much intrinsic interest in English, they know that a good result in the public exam is important for their future study and job prospects.

In Clara's lesson this afternoon she is working through a series of exercises from a book of practice tests. The particular exercise that she is checking consists of single-sentence multiple-choice grammar items in which the students have to identify the correct way to complete the sentence from four given alternatives.

One of the first items in the exercise reads:

He did very little work for his exam. He_____ (pass).

The desired completion according to the Teacher's Book is *can't have passed*. However, one of the students has selected another of the four possible options: *could have passed*. He asks Clara whether his chosen answer might also be correct . . .

This snapshot describes an episode that is likely to resonate with the experiences of most of us who have taught a second language. Not all of us will have worked with teenagers in the public sector (like Clara), but we have all been in situations where we find ourselves confronted with the unexpected – in Clara's case, a question from a student – and where we are forced to make a spontaneous and more-or-less instant decision about how to react.

Experience and an awareness of potential pitfalls may have taught us the benefits of caution, leading us to take the prudent step of deciding to defer a response so that we can buy ourselves some thinking time ('That's a very interesting question . . .!'). As part of this strategy, perhaps we refer the problem back to the individual student ('What do *you* think?'), and invite the other students to contribute to the problem-solving activity ('What do the rest of you think?'). Meanwhile, we attempt a smile of encouragement as we rack our brains to work out our own answer. If our antennae have warned us that the question is really tricky, we may well decide not to commit ourselves to an explanation there and then, undertaking instead to provide a more carefully considered reply shortly afterwards ('Let me think about that and get back to you in the next class').

Very often, however, we seem to end up improvising a response. We may do so for a variety of reasons, and often without being fully aware of them. For some of us, there may be times when we make a conscious, principled decision to exploit a learning opportunity and aim to provide the learners with knowledge at a moment when we sense that they may be especially receptive, i.e. (to use the contemporary jargon of second language acquisition) we think that our response to the learner's problem may trigger a restructuring of not only the interlanguage[1] of that learner but also potentially the interlanguage of others in the class.

For the majority of us, though, the reasons are likely to be less sophisticated and skilfully calculated, particularly when we are not so experienced and streetwise. We may improvise out of misplaced confidence, or naïveté – perhaps simply because our instinct when asked a question is to try to be helpful and provide a response. Or we may, of course, improvise for the opposite reason: out of fear and a lack of confidence. Perhaps we are worried that our students will judge us to be incompetent and deficient in basic knowledge if we do not provide them with an on-the-spot solution to their problem. We may be afraid that we will lose face as a result: that rather than perceiving our delaying strategy as the

---

[1] **Interlanguage** is defined by Thornbury (2006:109) as a term describing 'the grammatical system that a learner creates in the course of learning another language'. It is a constantly evolving system of rules. **Restructuring** refers to the process by which the learner's interlanguage appears to adapt in response to new information.

responsible action of a thinking professional teacher, the students will view such stalling tactics as signs of weakness and inadequacy.

Whatever blend of beliefs, emotions and anxieties influences our decision, once we have made a move to answer the question, it is very difficult to turn back. Even as it begins to dawn on us that the problem is perhaps not as straightforward as we had initially assumed, we usually carry on, possibly feeling that, having once started, there is no way out. In the worst case, it is only when it is far too late, as we observe (or try to ignore) the glazed incomprehension in the expressions of our students, that we realise how big a hole we may have dug for ourselves in our well-intentioned attempt to be of assistance.

In the case of Clara, and the lesson described in Snapshots 1a and 1b, we do not know what influenced her actions at this point. Unfortunately, there was no opportunity to interview her after the class, so we can only speculate. In the event, for whatever reason, Clara opted to provide a virtually instant response to her student's question, as described in the second part of the snapshot:

Snapshot 1b: Clara

Clara's face betrays no emotion, and she pauses for barely a couple of seconds before providing the following response:

> So in this case actually it's better to use *He can't have passed* because you are just predicting something to happen, but you are not sure whether he can pass or not. You just predict it. Since he is not working hard, so he has the chance of failing in the exam, OK? If the test paper was returned to that student, you can say *He could have passed* or *He couldn't have passed*

As we look at Snapshot 1b, we may have different reactions, both to Clara's choice of strategy, and to the content of her response. However, the reason for focusing on this incident and on Clara's behaviour is not to invite analysis of her motivations or any evaluation of the quality of her explanation. Our interest is in the general rather than the specific, and in this case Clara's experience is being presented in order to draw our attention to the challenges facing any L2 teacher in a similar situation.

When Clara produced the explanation in Snapshot 1b, electing to improvise in front of a class of 40 students (not to mention the video camera that was recording the lesson on this occasion), her skills as a teacher were being challenged in a number of ways and at a variety of levels. Some aspects of the challenge had little or no relation to the content of the lesson. For instance, the situation was demanding on an emotional and psychological level. Clara was new to the school, she had been teaching this class for only a few weeks and it was the first time in her career that she had taught a class preparing for a major public examination. The incident was therefore a genuine test of her ability to keep her nerve in front of a (potentially critical) student audience. The situation also presented a challenge to Clara's overall teaching competence, and whether, for example, she would be able to engage the attention of a class of students and retain their interest in what she was saying.

But the most significant aspects of the challenge for our present purposes are those that are language-related. The most obvious of these was the challenge to her knowledge of subject matter. The practice test item and the student's question concerned modality, a notoriously complex area for both students and teachers of L2 English. In addition, the question did not relate to a relatively straightforward formal feature of verb phrases involving modal auxiliaries: instead it focused on semantic interpretations of modalised verb phrases referring to past time, interpretations that were rendered that much more difficult and speculative because of the inevitable lack of context accompanying a single-sentence multiple-choice practice test item.

However, knowledge of subject matter represents just one aspect of the multifaceted language-related challenge facing Clara, or any of us when we find ourselves in similar situations in our teaching. A degree in Linguistics and an in-depth knowledge of the relevant area of grammar might (though not necessarily) equip us to cope with certain aspects of the challenge related specifically to subject matter, but there would be other language-related ways in which we might find ourselves challenged, going well beyond mere knowledge of subject matter, as the following observation from Michael Swan depicts so vividly.

> Good teaching involves a most mysterious feat – sitting, so to speak, on one's listener's shoulder, monitoring what one is saying with the listener's ears, and using this feedback to shape and adapt one's words from moment to moment so that the thread of communication never breaks. This is art, not science . . .
>
> (Swan, 1994:54–5)

Swan was actually writing about pedagogic language rules, and proposing a set of criteria for such rules, criteria that might be applied to the 'rules of thumb' that teachers produce on the spur of the moment, like Clara, just as much as to the more carefully honed statements appearing in textbooks. The quotation comes from the end of Swan's paper, when he provides a spirited defence of teachers' 'rules of thumb', arguing that the pedagogic focus of such rules may enable them to fit the need of a given classroom moment more successfully than other, more descriptively 'respectable' statements of that rule.

The significance of Swan's remarks in the context of the present discussion is that they highlight the paramount importance of the learner perspective in determining how we select and package the information and examples we make available to our students in the hopes of promoting learning. Snapshot 2 (see p. 6) illustrates this point. Like Clara in Snapshot 1, the teacher in this case (Pearl) is reacting to a student's contribution, and providing feedback, not only for the benefit of that student but also for the whole class. Unlike Snapshot 1, however, the area of language focus should not have posed any challenges to the teacher's knowledge of subject matter.

In this case, as we can see, the teacher adopts a different strategy from that employed by Clara in Snapshot 1. Pearl correctly identifies that there is a problem with the student's answer, but rather than providing a detailed explanation, drawing on her knowledge of the relevant subject matter, she tries to use a mixture of question and gesture in an apparent attempt to guide the student towards self-correction of the error. Given that these are young students with relatively limited English, this approach would seem to have much to commend it. However, it is a strategy that Pearl uses to little obvious effect. She may well have understood the confusion that was the likely basis of the student's error. But from the way she handles that error, there is little to indicate that she has made any real attempt to view the problem from the learner perspective. If she has, then somewhere in the 'real-time' process of analysing his problem and providing potentially useful feedback, there must have been a breakdown, because her correction conveys very little, either to the student making the error or to the rest of the class. The second student's correct response has nothing to do with Pearl's intervention: he is merely reading out what he has already written in his book.

There are, of course, a number of language-related questions to be considered when one attempts to evaluate a teacher's content-focused intervention from the learner perspective, whether that intervention is Pearl's, Clara's or any of our own. All of these considerations connect in some way to Swan's (1994) 'design criteria for pedagogic language rules'. Some of them relate exclusively to knowledge of subject matter, such as:

- Is the teacher's explanation an accurate representation of the 'truth'?

Snapshot 2: Pearl

Pearl works in a large co-educational secondary school (for 11- to 18-year-olds) in a residential district of Hong Kong Island. She teaches both English and Home Economics, and all her English teaching is with the junior forms in the school.

It is a Wednesday morning, and Pearl is teaching a group of Secondary 1 students (11- to 12-year-olds). The class size is small by Hong Kong standards – there are just 20 children – because it consists of so-called 'remedial' students (i.e. those in the form whose test scores label them as being among the weakest in English).

Pearl is going through a blank-filling exercise, which the students worked on in pairs earlier in the lesson. The exercise focuses on the Present Simple and Present Progressive.

One of the items in the exercise reads:

> *My brother _____ (swim) very well. Perhaps he can give you swimming lessons.*

When Pearl nominates one student to provide his answer, the boy says:

> *My brother is swimming very well. Perhaps he can give you swimming lessons.*

Pearl's immediate reaction is to laugh (in a slightly nervous, but not unfriendly way). She starts miming breast-stroke movements, saying '*My brother is swimming very well?*' as she does so. She then says '*He is swimming all the time?*' and laughs again, looking towards the student who gave the incorrect reply. The boy stares at his textbook, saying nothing. Pearl turns to another student, from whom she immediately elicits the correct sentence completion. She then moves on to the next item in the exercise.

Other considerations, however, involve a complex blend of language-related competences, including the teacher's ability to communicate effectively. For instance:

- Does the teacher's explanation provide the learners with what they need at that particular moment? (In other words, does the teacher appear to have diagnosed the learners' problem correctly?)
- Does the teacher's explanation provide the learners with the right amount of information (neither too much nor too little) to serve their immediate learning needs?

- Is the explanation pitched at the right level, in that it uses only concepts and terminology with which the learners are already familiar?
- Is the explanation expressed in a clear, coherent and fully intelligible way?

In focusing attention on such questions, we are in fact identifying many of the key characteristics of Teacher Language Awareness, which is the focus of this book. The quotation from Swan is especially useful as we consider the nature of TLA because it encapsulates many aspects of the challenges involved in being a language-aware teacher and highlights some of the associated complexities and paradoxes which we shall explore in more detail in the following chapters.

Swan's final words, in which he talks about the art involved in good teaching, are also highly significant in relation to TLA, if language awareness is (as I would argue) one of the attributes one would expect the 'good teacher' to possess, since those words remind us that TLA as exemplified in the act of teaching is both art and science. TLA is in one sense science, in that it is dependent upon the teacher's possession of an appropriate base of knowledge and understanding about language (in particular, the target language) and how it works. At the same time, however, TLA, when it is demonstrated in good classroom practice, is much more than the direct application of science, i.e. the teacher's knowledge of linguistics. It involves a complex blend of learning- and learner-related understanding and sensitivity, such that the teacher is able to provide the precise amount of knowledge the learner needs at a given point and to convey that knowledge in a form that creates no barriers to comprehension. The language-aware teacher therefore needs to be both scientist and artist, and therein lies much of the challenge.

Earl Stevick, writing in 1980 about grammatical explanation, captures the essence of this blend of science and artistry, at the same time providing a strong argument in support of the need for the L2 teacher to be language-aware:

> The explaining of grammar. . . casts light on the unfamiliar pathways
> and the arbitrary obstacles through which [the student] must
> eventually be able to run back and forth with his eyes shut. It can
> thus save him a certain amount of time, energy, and barked shins.
> It is for this same reason, of course, that the teacher needs to know
> these same pathways and obstacles – not only to run back and forth
> in them for herself, but also to see them as they look to a newcomer.
> On top of this are the skills of knowing when to turn on the spotlight
> of explanation and when to turn it off, and knowing just how to aim
> it so that it will help the student instead of blinding him.
>
> (Stevick, 1980:251)

At first sight, the message of a book on TLA might appear to be simply that it's a good idea for teachers of a language to know something about the subject (i.e. the language) they are teaching. If so, then the writer of such a book could with good reason be accused of what Basil Fawlty (in the TV comedy series *Fawlty Towers*) might describe as 'stating the bleeding obvious'.

I hope this book succeeds in doing rather more than that. There is in my view very little about language teaching and language learning that could justifiably be described as obvious, and it is the assumed truths about the processes we engage in as language teachers and about the qualities we require in order to be effective practitioners that are often most in need of interrogation and critical analysis. In the chapters that follow, an attempt is made to subject this particular assumed truth about language teaching and language teachers to questioning by exploring such issues as:

- What sort of knowledge about language do L2 teachers need?
- Why is knowledge of this kind important?
- How does such knowledge (or the lack of it) affect L2 teachers' handling of language-related issues in their teaching?

As far as possible, these issues are discussed and illustrated in relation to the lives and experiences of real teachers. As noted in the Introduction, the examples are drawn from one particular type of L2 teaching (the teaching of English as a Foreign Language) and a single macro-context, the Hong Kong secondary school, which has been the focus of my professional life since 1990. The problems and issues confronting the teachers in the book are, however, universal, and the experiences of these Hong Kong teachers (and the constraints they face) will, I am sure, be accessible and indeed familiar to L2 teachers around the world.

1 Language Awareness, 'Knowledge About Language' and TLA

1.1 Introduction

The aim of the present chapter is to provide a context for the book's focus on TLA: conceptually, by setting TLA within the broader framework of **Language Awareness** more generally, and historically, by situating the growing interest in TLA within the context of changing perspectives on grammar and L2 teaching. The chapter begins by briefly outlining the emergence of the Language Awareness 'movement', and examining what is understood by the terms 'Language Awareness' and '**Knowledge About Language**' (KAL) – the associated phrase which appears in much of the literature, particularly that concerned with the National Curriculum for English Language in the UK (see, e.g., Carter, 1990). The chapter then discusses the central concern of the Language Awareness 'movement' with **explicit knowledge** about language, and with the relationship between explicit and **implicit knowledge**. The debate about the interface between these two types of knowledge is linked to parallel discussions about **declarative/procedural knowledge** and learning/acquisition, as well as the related concept of **consciousness**. The relationship between Language Awareness, '**consciousness-raising**' and the language awareness of teachers is examined, and the chapter ends with a brief discussion of the increased attention to TLA within the context of recent trends in L2 education.

1.2 The Language Awareness 'movement'

Since the early 1980s, Language Awareness has become a major concern in language education. There has been much discussion of Language Awareness both in relation to the language development of students and, to a lesser extent, in connection with the study and analysis of language by teachers of language (see, e.g., Hawkins, 1984; Donmall, 1985; Sinclair, 1985; James and Garrett, 1991a; Fairclough, 1992; Carter, 1994; McCarthy and Carter, 1994; van Lier, 1995; 1996). The so-called Language Awareness 'movement', which has embraced both mother-tongue and second-/foreign-language teaching, has sought to find ways of improving the language awareness of students and of their teachers.

Initially the Language Awareness movement's focus was specifically on the language awareness of learners. An underlying belief behind the movement is that students who are able to analyse and describe language accurately are likely to be more effective users of the language. A direct relationship is assumed between explicit knowledge of formal aspects of language and performance in using the language. In the case of teachers, it is assumed that an understanding of the language they teach and the ability to analyse it will contribute directly to teaching effectiveness. This is the view expressed, for example, by Edge (1988:9): 'My position on this may seem over-conservative in some circles . . . but I want to argue that knowledge about language and language learning still has a central role to play in English language teacher training for speakers of other languages.' The language awareness development activities in Bolitho and Tomlinson (1980; 1995), Wright (1994) and Thornbury (1997) reflect such an assumption. Although these assumptions about learners and teachers may appear compelling, there was initially little or no empirical evidence produced to support them, at least as far as native English speakers are concerned. However, recent research (see, e.g., Andrews, 1999b; McNeill, 1999) suggests that TLA does have the potential to exert a powerful influence upon teaching effectiveness, at least as far as L2 teachers are concerned. Evidence from related studies is presented in subsequent chapters, particularly Chapters 5, 6 and 8.

1.3 Language Awareness and 'Knowledge About Language' (KAL)

The term 'Language Awareness' was put on the international agenda of language education as recently as 1992, with the formation of the Association for Language Awareness and the setting up of the journal *Language Awareness*. The association and the journal were the outcomes of a growing interest in language awareness, originating in the 1970s and burgeoning in the 1980s, especially in Britain (where Language Awareness is frequently referred to as 'Knowledge About Language', or KAL). Mitchell, Hooper and Brumfit (1994:2) describe KAL as a new title for an old concern: 'that pupils learning languages in formal settings should acquire some explicit understandings and knowledge of the nature of language, alongside the development of practical language skills'.

Much of the impetus for the British interest in Language Awareness / KAL stemmed from a widespread reaction to the poor language performance of children at school. According to James and Garrett (1991b:3), for example: 'It [Language Awareness] was initially and essentially a response to the notoriously dismal achievements in two areas of British education: foreign language learning and school-leavers' illiteracy.' Such concern is far from new, as Hawkins (1992) points out, charting the history of the debate about Language Awareness / KAL in the curriculum during the twentieth century. He sees the concerns about children's language performance as originating in dissatisfaction with the teaching of English as a mother tongue (L1), and developing subsequently into a perception that failure to foster 'awareness of language' (Halliday, 1971) was hindering children's progress in both the mother tongue and L2 (Hawkins, 1992).

In his review of the development of the Language Awareness movement, Gnutzmann (1997) argues, from a European perspective, that British protagonists of Language Awareness can be placed in the tradition of a deficit model of language behaviour, where educational failure is associated with cultural (in this case linguistic) deprivation, resulting from students not having learned the language in which the school curriculum is delivered and examined (Hawkins, 1999).

It could be argued, however, that it is somewhat of a caricature to portray the Language Awareness movement as being based on a deficit model. Much language awareness work focuses on the noticing of differences, without the necessary implication of a deficit. In the case, for example, of the relationship between the standard variety of a language and the dialect used by a particular speech community, the goal of language awareness, as viewed by many within the Language Awareness movement, would be to increase awareness of the differences between the two varieties, without the superiority of either being implied. One consequence of achieving this goal would be that enhanced awareness would empower those who are speakers of the dialect to succeed when following a school curriculum based upon the standard variety.

Although there has been great interest in Language Awareness / KAL in recent years, it is far from easy to find a useful definition of either. As van Lier (1996) points out, the definition of Language Awareness agreed by the 1982 Language Awareness Working Party – 'Language Awareness is a person's sensitivity to and conscious awareness of the nature of language and its role in human life' (Donmall, 1985:7) – is open to a wide range of interpretations. As a result, according to van Lier, it is difficult to decide whether the two terms – Language Awareness and Knowledge About Language – are synonymous or whether one is a subset of the other. The focus on KAL in the UK National Curriculum for English may have led to a narrow view of KAL in some quarters: 'in the media and elsewhere KAL is often interpreted as a renewed call for formal grammar teaching' (van Lier, 1996:80). However, van Lier (1996:80) suggests

11

that, 'In principle this term [KAL] should be compatible with any conception of LA, all the way along the continuum from the most utopian to the most utilitarian position.'

The variety of activity related to Language Awareness / KAL has also made it increasingly difficult to pin down the concept. As indicated by Mitchell, Hooper and Brumfit (1994:5), KAL-related concerns have now broadened to include the relationships between languages, language development in young children, the nature of social interaction, language-choice and personal identity, individual and societal bilingualism and multilingualism, language variation, and the (mis)uses of language for social control, as well as the more traditional questions (of central importance to both mother-tongue and L2 teachers) about the contribution made by explicit study of language to the learning of language, i.e. mastery of the system.

Carter's (1994) definition of Language Awareness reflects the breadth of the concerns encompassed by Language Awareness:

A general language awareness involves at least:

(a) awareness of some of the properties of language; creativity and playfulness; its double meanings.
(b) awareness of the embedding of language within culture. Learning to read the language is learning about the cultural properties of the language. Idioms and metaphors, in particular, reveal a lot about the culture.
(c) a greater self-consciousness about the forms of the language we use. We need to recognise that the relations between the forms and meanings of a language are sometimes arbitrary, but that language is a system and that it is for the most part systematically patterned.
(d) awareness of the close relationship between language and ideology. It involves 'seeing through language' in other words.

(Carter, 1994:5)

The definition would appear to be particularly appropriate to the language awareness of native speakers, with the emphasis on the creative properties of language and the importance attached to awareness of language and ideology, in (a) and (d), although (b) and especially (c) are highly relevant to the second language context. Traditionally, (c) has been the cornerstone of curricula in L2 education, where, whatever the disagreements about the role of explicit knowledge of grammar, a focus on the forms of language and the relationship between form and meaning is generally uncontroversial (see Chapter 3 for further discussion), even within less form-oriented approaches to language teaching, such as the Communicative Approach (see, e.g., Littlewood, 1981; Brumfit, 1984) and Task-based Language Teaching (see, e.g., Ellis, 2003; Nunan, 2004). By contrast, the teaching of English as a mother tongue has typically attached less importance to the formal aspects of language: this was particularly the case during the 1970s and 1980s.

As I have shown, the concept of Language Awareness is essentially broad in character. However, while the breadth of its coverage may give the impression of uniting scholars from different language backgrounds and from different disciplines in a common goal of promoting higher language standards, some underlying differences in focus do need to be clarified. For example, Gnutzmann (1997) argues that European scholars' interest in language awareness pre-dates the current British movement and points out that concepts such as *conscience métalinguistique, Reflexion über Sprache, Sprachbetrachtung, Sprachbewußtheit* and *Sprachbewußtsein* have been current in the language education literature for some time (see, e.g., Candelier, 1992; Gnutzmann, 1992; van Essen, 1992). The extent to which these various terms refer to the same concept is open to debate. For instance, Gnutzmann accounts for the different German terms by arguing that each reflects a slightly different topic of interest and that each was in vogue at a different time.

1.4 Language Awareness, TLA and the explicit/implicit knowledge dichotomy

If there is a single unifying feature of all the Language Awareness / KAL-inspired interests and activities outlined above, it appears to be concern with 'explicit knowledge about language', a phrase which appears in all three original aims of the journal *Language Awareness*. The implication in the repeated use of the word explicit is that there is a distinction between 'conscious or overt knowledge about language' and 'intuitive awareness that children demonstrate when they use language' (Goodman, 1990), i.e. between explicit and implicit knowledge.

In the L2 context, explicit knowledge is defined by Ellis (2004:244) as declarative knowledge of 'the phonological, lexical, grammatical, pragmatic and socio-critical features of an L2'. According to Ellis, such knowledge 'is held consciously and is learnable and verbalisable. It is typically accessed through controlled processing when L2 learners experience some kind of difficulty in the use of the L2' (2004:245). Explicit knowledge includes what Ellis calls 'metalingual knowledge' – knowledge of the technical terminology for labelling those linguistic and socio-critical features.

However, the two terms are not synonymous, since learners may make their knowledge explicit with or without the use of such terminology. Nevertheless, as Alderson, Clapham and Steel (1996:2) point out, 'it would appear that whatever . . . explicit knowledge consists of, it must include metalanguage, and this metalanguage must include words for grammatical categories and functions'.

Implicit knowledge, by contrast, is 'procedural, is held unconsciously and can only be verbalized if it is made explicit. It is accessed rapidly and easily and thus is available for use in rapid, fluent communication' (Ellis, 2005:214). Ellis (1994) characterises two types of implicit knowledge – formulaic knowledge (ready-made chunks of language) and rule-based implicit knowledge. In both cases, according to Ellis (1994:356), 'the knowledge is intuitive and, therefore, largely hidden; learners are not conscious of what they know. It becomes manifest only in actual performance.'

Implicit knowledge is generally agreed to be the type of knowledge that enables a language user to communicate with confidence and fluency. The development of such knowledge and the role, if any, that explicit know-ledge might play in that process have been the focus of considerable debate and research. The nature of the relationship between these two types of knowledge/awareness has also been a long-standing concern of those interested in Language Awareness (see, e.g., Little, 1997). The research evidence has not always provided consistent support for the strength of that relationship. For example, Alderson, Clapham and Steel, in their 1996 study referred to above, conclude that 'Whilst knowledge about language may be worthwhile in its own right, there is no evidence from this study to justify the teaching of metalinguistic knowledge as a means of improving students' linguistic proficiency' (p. 14).

The contrast between explicit and implicit knowledge is closely connected to the distinction between **declarative** and **procedural knowledge**, which, according to Robinson (1997), has been the subject of much recent debate in cognitive psychology about general theories of human learning. For example, Anderson (1983) claims that 'separate systems are responsible for declarative (factual) knowledge and procedural knowledge of how to apply factual knowledge during skilled performance' (Robinson, 1997:47). According to Anderson (1995:308), 'Declarative knowledge is explicit knowledge that we can report and of which we are consciously aware. Procedural knowledge is knowledge of how to do things, and it is often implicit.' However, the relationship between these two systems is controversial. Anderson argues that there is an interface between the two systems and describes mechanisms responsible for converting declarative knowledge into procedural knowledge, while other cognitive psychologists (see, e.g., Willingham, Nissen and Bullemer,

1989; Squire, 1992) claim that 'the two knowledge bases are qualitatively different and non-interfaced' (Robinson, 1997:47).

In relation to the controversy surrounding the interface between explicit and implicit knowledge in the L2 teaching context, there are, as Ellis (2005) points out, three basic positions. The first is that espoused by Krashen (1981). According to Krashen, 'acquisition' and 'learning' are two separate processes. 'Acquisition' (of implicit knowledge) is a subconscious process which takes place only when the learner is focused on conveying meaning – it is unaffected by practice, error correction or any other form-focused activities. Such activities may, however, give rise to conscious 'learning'. The 'learned system' (i.e. explicit knowledge) resulting from the latter process is, in Krashen's opinion, of use only when the learner has time to monitor the output from his/her 'acquired system'. Krashen asserts that 'learned knowledge' (explicit knowledge) cannot be converted into 'acquired knowledge' (implicit knowledge). This position is frequently referred to as the **non-interface position**.

In direct contrast with the view adopted by Krashen, there are others (see, e.g., Johnson, 1996; DeKeyser, 1998) who argue, based on skill-learning theory, that if learners have plenty of opportunity for communicative practice, then explicit knowledge can become implicit knowledge. This is the **interface position.** Johnson (1996) provides a book-length exploration of the relationship between language acquisition and skill learning. He argues (pp. 170–7) that skill learning provides a justification for the P-P-P (Presentation-Practice-Production) approach to L2 teaching associated with the 'weak' form of communicative language teaching (CLT), the argument being that grammar rules presented explicitly can become proceduralised (i.e. converted into implicit knowledge) as a result of extensive communicative practice with a 'form defocus'.

Ellis (2005) describes a third position, which he labels the **weak interface position**. Those who take this position believe that explicit knowledge facilitates processes such as **'noticing'** and **'noticing the gap'** (Schmidt, 1994), which have been claimed to be crucial to L2 acquisition. In other words, rather than justifying the explicit presentation and practice of grammar on the grounds that practice will promote proceduralisation (the interface position), the weak interface position is that 'explicit knowledge of a grammatical structure makes it more likely learners will attend to the structure in the input and carry out the cognitive comparison between what they observe in the input and their own output' (Ellis, 2005:215).

Whichever view is taken on the possibility of there being an interface between implicit and explicit L2 knowledge (and it is a debate that continues to preoccupy L2 acquisition theorists and researchers), the distinction between on the one hand applying rules of grammar successfully in production and comprehension, and on the other hand being able to explain those rules is of considerable significance for the L2 teacher. Conventional wisdom would suggest that both types of knowledge are essential parts of the L2 teacher's TLA, an argument that is developed further in Chapter 2. Indeed, this book argues that it is important for the L2 teacher to possess a high level of explicit knowledge of grammar whether or not that teacher believes in the value of learners' developing such knowledge (see 2.4 below). Equally, however, the L2 teacher faces potential problems with both types of knowledge, as we shall see in a number of the snapshots in succeeding chapters.

1.5 Language Awareness, TLA and 'consciousness-raising'

As Ellis (2002a:162) reminds us, the distinction between implicit and explicit knowledge should not be confused with the distinction between implicit and explicit learning, i.e.: 'whether a person is able to learn a language without consciousness . . . needs to be considered independently of the kind of knowledge they develop'. Nevertheless, 'underlying the whole question of the relationship between explicit and implicit knowledge and how they are internalised is the question of "**consciousness**" in language learning' (Ellis, 1994:361). The concept of consciousness and the nature of the role played by the learner's conscious mental processes in L2 acquisition have been widely discussed in the literature (see, e.g., the studies cited in Schmidt, 1993:207).

Schmidt (1990), in exploring the role of consciousness in L2 learning, adopts the view that the importance of unconscious learning (i.e. Krashen's 'acquisition') has been exaggerated. He argues instead that learners have to pay some kind of attention to language forms in order for acquisition to occur. Schmidt distinguishes between three senses of the word 'conscious': 'consciousness as awareness', 'consciousness as intention' and 'consciousness as knowledge'. He also differentiates between levels of awareness – which he labels 'perception', 'noticing' and 'understanding'. **Noticing** – i.e. 'the process of bringing some stimulus into focal attention, . . . registering its simple occurrence, whether voluntarily or involuntarily' (Mitchell and Myles, 1998:139) – is seen by Ellis (1994:361) as being 'of considerable theoretical importance because it accounts for which features in the input are attended to and so become intake'.[1]

---

[1] Ellis (1990:96) defines **input** as 'the target language samples to which the learner is exposed', while **intake** is 'that portion of the input which the learner actively attends to and is, therefore, used for acquisition'. In other words, intake refers to that subset of the available input which is taken into the learner's short-term memory, 'the first step in the process of accommodating it into the learner's developing interlanguage system' (Thornbury, 2006:106).

As Ellis (2005) points out, however, the extent to which 'noticing' is necessary for learning is controversial. Swan (2001:204), for example, suggests that regarding 'noticing' as a prerequisite for acquiring grammatical features is 'an extreme and decidedly eccentric notion'. Harmer (2003) is also sceptical about the more extreme claim being made for 'noticing': that we can acquire a language feature only if we have consciously noticed it. He comments from experience that 'some language is clearly acquired subconsciously without any conscious attention being drawn to it either by the learner or by some other agent (such as the teacher)' (Harmer, 2003:10). Such views are supported by evidence from research. For instance, Williams's (2005) study suggests that the learning of some form–meaning relationships can take place without awareness. Ellis (2005) notes that Schmidt has modified his position to acknowledge that there may be some non-conscious registration of linguistic form. Nevertheless, Schmidt (2001:30) still argues that 'more attention results in more learning'.

One term which has come to the fore in relation to these reassessments of the role of consciousness and of explicit knowledge of grammar in L2 acquisition is **consciousness-raising** (see, e.g., Sharwood Smith, 1981; Rutherford and Sharwood Smith, 1985; Rutherford, 1987). Consciousness-raising, for Rutherford and Sharwood Smith (1988), is not seen as referring just to one type of classroom activity, or one set of roles for teacher and learner. Instead, the term applies to activities on a continuum ranging from, at one end, the intensive promotion of conscious awareness via the articulation of pedagogical rules through to, at the other end, simply exposing the learner to specific grammatical phenomena. This broad conceptualisation of consciousness-raising therefore incorporates varying degrees of explicitness and elaboration by the teacher, and the possibility, but not the necessity, of learners' 'verbalising' or 'articulating' what they have become aware of (Sharwood Smith, 1981:162).

In Sharwood Smith's subsequent work (see, e.g., Sharwood Smith, 1991:119–20), he abandons the term consciousness-raising in favour of '**input enhancement**', on the grounds that as a teacher it is not possible to know whether the learner's consciousness has been raised, only that aspects of the input have been highlighted in some way. Sharwood Smith also distinguishes between what he calls 'externally created salience' (e.g., by the teacher) and 'internally created salience' (by learning mechanisms), to bring out the point that 'what is made salient by the teacher may not be perceived as salient by the learner' (1991:120–1).

James (1992; 1996) explicitly addresses the relationship between consciousness-raising and Language Awareness. He argues that they are in fact two contrasting manifestations of linguistic metacognitions. For James, consciousness-raising is for L2 learners and is intended to facilitate a move from the explicit to the implicit. As James (1992:184) puts it, 'Consciousness gives the learner insight into what he [*sic*] does not know and therefore needs to learn. That is, consciousness-raising defines a set of learning objectives, what needs to be done to put a deficiency right.' By contrast, Language Awareness, according to James (1996:223), is 'an ability to contemplate metacognitively language over which one already has a high degree of skilled control and inexplicit intuitions', i.e. it is 'implicit knowledge that has become explicit' (Levelt et al., 1978:5, cited in James, 1996). James (1996) draws the conclusion that logically Language Awareness applies more to knowledge of the mother tongue, while consciousness-raising is for L2 learners.

It could be argued that James presents a rather narrow view of consciousness-raising, emphasising the remedying of deficiencies (i.e. the corrective function) rather than the broadening of the learner's linguistic repertoire that may also result from activities in which specific features of the input have been made salient by the teacher (i.e. the additive function). It is also something of an over-simplification to associate Language Awareness primarily with knowledge of the mother tongue, since language awareness work with intermediate and advanced L2 learners and with L2 teachers often involves reflection on and analysis of language where the learner/teacher already has a measure of implicit knowledge and skilled control.

Certainly, though, for the L2 teacher (whether a native speaker or non-native speaker of the language being taught), both sorts of linguistic metacognition mentioned by James are important. For instance, any pedagogical decision relating to the language content of one's teaching undoubtedly involves metacognitions about language over which the teacher has, to a greater or lesser extent, 'skilled control and inexplicit intuitions', a point which is discussed at greater length in 2.2. At the same time, it is clear that consciousness-raising (or input enhancement / creating salience) – indeed any structuring ('tuning' or mediation) of language input for pedagogical purposes – places significant demands on the L2 teacher's language awareness. The nature of these demands is discussed further in 2.4. Examples of teachers' responses to such demands can be found in snapshots throughout the book, but particularly in Chapter 5, which focuses on TLA and pedagogical practice.

1.6 TLA and recent perspectives on L2 education

The role of grammar in L2 pedagogy will be discussed in detail in Chapter 3, with a historical review and an examination of the major areas of debate. At this point, the aim is simply to place TLA and the development of interest in this specific area of L2 teacher competence within the context of recent perspectives on grammar and L2 teaching.

The debate about the importance of grammar and whether it should be taught explicitly has a long history, with different views prevailing, at least in certain sectors of L2 education, at various times. Contrasting traditions seem to have developed, for instance, in ESL and EFL contexts – with the latter exhibiting a greater tendency to retain an explicit focus on the teaching of grammar (Celce-Murcia, Dörnyei and Thurrell, 1997).

In the latter part of the twentieth century, the role of form-focused instruction in L2 education (i.e. explicit teaching of grammar) was challenged in a number of ways, but particularly as a result of the advent of the Communicative Approach to language teaching (CLT), which prompted a re-evaluation of the role of grammar, causing a 'switch of attention from teaching the language system to teaching the language as communication' (Howatt, 1984:277). As Roberts (1998:150) observes, it is a myth to assert that CLT 'has no place for grammar in the formal sense'. Nevertheless, according to Tonkyn (1994:4), pedagogical practice in many CLT classrooms 'tended to play down the value of grammar teaching. Communicative success, it was suggested, did not necessarily require grammar.'

The rise of CLT, and the accompanying switch of focus from the teacher to the learner, led not only to a changed perception of the value of grammar-focused teaching, but also to an altered view of the teacher's role, which very often became primarily that of facilitator. If the L2 teacher's main role was to facilitate learning, then this was frequently taken to imply that the principal need of such a teacher was familiarity with CLT techniques and the skills of managing pair- and group work, rather than knowledge of subject matter (i.e. knowledge about the specific language being taught). The methodological enrichment accompanying CLT had a significant impact on many training courses of the time, and the extent to which they moderated their focus on such traditional concerns as how to teach grammar.

Nevertheless, courses of language teacher training such as those leading to the Royal Society of Arts (RSA) Certificates and Diplomas in the Teaching of English as a Foreign Language (TEFL)[2] continued to pay

---

[2] Administration of the RSA TEFL schemes was taken over by the University of Cambridge Local Examinations Syndicate (UCLES) in the late 1980s,when they became known as the RSA/UCLES schemes. UCLES is now re-branded as Cambridge Assessment, with a subsidiary department known as Cambridge ESOL. The Certificate and Diploma in the Teaching of English as a Foreign Language to Adults (CTEFLA and DTEFLA) and their counterpart schemes aimed at non-native-speaker teachers (the Certificate and Diploma for Overseas Teachers of English, COTE and DOTE) have been replaced by a certificate and diploma targeted at both native-speaker and non-native-speaker teachers of English: the Certificate and Diploma in English Language Teaching to Adults (known as CELTA and DELTA).

at least some attention to 'Language Awareness', following the practice established by John and Brita Haycraft on their pioneering four-week pre-service courses for native speakers at International House, London, in the 1960s. Also during this period, Bolitho and Tomlinson's book *Discover English* (1980) appeared, the first published materials to focus on developing teachers' awareness about language, and there were others who were still prepared to advocate the importance of teachers' subject-matter knowledge. However, it is noticeable that when Edge (1988), for example, makes his case for language study as part of L2 teacher education programmes (see 1.2), he does so somewhat apologetically, in acknowledgement of the continuing anti-grammar sentiment in some sectors of the ELT profession in the 1980s.

More recently, coinciding with what is sometimes characterised (perhaps over-simplistically) as a grammar revival, and with the best-selling ELT textbooks once again mainly having grammatical syllabuses as their primary organising principle (Thornbury, 1998), there have been more forthright assertions about the importance of focusing on language awareness in L2 teacher development courses. Wright and Bolitho (1993:292), for instance, make the point very simply: 'the more aware a teacher is of language and how it works, the better'.

It should be emphasised that, in making such claims, Wright and Bolitho (1993) were not in any way implying that the primary focus of language awareness activity should be on grammar, nor that such activity necessarily entailed a traditional view of grammar. Many of the grammar-related language analysis tasks in TLA-related books and on teacher development courses have focused on grammar in context, drawing increasingly on insights from research (often corpus-based) on grammar and lexis, discourse grammar, and spoken and written grammar (as discussed further in 3.5).

Since the early 1990s, there has been growing attention to TLA, both in books and in such journals as the *English Language Teaching Journal* and *Language Awareness*. TLA has also become an increasingly important component of the professional standards expected of the L2 teacher, as indicated, for instance, by the greater emphasis accorded to the teaching and assessment of language awareness within the RSA/UCLES TEFL programmes referred to above (UCLES, 1996; 1998). However, much of what has been written on the subject has tended to concentrate in the main on methods of promoting TLA, as, for example, in the works mentioned earlier (Bolitho and Tomlinson, 1980; 1995; Wright, 1994; Thornbury, 1997).

Although form-focused language instruction is a major part of so much L2 teaching, many teachers, particularly those with some exposure to the debates of recent years, remain uncertain about the role of grammar, and how it is best taught and learned. For many teachers, especially those native-speaker teachers who went through an education system in which they themselves did not experience formal grammar teaching, such uncertainty is accompanied by feelings of doubt and insecurity about their own TLA. However, as the discussion in later chapters reveals, teacher uncertainty about grammar is not confined to the native-speaker teacher. Chapter 7 explores the TLA of native-speaker and non-native-speaker L2 teachers.

Perhaps surprisingly, despite all the attention given to Language Awareness / KAL in recent years, it has taken some time for TLA to find its way on to the research agenda. The interest in Language Awareness / KAL referred to earlier in the chapter has focused primarily on the awareness/knowledge required by children, and although it has been acknowledged that any changes in expectations about the knowledge to be acquired by learners have implications for the knowledge base needed by teachers, there has been relatively little research into the nature of that knowledge base. Meanwhile, in L2 education, as noted above, attention seems to have centred mainly on ways of helping teachers to develop that knowledge base and enhance their language awareness, rather than on investigating the nature of TLA or its impact on pedagogical practice.

In recent years, however, a certain amount of research has been conducted, initially mainly in the UK, related to the language awareness of teachers of both L1 and L2 (see, e.g., Brumfit, 1988; Chandler, Robinson and Noyes, 1988; Mitchell and Hooper, 1991; Wray, 1993; Mitchell, Hooper and Brumfit, 1994; Brumfit and Mitchell, 1995; Williamson and Hardman, 1995; Brumfit, Mitchell and Hooper, 1996; Berry, 1997; Murray, 1998; McNeill, 1999; Andrews, 1999b; Walsh, 2001; Morris, 2002; 2003). There is also a growing body of research specifically on L2 teacher cognitions about grammar (see, e.g., Palfreyman, 1993; Borg, 1998; 1999a; 1999b; Johnston and Goettsch, 2000; and the review of such research in Borg, 2003a; 2006). The strength of current research interest in the language awareness and subject-matter cognitions of teachers of language, particularly L2 teachers, is demonstrated by two recent volumes reporting a wide range of related studies (Trappes-Lomax and Ferguson, 2002; Bartels, 2005a)[3]. The data discussed in the following chapters are drawn largely from my own research.

1.7 Conclusion

In the present chapter, I have attempted to provide a historical and conceptual background to the book's specific focus on Teacher Language

---

[3] The papers in Bartels (2005a) all use the term 'Knowledge About Language' (KAL).

Awareness by setting the discussion within the context of the general growth of interest in Language Awareness or 'Knowledge About Language' since the 1980s. The chapter has noted the following:

- the emergence (particularly in the UK) of the Language Awareness movement as a response to the poor language performance in the L1 and also L2 of children at school;
- the broad (and generally similar) focus of Language Awareness and 'Knowledge About Language' (KAL);
- the central importance for the Language Awareness movement of 'explicit knowledge about language';
- contrasting views in the literature about the relationship between explicit and implicit language knowledge and about the role of 'consciousness';
- the demands that any explicit attention to features of language in L2 teaching places on the L2 teacher's language awareness;
- recent perspectives in L2 education on grammar pedagogy and an explicit focus on grammar, and their implications for the L2 teacher's language awareness.

The following chapter attempts to explore the precise nature of Teacher Language Awareness.

Questions for discussion and reflection

1) How would you rate your own language awareness?
2) How do you feel that it affects your performance as a teacher?
3) Do you feel more confident about your language awareness in some areas (of the language generally, and of grammar specifically) than others? If so, in which areas are you most confident, and why? In which areas are you least confident, and why?
4) Based on your experiences as L2 teacher and learner, what are your own views on the question of the interface (if any) between explicit and implicit language knowledge?
5) In your own teaching, to what extent do you seek to promote the development of your students' explicit knowledge about language? What is your rationale for the approach you adopt?
6) In your previous experience of L2 teacher education courses (e.g., your initial training), was there a component focusing on 'Language Awareness' or 'Language Analysis'? What form did that component take? What impact, if any, did it have on (a) your knowledge, and (b) your confidence?

2 TLA and the teaching of language

2.1 Introduction

The previous chapter provided a brief overview of the history of interest in Teacher Language Awareness (TLA), in the context of the renewed attention given since the late 1970s to issues relating to 'Language Awareness' / 'Knowledge About Language', and in particular to the role of explicit language knowledge in language learning. The aim of the present chapter is to examine the language awareness of the teacher more closely, and to consider the nature of the role it plays in the context of language teaching and learning. The focus of the chapter is on L2 teaching and learning, with particular reference to TLA as it relates to grammar. However, many of the issues raised may be equally relevant to L1 teaching, and, as I have already noted, the TLA construct is seen as applying in principle to the full range of a teacher's language knowledge and awareness, not just to grammar.

The chapter begins by asking **What is Teacher Language Awareness?** The complex nature of TLA is explored, including its relationship with language proficiency and with the generic construct **pedagogical content knowledge**. The chapter then goes on to ask whether TLA is important for all L2 teachers and why, by examining the relevance of TLA within different approaches to L2 pedagogy. This is followed by discussion of how TLA can affect teacher behaviour, particularly through its impact on the ways in which target language **input** is made available to learners in the L2 classroom. The chapter concludes with an analysis of the factors that can affect the application of TLA in pedagogical practice, and of the potential impact of TLA on the teacher's handling of language-related issues both before the lesson and in the classroom.

2.2 What is Teacher Language Awareness?

Let us begin our examination of the nature of TLA by looking again at Thornbury's (1997:x) definition, quoted in the Introduction, which describes TLA as 'the knowledge that teachers have of the underlying systems of the language that enables them to teach effectively'.

According to such a view, TLA is essentially concerned with subject-matter knowledge and its impact upon teaching. In other words, it relates to the L2 teacher's need to be able to function effectively as an *analyst* of the language, with the ability 'to talk about the language itself, to analyse it, to understand how it works and to make judgements about acceptability in doubtful cases' (Edge, 1988:10). Hales's (1997:217) definition shows a similar focus on subject-matter knowledge: 'Language awareness could be glossed as a sensitivity to grammatical, lexical, or phonological features, and the effect on meaning brought about by the use of different forms.'

Snapshot 3 provides a clear illustration of the central role of subject-matter knowledge in any teacher's language awareness. It also highlights the sorts of problems that can arise when teacher subject-matter knowledge is lacking.

In the classroom episode that Rose describes, she and her students apparently have no problems dealing with mechanical exercises transforming active sentences to passive and vice versa. However, once attention switches to the meaning of passive voice, and the reasons for selecting active or passive, i.e. what Hales (1997:217) refers to as 'the effect on meaning brought about by the use of different forms', Rose admits that she is unable to resolve her students' difficulties, because she lacks the relevant knowledge of the underlying systems of the language. From Rose's comments, it appears that she is not alone: other English teachers in her school find her query equally challenging.

From Rose's comments, subject-matter knowledge is evidently an important, indeed necessary, part of TLA, a point we noted in the Prologue. However, when we look at examples of how teachers handle grammar-related issues in the classroom itself, it becomes apparent that the relationship between subject-matter knowledge and classroom teaching is very complex, and that subject-matter knowledge alone is not sufficient to ensure the effective application of TLA in pedagogical practice, as Snapshot 4 confirms.

From the learners' perspective, there seem to be a number of potential problems with Karen's explanation in Snapshot 4 (see p. 26). However, the inadequacies of Karen's explanation are much less obviously the result of a gap in subject-matter knowledge than are the problems reported by Rose in Snapshot 3. Indeed, Karen, over a series of observed lessons, revealed no major weaknesses in subject-matter knowledge per se. There were, though, a number of similar instances in those lessons where Karen's output in the classroom seemed to be inadequately monitored, where she tended to say too much about grammar-related issues with arguably insufficient reflection upon the intelligibility or usefulness of what she was saying. In other words, it appeared that Karen was not really

Snapshot 3: Rose

Rose teaches English in a very academic Catholic secondary school for girls in Kowloon. Rose has received all her education in Hong Kong, almost all of it through the medium of English, both at secondary school and at university, where she majored in English Literature. As a result of her background, she is a very fluent and confident communicator in English. However, she finds the handling of grammar in her teaching extremely challenging. She attributes this to her experience as a learner, an experience she describes as 'self-learning' and which seems to have involved little or no explicit teaching of grammar.

Perhaps because of her own uncertainties about grammar, Rose claims to be wholeheartedly committed to the school's 'traditional' approach, in which the textbook is supplemented by deductive form-focused teaching of discrete grammar points, using 'standardised exercises for the whole form prepared by the teacher' with set answers.

Rose has just been observed giving a lesson during which the entire 35 minutes were spent on a set of 'standardised grammar exercises'. During the post-lesson interview, she reflects on the challenges she faces whenever she deals with grammar. As an illustration, she recounts the difficulties she experienced in a recent lesson teaching passive voice:

> It's easy if you ask them to rewrite the sentences, because they find it easy to follow. However . . . they just don't know when we are supposed to use passive voice and when we are supposed to use active voice. And one of the students even asked me, 'Miss Wong, why do we have to use passive voice in our daily life?' and I find this question difficult to answer, ha, and I said, 'Oh, I'll tell you next time' . . . and then I asked my colleagues, 'Why do we use and teach passive voice?' and no one can give me the correct answer. And then I go home and think about it. But even now I really don't know how to handle that student's questions. I finish the worksheets with them and they know how to rewrite the sentences. But I don't know how to explain to them.

Snapshot 4: Karen

Karen has been teaching English for three years. She is currently in her second school, a co-educational secondary school in the New Territories. She is happy and less stressed than in her previous job: although the students in her present school are rather passive, they are generally well intentioned and pleasant.

Karen teaches three classes of English this year. One of them is a Secondary 4 (Year 10) class: a group of forty-two 15-year-olds who will be taking the HKCEE public examination towards the end of the following school year. Karen enjoys teaching this class. As she says of them herself: 'Most of them are very nice . . . and I really want to help them.'

One Thursday morning, Karen and her Secondary 4 students are spending the whole of a 40-minute lesson revising the formation of questions in English. The students have just been focusing on the order of the words in the question *Will you come at 8 am?* Karen feels that her students may not be learning much from their analysis of such a sentence, given that the simple subject–verb inversion is of the type they learned in primary school. She therefore attempts to extend their opportunities for learning by explaining some of the complexities of meaning associated with the modal auxiliary *will*, as used in the question *Will you come at 8 am?* In doing so, Karen gives her students the following explanation:

> For this word *will* we have two kinds of meaning. Number 1 you can say that it's about future tense . . . maybe it's now 4 am, and then *Will you come at 8 am?* Future tense . . . Or another one maybe . . . Do you know that traditionally if I say *I shall go / I will go*, they are different? Can you remember? *I shall go* is about future, *I shall go* future tense. And then *I will go* – maybe the underlying meaning is like this: *I must go / I have to go*. And then for this one again it's the same, *Will you come at 8 am?* Maybe it's about the future and secondly you can say that *Do you have to come?* Or *Will you really come? Because I hope that you can come.* And then *Yes, I will come, I must come, I will come* . . . something like that.

thinking about the language content from the viewpoint of the learners, taking into account their potential difficulties. Analysing language from the learner/learning perspective is clearly an important aspect of TLA, as we saw in the Prologue. Karen's problems in this regard offer confirmation of the point made earlier, that the successful application of TLA in practice is dependent not only on a sound language systems knowledge base.

The extract from Karen's lesson in Snapshot 4 suggests that there are a number of elements that contribute to the complexity of TLA. Of particular significance is the relationship between teachers' subject-matter knowledge and their language proficiency, or 'communicative language ability' (CLA) in Bachman's terms. Bachman's model of CLA consists of 'both knowledge, or competence, and the capacity for implementing, or executing, that competence in appropriate, contextualised communicative language use' (Bachman, 1990:84). A major part of CLA is what Bachman calls language competence. This includes organisational competence (covering grammatical and textual competences) and pragmatic competence (illocutionary and sociolinguistic competences). The second major part of CLA is strategic competence, which refers to the higher-order processes that enable the language user to determine communicative goals, assess communicative resources, plan communication and execute that plan. The third part of Bachman's model of CLA is what he refers to as psychophysiological mechanisms: the auditory, articulatory and neurological processes that are part of human communication. The problems with Karen's explanation in Snapshot 4 appear to be linked, at least in part, to her strategic competence, and the extent to which she is able to draw on her communicative resources and convey her intended message effectively.

The closeness and pervasiveness of the interconnections between subject-matter knowledge and language proficiency become clear if we stop to consider the nature of teachers' content-related activity both pre-lesson and in-lesson. In preparing for lessons with a grammar focus, for example, language-aware teachers' reflections on lesson content (their **metacognitions**) are likely to encompass both their explicit knowledge of the relevant grammar rules and their own communicative use of the grammar item. Then, once teachers are in the classroom, anything they say about grammar during the lesson not only will draw on their subject-matter knowledge, but will also be mediated through their language proficiency, assuming that the medium of instruction is the L2. From this, then, it seems reasonable to argue that much of the complexity of TLA derives from the uniqueness of the situation in language teaching (as compared with the teaching of other subjects), where content and medium of instruction (MOI) are inextricably intertwined. Even in L2 teaching contexts where there is considerable classroom use of the L1, this observation still applies to those parts of the lesson in which the L2 is the MOI.

A second element contributing to the complexity of TLA, as noted above, is the need for teachers to be aware of the learners, to be aware (to the extent that such awareness is possible) of the learners' present level of language development (their **interlanguage**), and to tailor their handling of grammar-related input to that level. As Wright (2002:115) observes, 'A linguistically aware teacher not only understands how language works, but understands the student's struggle with language and is sensitive to errors and other interlanguage features.' Given that any class of learners will contain as many interlanguages as there are learners, all at different stages of development, this presents the teacher with particular challenges.

Based on all the above, it would seem that any model of TLA would need to take account of the following:

- The language knowledge/awareness of the teacher embraces both knowledge of subject matter and language proficiency, since it involves reflections on both and entails the mediation of the former through the latter.
- The language knowledge/awareness required by the teacher of a language is qualitatively different from that of the educated user of that language. As I have argued elsewhere (see, e.g., Andrews, 1999a), teachers of a language, like any educated users of that language, undoubtedly need sufficiently high levels of implicit and explicit knowledge of grammar to facilitate effective communication. In the case of teachers, their effectiveness as communicators is directly linked to their adequacy as models for their students. At the same time, however: 'effective L2 teaching requires of the teacher more than just the possession of such knowledge and the ability to draw upon it for communicative purposes. The L2 teacher also needs to reflect upon that knowledge and ability, and upon her [sic] knowledge of the underlying systems of the language, in order to ensure that her students receive maximally useful input for learning' (Andrews, 1999a:163).
- The language knowledge/awareness of the teacher is therefore '**metacognitive**', i.e. it involves 'cognition about cognition' (Flavell, 1981, quoted by Gombert, 1992:7). In other words, TLA is not just knowledge of subject matter mediated through a teacher's language proficiency, but rather, as suggested above, it also involves an extra cognitive dimension of reflections upon both knowledge of subject-matter and language proficiency, which provides a basis for the tasks of planning and teaching. (See, e.g., Andrews, 1997, and 1999a, where

the term 'teacher **meta**linguistic awareness' is used to emphasise the importance of this metacognitive dimension.)

- The language knowledge/awareness of the teacher also encompasses an awareness of language from the learner's perspective, incorporating awareness of the learner's developing interlanguage. Such awareness would include an appreciation of the current state of each learner's interlanguage and of its likely developmental path, as well as an awareness of the processes of interlingual development. Awareness of the learner and the learner's perspective also includes an awareness of the extent to which the language content of the materials/lessons poses difficulties for learners.

2.3 TLA and pedagogical content knowledge

There are clearly close connections between this conception of TLA and the more generic construct **pedagogical content knowledge,** or PCK (see, e.g., Shulman, 1987; Brophy, 1991; Gess-Newsome and Lederman, 1999; and Turner-Bisset, 1999 and 2001). Brophy (1991:xii) describes PCK as 'a special form of professional understanding that is unique to teachers and combines knowledge of the content to be taught with knowledge of what students know or think they know about this content and knowledge of how this content can be represented to the students through examples, analogies, etc. in ways that are most likely to be effective in helping them to attain the intended outcomes of instruction'.

Shulman developed the original conceptualisation of PCK in a series of papers (e.g., Shulman, 1986a; 1986b; 1987) in which he focused on the need for educational researchers to engage in the study of 'teachers' cognitive understanding of subject matter content and the relationships between such understanding and the instruction teachers provide for students' (Shulman, 1986a:25). Shulman (1987:15) identified a number of possible categories of a knowledge base for teaching, but he saw the relationship between content and pedagogy as centrally important: 'the key to distinguishing the knowledge base of teaching lies at the intersection of content and pedagogy, in the capacity of a teacher to transform the content knowledge he or she possesses into forms that are pedagogically powerful and yet adaptive to the variations in ability and background presented by the students'.

More recent attempts to describe teacher knowledge have used the term PCK slightly differently. Turner-Bisset (2001), for example, uses PCK as an overarching term to describe all the knowledge bases that underpin effective teaching. This use of the term acknowledges the central importance of the content–pedagogy relationship and, as the quote from

29

Shulman (1987) suggests, its close interrelationship with other categories of the knowledge base of teaching, such as knowledge of the learners. Turner-Bisset identifies several knowledge bases (e.g., subject knowledge, beliefs about the subject, curriculum knowledge, beliefs about teaching and learning, knowledge of learners, knowledge of self, and contextual knowledge) and speaks of them as interacting sets: at times only some work together, but in acts of expert teaching they blend together.

Freeman (2002) has described PCK as a messy, even unworkable concept to apply to language as subject matter. Freeman argues that in L2 teaching, the teacher's knowledge of subject matter would probably be defined in linguistic terms, while students' prior knowledge and conceptions of language would most likely be based on their L1. The meeting of these teacher and student conceptions in the L2 classroom would therefore take place in a mixture of L1 and L2, creating, as Freeman (2002:6) put it, 'at least three, potentially conflicting, levels of representation: the teacher's linguistic knowledge, the students' first language background, and the classroom language interactions'. The situation pointed out by Freeman does indeed (as Tsui has pointed out in a personal communication) illustrate the complexity of the L2 teacher's PCK, which necessarily involves knowledge about students' conceptions and misconceptions about both the L2 and the L1. However, rather than taking such arguments as grounds for rejecting PCK as an unworkable concept in L2 teaching, I would argue that it is precisely at the interface Freeman describes that TLA comes into play, with the language-aware teacher being equipped to resolve what Freeman sees as potential conflicts. As a result, I have preferred to interpret issues of the sort mentioned by Freeman as lending support to the arguments outlined here and elsewhere (see, e.g., Andrews, 2001; 2003) for a modified model of PCK incorporating the TLA construct. As such, PCK is seen as the overarching knowledge base, and TLA is seen as one subset of the teacher's knowledge bases (a knowledge base subset that is unique to the L2 teacher), which interacts with others and blends with them in acts of expert L2 teaching.

The model below (Figure 1) reflects the characteristics of TLA outlined in 2.2 above, by representing TLA as forming a bridge between language proficiency and knowledge of subject matter. This enables TLA to be seen both as a pedagogically related reflective dimension of language proficiency, and also as a sub-component of the L2 teacher's PCK, which interacts with the other sub-components. Figure 1 is a modified version of the model in Andrews, 1999b and 2001. The present model differs from the earlier versions in a number of ways, but primarily in that knowledge of the learners has been incorporated as an integral component of TLA, and knowledge of subject matter has been replaced with the broader heading 'subject-matter **cognitions**' in order to reflect the close interrelationship

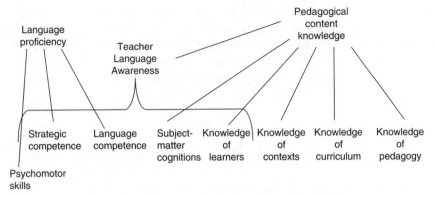

Figure 1: Teacher Language Awareness, language proficiency and pedagogical content knowledge (modified from Andrews, 1999b; 2001)

of knowledge and beliefs (see, e.g., Woods, 1996). The categories into which teacher cognitions are divided in any such model are, as Tsui (2003:137) has pointed out, more analytic than real. The model is nevertheless included here in an attempt to focus attention on those aspects of the L2 teacher's professional knowledge base which seem to intermesh particularly closely whenever pedagogical practice is specifically engaged with the content of learning, i.e. the language itself. Chapter 4 contains further discussion of TLA and teachers' subject-matter cognitions.

One other point that needs to be emphasised in any discussion of the nature of TLA is the use of the word 'awareness' in preference to 'knowledge'. This underlines both the dynamism of the construct, and also the important difference between the possession of knowledge and the use made of such knowledge: i.e. the declarative and procedural dimensions. I would argue that TLA incorporates a procedural as well as a declarative dimension, with knowledge of subject matter (i.e. the language systems knowledge base) at the core of the declarative dimension. If I began using the word 'awareness' in part for historical reasons (since the term 'language awareness' has been extensively used in discussions of L2 teacher development, especially in relation to TEFL/TESL, for a number of years), it was retained deliberately, in order to emphasise the difference between the possession of subject-matter knowledge and 'knowledge-in-action' (i.e. awareness). Knowledge and awareness are, of course, interlinked. As Duff (1988) has observed, the L2 teacher needs a deep and wide-ranging knowledge of the language being taught, since this knowledge informs the teacher's awareness. Duff (1988:72) suggests that an awareness 'that is not sustained by knowledge is inadequate'. I would concur with Duff's position, since subject-matter knowledge forms the core of the conception of TLA as set out in this chapter. At the same time, however, I would argue that, for the L2 teacher, knowledge without an accompanying awareness may be equally inadequate, leading, for example, to the type of lesson in which the teacher seems to be intent upon displaying his/her own knowledge about language rather than drawing upon that knowledge selectively in order to facilitate the learners' acquisition of language.

2.4 Is TLA important, and if so, why?

In the previous chapter (section 1.6), the changing perceptions of the importance of grammar in L2 teaching were briefly outlined. Although an explicit focus on grammar seems to form part of much L2 teaching around the world, there are still lingering uncertainties (at the theoretical level at least) about the importance and role of grammar teaching within L2 pedagogy. We therefore need to look closely at any assertion that TLA is important for the L2 teacher and consider the supporting arguments with care. Wright and Bolitho (1993:292), for example, may claim (as noted in Chapter 1) that 'the more aware a teacher is of language and how it works, the better', but what are the justifications for such a claim?

In attempting to examine those justifications, it may be helpful to consider the relevance of TLA to each of the three options in language teaching outlined by Long and Robinson (1998) – '**focus on formS**', '**focus on form**' and '**focus on meaning**' – options which are linked to different teaching/learning foci. The first option, '**focus on formS**', is the label applied by Long and Robinson to 'synthetic' approaches to language teaching (Wilkins, 1976), i.e. those which focus on the teaching of discrete points of language in accordance with what Rutherford (1987:4) describes as the 'accumulated entities' view of language learning. These 'synthetic' approaches have predominated throughout most of the history of L2 education.

Long and Robinson call the second of their options '**focus on form**'. As Ellis (2005) points out, there are a number of possible interpretations of the term 'focus on form' (including the interpretation which Long and Robinson label 'focus on formS'). However, Long (1991:45–6) specifically defines 'focus on form' as an approach which 'overtly draws students' attention to linguistic elements as they arise incidentally in lessons whose overriding focus is on meaning or communication'. In other words, 'focus on form' refers to approaches where the students' primary engagement is with meaning-focused activity, as in 'strong' versions of a task-based approach. Within such approaches, 'focus on form' occurs as attention switches to language when the need/opportunity arises in the course of communication, and not as part of a predetermined plan to teach specific language features.

The final option, '**focus on meaning**', refers to the range of approaches which Long and Robinson (1998:18) call 'non-interventionist'. These approaches (often referred to as 'natural', and associated in more recent years with, e.g., Newmark, 1966; Krashen, 1985; and Prabhu, 1987) advocate abandoning a focus on language formS. Instead, they seek to replicate the processes of L1 development in the belief that 'classroom language learning will proceed more effectively if language learners are allowed to construct their interlanguages "naturally", in the same way as they would if they were learning grammar through the process of learning to communicate' (Ellis, 1994:652).

If we take the first of these options, it should be clear from the pre-ceding discussion that Teacher Language Awareness can potentially play a crucial role in determining the success of any 'focus-on-formS' approach designed to help develop learners' explicit knowledge. Whatever the nature of the focus-on-formS approach adopted – whether it is based upon the traditional P-P-P (Presentation-Practice-Production) teaching sequence, or on a less production-focused approach such as 'consciousness-raising' (Rutherford and Sharwood Smith, 1985) or 'input enhancement' (Sharwood Smith, 1991) – if the syllabus is broadly linguistic, then TLA will necessarily be a significant factor at each stage from lesson preparation through to the provision of corrective feedback.

The type of demand which might be exerted on TLA within teaching that corresponds to the second of these options, 'focus on form', would vary according to the precise nature of the approach adopted. The approach most commonly identified with 'focus on form' is Task-based Language Teaching (TBLT). However, as Skehan (1996; 2003) has pointed out, there are strong and weak forms of TBLT, a distinction reflecting that made by Howatt (1984) in relation to Communicative Language Teaching (CLT) (see Chapter 3). Skehan's strong form of TBLT (which corresponds more closely to Long and Robinson's 'focus on form') sees the task as the basic unit of teaching, in which acquisition of form takes care of itself with relatively little intervention by the teacher. A weak form of TBLT would still have tasks at its core, but these may be preceded and/or followed by focused instruction, the post-task instruction usually depending on the quality of the students' performance of the task.

Whichever type of 'focus-on-form' approach is adopted, however, it seems that 'focus on form' in fact poses no less of a challenge to a teacher's language awareness than 'focus on formS'. For example, even the strong form of TBLT would entail the selection of suitable learning tasks, which would involve considering such factors as the potential lin-guistic demands of the task and the linguistic capacity of the learners to cope with those demands. In addition, and perhaps most signifi-cantly, a strong 'focus-on-form' approach might actually increase the demands on a teacher's language awareness, because of the emphasis on language-related activity arising spontaneously out of the tasks rather than being determined in advance. TLA would significantly affect both the teacher's judgement of whether and when to intervene, and also the ability to intervene in ways likely to promote learning. With the weaker form of TBLT, the demands on TLA are that much more apparent, as the teacher is confronted with the need to make decisions about whether and how to address grammar issues before, during, and after the task (for further discussion, see Richards, 2002, and Nunan, 2004).

It is with the third option, 'focus on meaning', that the importance of TLA is perhaps the least obvious. After all, if the emphasis is on non-intervention, then it might be assumed that the demands on a teacher's language awareness would be greatly reduced, if not entirely eliminated. However, even within those approaches which are the least sympathetic to form-focused instruction (such as those inspired by the work of Krashen), one could argue that TLA plays a significant part in the effectiveness or otherwise of what takes place in the classroom. Krashen's 'input hypothesis' (1981; 1985), for example, proposes that comprehensible input is a major causative factor in L2 acquisition. If a teacher wanted the classroom to be a major source of comprehensible input and therefore an 'acquisition-rich' environment, then he/she would presumably need to make decisions about the current stage of development of the students' 'acquired systems', and

(a) select texts providing comprehensible input;
(b) devise tasks entailing an appropriate level of linguistic challenge; and
(c) control his/her own language to a level a little beyond the students' current level of competence.

All of these tasks would pose considerable challenges to the teacher's language awareness.

From this it would appear that although TLA is of particular importance where teachers are employing 'focus-on-formS' or 'focus-on-form' approaches, it can also impact upon a teacher's effectiveness even within the most extreme of meaning-focused approaches. It therefore seems reasonable to argue that TLA is an essential part of any language teacher's knowledge/skills base.

2.5 How does TLA affect teacher behaviour?

In recent years, there have been various attempts to characterise how Teacher Language Awareness affects teacher behaviour. Thornbury

(1997), for example, lists a number of potential consequences of weakness in the area of language awareness:

> - a failure on the part of the teacher to anticipate learners' learning problems and a consequent inability to plan lessons that are pitched at the right level;
> - an inability to interpret coursebook syllabuses and materials and to adapt these to the specific needs of the learners;
> - an inability to deal satisfactorily with errors, or to field learners' queries; and
> - a general failure to earn the confidence of the learners due to a lack of basic terminology and ability to present new language clearly and efficiently
>
> (Thornbury, 1997:xii)

Wright and Bolitho (1993) identify a number of pedagogic tasks where TLA may have a significant positive impact, including preparing lessons; evaluating, adapting and writing materials; understanding, interpreting and designing syllabuses; and assessing learners' performance. They suggest that a lack of awareness most typically shows itself at the classroom level: 'for example when a teacher is unable to identify and compensate for shortcomings in a coursebook, or is "caught out" by a learner's question on the language' (Wright and Bolitho, 1993:292). They emphasise that these points about TLA apply equally to NS and NNS teachers, a point we shall discuss further in Chapter 7.

In an early investigation of TLA (Andrews, 1994), I asked trainers of English native-speaker teachers of EFL to characterise the grammatical knowledge and awareness required of teachers. The list below gives an indication of the range of aspects mentioned by the trainers and represents one view of how TLA might ideally manifest itself in teacher behaviour.

> 1) Knowledge of grammatical terminology
> 2) Understanding of the concepts associated with terms
> 3) Awareness of meaning/language in communication
> 4) Ability to reflect on language and analyse language forms
> 5) Ability to select/grade language and break down grammar points for teaching purposes
> 6) Ability to analyse grammar from learners' perspective
> 7) Ability to anticipate learners' grammatical difficulties
> 8) Ability to deal confidently with spontaneous grammar questions
> 9) Ability to think on one's feet in dealing with grammar problems
> 10) Ability to explain grammar to students without complex metalanguage
> 11) Awareness of 'correctness' and ability to justify an opinion about what is acceptable usage and what is not
> 12) Sensitivity to language/awareness of how language works
>
> (Andrews, 1994:75)

It is interesting to note how many of the ideal characteristics listed mirror the deficiencies mentioned by Thornbury, and by Wright and Bolitho.

A comparable list of qualities, taken from Leech (1994), and forming part of his discussion of the 'mature communicative knowledge' of grammar required by the teacher, is set out below.

A 'model' teacher of languages should:

a) be capable of putting across a sense of how grammar interacts with the lexicon as a communicative system;
b) be able to analyse the grammatical problems that learners encounter;
c) have the ability and confidence to evaluate the use of grammar, especially by learners, against criteria of accuracy, appropriateness and expressiveness;
d) be aware of the contrastive relations between native language and foreign language;
e) understand and implement the processes of simplification by which overt knowledge of grammar can best be presented to learners at different stages of learning.   (Leech, 1994:18)

The lists from Andrews (1994) and Leech (1994) have their limitations. The former raises as many questions as it answers. We might ask, for example, what precisely is meant by 'complex metalanguage' (point 10). Presumably the point at issue is whether the metalanguage actually means something to the learners, rather than any inherent complexity in the terminology employed. With the Leech list, too, we might wish to suggest certain modifications and make explicit certain ideas which are perhaps implicit. For instance, in relation to (a), one would want to emphasise that this interaction of the grammar and the lexicon should relate not only to such interaction within the sentence – Leech (1994:19) refers to 'words, phrases, sentences, and their categories and structures' – but also to the interaction of form and meaning in longer stretches of text. With reference to (b), we might wish to add the qualifying comment 'from the learners' perspective', while with (e) one would want to highlight Leech's further comment, 'whatever the level of learning, the degree of explicit explanation needs to be reduced to the simplest level consistent with its pedagogical purpose' (1994:21), and also to add another aspect of simplification, that teachers should control their own use of language. We might also want to argue that the scope of the knowledge characterised in both lists should be broadened to include an awareness of the distinctive features of spoken grammar (see, e.g., Carter and McCarthy, 1997; 2006). Whatever minor adjustments one might feel inclined to make to both these lists, however, they provide a useful inventory of facets of teacher behaviour to look out for when observing instances of Teacher Language Awareness in the context of grammar-related pedagogical activity.

Both of the lists above are concerned with the knowledge, awareness and ability the teacher brings to the task of dealing with issues relating to 'input' – 'the target language samples to which the learner is exposed' (Ellis, 1990:96). Although there are different views among researchers into second language acquisition as to how languages are learned or acquired (see Chapter 3 for discussion of some of the research relating to form-focused instruction), one thing that is clear is that it is a precondition for learning that learners should be exposed to input. The L2 learner, whether in the instructed learning or the immersion setting, learns the target language from the samples of that language to which he/she is exposed, either deliberately or incidentally. The sixth of Ellis's (2005) ten principles of instructed language learning, offered as 'provisional specifications' for a learning-centred language pedagogy, states that '[s]uccessful instructed language learning requires extensive L2 input' (p. 217). The significance of Teacher Language Awareness is therefore likely to come primarily from its impact upon the ways in which input is made available to learners in the classroom setting.

In relating TLA to input, however, it should not be assumed that TLA as a construct has a place only within a cognitive, information-processing view of L2 learning. On the contrary, I would argue that the significance of TLA is equally obvious within a sociocultural view of L2 learning, which sees such learning as socially constructed through both interpersonal and intrapersonal interactions (see, e.g., Lantolf, 2000). For instance, TLA clearly has the potential to influence both the decisions the teacher makes about whether to withhold or provide **scaffolding** (i.e. interactional support) to assist in the co-construction with the learner(s) of new knowledge, and also the strategies and the language used by the teacher in providing and then gradually withdrawing that scaffolding. The mediating role of the teacher in relation both to the provision of input (or **affordances**[1]) and to the processes that might promote the assimilation of new information into the learner's interlanguage is therefore potentially crucial when viewed from either perspective.

---

[1] Sociocultural theory would use the term affordances in preference to input. Affordances are those 'language learning opportunities that exist in the learner's linguistic "environment"' (Thornbury, 2006:9).

When the L2 learner is studying language formally, learning may still take place outside the classroom, depending on the extent to which the learner has the opportunity and motivation to become involved in any L2 immersion. For many L2 learners worldwide, however, their major opportunities for exposure to L2 input occur within the classroom and as a result of any related activities that may take place outside the classroom setting. In the context of any L2 classroom, the three main sources of target language input for learners are materials, other learners and the teacher him-/herself. The model in Figure 2 below (adapted from Andrews, 1999a) is intended to show how a teacher's language awareness can interact with the language output from all three sources, operating as a kind of 'filter' affecting the way in which each source of input is made available to the learner.

As Figure 2 suggests, learners may encounter L2 input direct (i.e. unfiltered) from sources such as the textbook (if they study any of it by themselves) and other students (if, e.g., they take part in any unmonitored classroom exchanges involving the L2), but their exposure to output from these sources may also be mediated, or 'shaped', by the teacher (via the TLA 'filter'). In making use of the textbook, for instance, the teacher might modify (however slightly) the textbook's presentation or practice of a grammar point, or draw learners' attention to the occurrence and significance of a particular grammatical structure within a reading comprehension text. When encountering language produced by the learners, orally or in writing, the teacher has a range of options for handling that output, but very often the feedback provided by the teacher will constitute an additional source of input for learning (for the class or for the individual learner) as the student's original output is modified by the teacher.

As Figure 2 illustrates, the teacher is also the producer of target language input. This may occur with the specific intention to induce learning, as in, for example, the presentation of new language, or, less deliberately, through any communicative use the teacher makes of the L2 in the classroom, such as for classroom management. Awareness of the potential of self-produced language as input for learning may lead the teacher to pay careful attention to the structuring of his/her utterances (which may, in other words, be 'filtered' through the teacher's language awareness). In the same lesson, however, there will almost certainly be many teacher utterances which are less consciously monitored, and which are not intended by the teacher to lead to learning, but which are nevertheless potentially available to the learner as 'unfiltered' input.

The point being made here is that the TLA 'filter' inevitably influences the decisions and choices the teacher makes in mediating, or 'shaping', the language input that is made available to learners in the classroom:

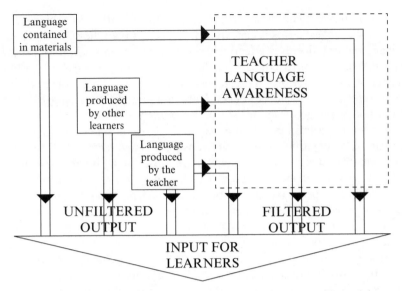

Figure 2: The role of TLA in structuring input for learners (adapted from Andrews, 1999a:166)

the language contained in materials, the language produced by other learners and the language produced by the teacher. With hindsight, the 'filter' metaphor is not ideal, because it may be misconceived as placing undue emphasis on TLA's defensive, 'risk limitation' role, and the ability of the language-aware teacher to spot and then filter out problems, errors and potential sources of misunderstanding. That role may indeed be important, but the TLA 'filter' is actually concerned at least as much with the more positive goal of sifting through input (potential or actual) in order to spot opportunities for learning. Such opportunities may, of course, occur because of a problem (for instance, a communication breakdown in a meaning-focused oral activity) or a student's misunderstanding or error. But they may also arise as a result of the teacher's openness to teaching/learning potential. As Wright (2002:115) notes: 'The linguistically aware teacher can spot opportunities to generate discussion and exploration of language, for example by noticing features of texts which suggest a particular language activity.'

2.6 The impact of TLA on pedagogical practice

It is evident from the preceding discussion that there are two factors specific to language that are seen as central to the operation of the TLA 'filter' described above. The first of these is subject-matter knowledge. As Thornbury suggests, this is crucial to the successful application of TLA in pedagogical practice: it is effectively the declarative dimension of TLA. In relation to grammar teaching, for instance, the quality of a teacher's thinking, actions and reactions at all stages – in preparation, teaching and postlesson reflection – is clearly dependent on a sound underlying language systems knowledge base. It is equally evident, however, that explicit knowledge of grammar, while a necessary part of a teacher's language awareness, is not sufficient by itself to ensure that any teacher will deal with grammar-related issues in ways which are most conducive to learning.

The second language-specific factor that plays a vital role in the application of TLA in pedagogical practice is language proficiency. This not only affects the quality of the teacher's reflections about language. It also has a direct effect upon the structural accuracy and functional appropriateness of the teacher's mediation of all three potential sources of language input.

These two language-related factors undoubtedly have a major influence on the quality of teacher-produced input and the effectiveness of the teacher's mediation of other potential input sources. As noted in 2.2 above, a third crucial factor is the teacher's awareness of the learner, and of the learner's developing interlanguage. These three factors may for our present purposes be subsumed under the heading of 'professional factors', together with, for instance, the teacher's beliefs about grammar and his/her previous experience of grammar teaching.

However, there are other factors – other cognitions, relating to attitude and to context – which interact with professional factors (including subject-matter knowledge) to exert a powerful influence upon the application of TLA in pedagogical practice. One key attitudinal factor is the teacher's self-confidence, or lack of confidence, about grammar. Another concerns the relative importance that the teacher (for whatever reason) accords to content issues rather than questions of methodology, classroom organisation and student responsiveness. As well as being influenced by professional factors, these attitudinal factors may also be influenced by the teacher's perceptions of and responses to contextual factors in the particular work situation, such as pressure of time and the need to follow a prescribed syllabus. These issues are explored further in Chapters 4 and 5.

Together these various influences have a substantial effect upon the teacher's willingness to engage with language-related issues, and upon the capacity for 'reflection-on-action' and 'reflection-in-action' (Schon, 1983), as well as on the feasibility of each teacher's personal engagement with and reflection on language-related issues in their teaching. Figure 3 illustrates the major interacting influences on TLA in pedagogical practice: the procedural dimension of TLA. It should be noted, however, that

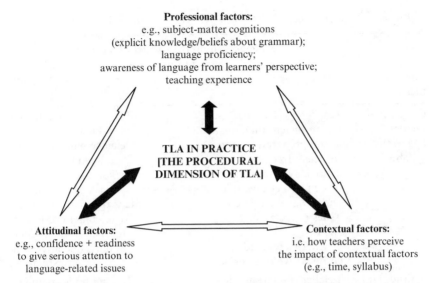

Figure 3: Key influences on the operation of TLA (modified from Andrews, 1999b; 2001)

within each individual teacher, these factors will interact in a variety of ways, with differing consequences. Just as the precise combination of factors may vary from individual to individual, so one should not expect the interaction of the factors to be stable and constant for each teacher on every occasion. Attitudinal and contextual factors may well differ from day to day, and even from class to class. Even the impact of professional factors such as explicit knowledge of grammar may vary to a certain extent, depending on the particular grammatical structure.

To analyse the impact of TLA on pedagogical practice, the simplest way is to itemise the range of grammar-related tasks that the teacher might perform with the intention of facilitating learning, since each of these tasks is potentially affected by the quality of that teacher's language awareness. The major pre-lesson task in which TLA plays a part involves analysing the grammatical area from the learner and learning perspectives. TLA affects the teacher's ability to identify the key features of the grammar area for learning and to make them salient within the prepared input. It also affects the teacher's ability to specify the most appropriate learning objectives, and to select materials and tasks which are most likely to serve those objectives, ensuring that they are appropriate in terms of the learners' age, previous learning and present stage of inter-lingual development, and that they serve the desired learning outcomes.

Table 1 (adapted from Andrews, 1999b) summarises the influences exerted by a number of different factors, singly or in combination, on

41

Table 1: The impact of TLA on lesson preparation – influential factors

Influential factors	Influences upon the impact of TLA on lesson preparation	
	Positive ◄─────────────────────► Negative	
Contextual factors (e.g. time/ syllabus)	Teacher feels he/she has, e.g., sufficient time for lesson preparation, and sufficient freedom/ control over content of teaching to engage fully ⇔ with language-related issues of lesson before entering classroom. Teacher views students as co-operative/responsive.	Teacher feels he/she has limited chances to engage with language-related issues before lesson because of, e.g., lack of time and/or lack of personal control over content of lesson. Teacher views students as unco-operative and/ or unresponsive.
Attitudinal factors (e.g. interest/ confidence)	Teacher is interested in language-related issues and considers it important to engage with them personally and directly. Teacher has confidence in own explicit grammar knowledge, and ⇔ communicative language ability. Teacher is also confident about assuming responsibility for shaping the language-related content of the lesson.	Teacher finds language-related issues uninteresting and perceives no need to engage with them personally and directly. Teacher lacks confidence in own explicit grammar knowledge and communicative language ability and may be frightened by grammar. As a result, teacher may adopt avoidance strategies, such as abdicating language content responsibility to textbooks.
Professional factors (e.g. knowledge/ experience)	Teacher has good explicit grammar knowledge, good communicative language ability and is ⇔ aware of the importance of the learner perspective on language-related issues. Teacher also has	Teacher has limited explicit grammar knowledge, and/or weaknesses in communicative language ability. Teacher has limited awareness of language from the learner perspective, and limited

Table 1: (cont.)

Influential factors	Influences upon the impact of TLA on lesson preparation	
	Positive ⟵ ⟶ Negative	
	positive previous experiences of grammar teaching. These factors combine to inform pre-lesson reflections about language-related issues, and therefore to influence language-related aspects of preparation, e.g. 1 Identifying key features for learning 2 Making them salient in prepared input 3 Matching practice tasks to learners' level and lesson objectives	and/or negative previous experiences of grammar teaching. Any one or more of these can have a potentially negative impact on pre-lesson reflections and language-related aspects of preparation, e.g. 1 Identifying key features for learning 2 Making them salient in prepared input 3 Matching practice tasks to learners' level and lesson objectives

the potential impact of TLA on the preparation of lessons. The table distinguishes between the positive and negative impacts of each influential factor. However, as the arrows indicate, the influence of each factor is a matter of degree, with the descriptors outlining the opposite extremes.

Within the classroom, as suggested in 2.4 and 2.5 above, TLA has the potential to exert a profound influence upon the teacher's performance of a range of tasks. These tasks include (i) mediating what is made available to learners as input; (ii) making salient the key grammatical features within that input; (iii) providing exemplification, clarification and feedback, as appropriate; (iv) monitoring students' output; (v) monitoring one's own output; (vi) helping the students to make useful generalisations based upon the input; and (vii) limiting the potential sources of learner confusion in the input; while all the time (viii) reflecting on the potential impact of all such mediation on the learners' understanding.

Careful preparation can, to some extent, help the teacher to meet these challenges. However, in the classroom, many of these tasks need to be performed spontaneously and in 'real time'. This means that effective operation of the procedural dimension of TLA involves a variety of personal qualities: vision, perception, sensitivity and reflectiveness. It also demands alertness and quick thinking, ease of access to the subject-matter knowledge base, a good level of communicative language ability and constant awareness of the learner. The experiences of both Karen and Rose (discussed in 2.2 above) illustrate the difficulties experienced by many teachers confronted with such demands. Although Karen and Rose are non-native-speaker (NNS) teachers of English, the challenges of TLA apply to NS (native-speaker) as well as NNS teachers, as discussed further in Chapter 7.

Table 2: The impact of TLA in the classroom

Impact of TLA in the classroom	
Positive ◄─────────────────────────────► Negative	
Teacher acts as a bridge between the language content of the materials and the learners, making salient the key features of the grammar area.	Teacher does little or nothing to act as a bridge / make salient the key features of the grammar area (e.g. doesn't go beyond the language content as presented in the materials).
Teacher 'filters' the content of published materials and notices/avoids potential pitfalls.	Teacher is unwilling/unable to 'filter' content. As a result, teacher may overlook or accept misconceptions and/or inaccuracies in materials.
Teacher 'filters' own classroom output (spoken and written) to ensure that it is 1 structurally accurate 2 functionally appropriate 3 clearly expressed 4 pitched at the learners' level 5 an adequate basis for learner generalisations	Teacher does not appear to 'filter' own classroom output (spoken and/or written). As a result, teacher's output may be 1 structurally inaccurate 2 functionally inappropriate 3 confusingly expressed 4 pitched at an inappropriate level for the learners 5 an inadequate basis for learner generalisations
Teacher 'filters' learner output (as appropriate in the context	Teacher's mediation of learner output in form-focused activity

Table 2: (cont.)

Impact of TLA in the classroom	
Positive ◄───────────────────────► Negative	
of form-focused activity). Mediation takes the learners' perspective into account and is ◄═══►	is inadequate. As a result, incorrect learner output may be ignored, the learners' perspective may not be taken into account and teacher mediation may be
1 correct, precise and intelligible	1 incorrect, imprecise and/or unintelligible
2 structurally accurate	2 structurally inaccurate
3 functionally appropriate	3 functionally inappropriate
4 pitched at the learners' level	4 pitched at an inappropriate level for the learners
5 an adequate basis for learner generalisations	5 an inadequate basis for learner generalisations
Teacher is able to operate 'filter' in 'real time', reacting spontaneously and constructively ◄═══► to issues of language content as they arise in class.	Teacher has difficulty in operating 'filter' in 'real time', and in reacting spontaneously and constructively to issues of language content as they araise in class.
Teacher is able to employ metalanguage to support learning correctly and ◄═══► appropriately	Teacher's use of metalanguage to support learning is incorrect and/or inappropriate (e.g. excessive, or at a level beyond the learners' comprehension).

Table 2 (from Andrews, 2001) summarises the potential impact of TLA, positive and negative, upon pedagogical practice. As in Table 1, the descriptors outline the opposite extremes, when each potential impact is in fact a matter of degree.

2.7 Conclusion

Teacher Language Awareness is an area of growing concern to language educators and to those attempting to set professional standards for L2

45

teachers. However, when concerns are expressed about L2 teachers' knowledge of/about language and reference is made to their language awareness, it seems to be assumed that there is a clear and shared understanding of what the term means. The view underlying the present chapter, however, is that TLA is often discussed in ways that overlook its complexity. In this chapter, therefore, an attempt has been made to analyse what TLA is, and to examine its impact on pedagogical practice. During the discussion, the following points have been noted:

- the central importance of subject-matter knowledge in any teacher's language awareness;
- the complexity of TLA, and its association with the close interrelationship between any teacher's subject-matter knowledge and language proficiency, particularly when the L2 is both the content and medium of instruction;
- the importance within TLA of the teacher's awareness of language from the learner's perspective;
- the relationship between TLA and the broader, more generic construct 'pedagogical content knowledge', of which TLA may be seen as a subcomponent;
- the importance of the declarative and procedural dimensions of TLA (i.e. the possession of subject-matter knowledge and the use the teacher makes of that knowledge);
- the relevance of TLA to all three options in language teaching discussed by Long and Robinson (1998): 'focus on formS', 'focus on form' and 'focus on meaning', with TLA viewed as being especially important when either of the first two options are employed, but also having the potential to impact on a teacher's effectiveness even when the 'focus-on-meaning' option has been selected;
- the positive and negative ways in which TLA may affect teacher behaviour;
- the influential role of TLA in the teacher's mediation of language input that is made available to learners in the classroom: the language contained in materials, the language produced by other learners and the language produced by the teacher;
- the factors that affect the application of TLA in pedagogical practice: language-related factors (the quality of a teacher's subject-matter knowledge and language proficiency); awareness of the learner; other 'professional' factors such as the teacher's beliefs about grammar and experience of teaching grammar; 'attitudinal' factors (for instance, self-confidence or lack of confidence about grammar, and readiness to engage seriously with content-related issues); and the teacher's perception of and response to 'contextual' factors in the work situation;

- how these factors might affect the impact of TLA on lesson preparation;
- the potential impact of TLA upon pedagogical practice.

The impact of TLA on pedagogical practice will be examined in greater detail in Chapter 5. In the meantime, the next chapter revisits a topic discussed briefly in chapter 1: the relationship between TLA, the centuries-old debate about the role and usefulness of explicit grammar teaching, and the more recent debate about the scope and nature of grammar.

Questions for discussion and reflection

1) How does a teacher's language awareness differ from his/her language proficiency? How are they interconnected in L2 teaching?
2) How far is it feasible to be aware of learner language development when you are dealing with a whole class? In your own teaching, can you think of a recent example when your (lack of) awareness of learner language development affected your handling of grammar?
3) What is the difference between the declarative and the procedural dimensions of Teacher Language Awareness? Why is the difference important?
4) Which of Long and Robinson's three 'options in language teaching' best describes the approach to L2 pedagogy that you are most familiar with? To what extent do you think TLA plays a role in the effective implementation of that approach?
5) Can you think of any examples from your recent teaching where your language awareness led you to make specific decisions about
    - your handling of language content in materials?
    - your treatment of language produced by learners?
    - the structuring of your own classroom utterances?
   With hindsight, do you think you made appropriate decisions? If not, why not?
6) How might contextual factors affect the application of the individual teacher's language awareness in pedagogical practice? In your own teaching situation, which contextual factors are most important, and what is their impact on TLA in practice?

---

3 TLA and the 'grammar debate'

3.1 Introduction

Chapter 1 spoke of the growing interest in Language Awareness since the 1980s and of the various attempts to develop ways of improving the language awareness of both learners and teachers. This interest and the educational initiatives associated with it are based upon a belief in the value of explicit knowledge about the formal aspects of the language: the language systems. Not surprisingly, therefore, a book with the title *Teacher Language Awareness* is already taking a position on one of the major issues in L2 education over the years: the explicit/implicit knowledge dichotomy (see 1.4). However, it should not be assumed that the case for learners' needing explicit knowledge of language is open and shut: that issue and the role of form-focused teaching (see 2.4) have been keenly debated subjects over the years.

Whatever the individual teacher's cognitions about such issues, the earlier discussion suggested that they are among the professional factors that affect that teacher's language awareness in pedagogical practice, i.e. the procedural dimension of TLA. In addition, the views on these issues prevailing in the time and place in which the L2 teacher is working exert a profound influence on contextual factors such as the syllabus and teaching materials, which also affect the operation of that teacher's language awareness in the language classroom (as illustrated in Chapter 2, Figure 3). The role of form-focused instruction is not, however, the only aspect of the 'grammar debate' of relevance to the L2 teacher. Of equal importance are the changing views about grammar itself, the scope of grammar and what should be included in the description, and therefore potentially in the teaching and learning, of grammar. In the present chapter, these various issues and the debates surrounding them will be examined, together with the implications for TLA.

The chapter begins by outlining the history of the debate about the importance of grammar in language teaching and the role of form-focused instruction, focusing particularly on the challenges to that role that have emerged in the past 30 to 40 years. The chapter then examines the rationale behind those challenges, before going on to reassess the value and the role of form-focused instruction in the light of Second Language

Acquisition (SLA) theory and research. The discussion then turns to another aspect of the 'grammar debate', concerning the scope of grammar and what should be included in any description of the grammar of a language, before considering the implications for TLA of these issues and of the insights emerging from these different aspects of the 'grammar debate'.

3.2 The history of form-focused instruction

As outlined in 1.6 above, grammar, and a focus on language forms, have been at the heart of language teaching for hundreds of years. According to Howatt (1984:32), in the sixteenth and seventeenth centuries '[y]oung children arrived at the grammar school at about the age of eight . . . and were immediately force-fed with a diet of unrelenting Latin grammar rules and definitions'. However, explicit teaching of grammar was not the only language instruction strategy employed by the grammar schools. As Hawkins (1994) has noted, up until the seventeenth century, immersion learning of Latin outside the classroom also played a significant role in the language learning experience of pupils in such schools. Hawkins cites the charter of King James Grammar School in Knaresborough, North Yorkshire, which stipulated that 'after three years in the school, any boy caught using English, even in the playground, was to be beaten by the Headmaster' (1994:111). Also, as Roberts (1998:146) emphasises, traditional grammar 'has rarely, if ever, served as an object of study for its own sake; rather, it has been used as a tool intended to facilitate practical but accurate mastery of the mother tongue and of foreign languages'. In the Tudor grammar schools, for example, Latin was being learned as a vocational subject, preparing students for service to the church and state.

The debate about the centrality of the role of grammar in language teaching is as old as language teaching itself. Kelly (1969) notes that

> since the beginning of language teaching the manner of learning the syntax and flexions of language has been disputed. Accepted methods have ranged from the inductive, by which the pupil himself [sic] arrives at rules from examples, to the deductive, whereby one proceeds from rules to a knowledge of the language. At all periods of language teaching both have existed, but never on an equal footing. Inductive methods were most fashionable during the late Renaissance and early twentieth century, while deductive approaches reached their greatest development during the late Middle Ages and the eighteenth century.

(Kelly, 1969:34, cited in Rutherford, 1987:34)

As Kelly points out, arguments about the value of explicit grammar-based language teaching go back several centuries, with the deductive pedagogy of the Middle Ages being challenged by the ideas of such innovators as Ascham (1515–68), Webbe (*c.*1560–1633) and Comenius (1592–1670). Of these, Webbe's views were the most extreme: Howatt describes how Webbe dispensed with grammar completely, stating that 'no man can run speedily to the mark of language that is shackled and ingiv'd with grammar precepts' (Webbe, 1622, cited in Howatt, 1984:34). Comenius, too, is often referred to as an advocate of an anti-grammar viewpoint, because of statements like 'All languages are easier to learn by practice than from rules.' However, as Stern (1983:78) points out, such statements should be treated with caution, since 'this proposition . . . is . . . followed by another less frequently quoted statement "But rules assist and strengthen the knowledge derived from practice" '. In fact, language teaching during the Renaissance was characterised by a range of positions on the role of grammar. According to Roberts (1998), while there were a number of teachers who, in reaction against the grammar-oriented traditionalists, advocated, like Webbe, the 'total abandonment of overt reference to grammar' (1998:147), there were others who sought a middle path, combining deductive and inductive approaches (i.e. focusing on explicit and implicit knowledge) in their teaching.

The debate about the importance of grammar in language teaching and the role of form-focused instruction has continued on and off ever since, with the different viewpoints in many ways paralleling those of earlier times. In the nineteenth century, for example, the Grammar-Translation method (firmly established in the grammar schools as the favoured approach for foreign-language teaching) had much in common with the way classical languages had been taught in the past; the late-nineteenth-century 'Reform Movement', with its text-based inductive approach to the teaching of grammar, had similarities with Ascham's inductive grammar; while the various 'natural methods' of the late nineteenth and early twentieth centuries (often collectively described as Direct Method), with their advocacy of learning via assimilation and interaction, reflected many of the ideas expressed by Webbe 250 years earlier.

In the twentieth century and into the twenty-first, too, the debate has gone on, against a background of increased interest in research and 'the scientific study of language problems' (Stern, 1983:103). In Britain the first divisions between ELT and foreign-language teaching became apparent, with the monolingual approach of the Direct Method becoming the consensus in ELT, while Grammar-Translation continued to hold sway in the teaching of most other languages. The role of grammar was still seen as central to L2 teaching – although several of Palmer's ideas, such as his 'subconscious assimilation' (1917), foreshadowed Krashen's

Monitor Model – and as late as the 1950s and 1960s, the differences with regard to grammar centred much more upon *how* it should be taught than on *whether* it should be taught. Thus, for example, while Hornby's 'Situational Approach' (1950), the audiolingual approach (see, e.g., Brooks, 1964) and the cognitive code learning theory (as outlined, for instance, by Chastain, 1971) may have differed significantly in their recommended treatment of grammar and as to whether rules should be taught inductively or deductively, none of them denied the importance of form-focused instruction. The audio-lingual approach, for instance, may have been essentially inductive, but it was nevertheless based upon a structural syllabus, with sentence patterns taught one by one (the 'accumulated entities' approach referred to in 2.4 above), it concentrated on promoting accuracy of production through the repeated practice of each new sentence pattern and it even allowed for a brief summary of the rule once learners had practised the pattern.

More recently, within the range of approaches emerging in the era of the Communicative 'movement', grammar has passed through a period in which its importance as the central focus for instruction has been challenged perhaps more fundamentally than at any time before. This has been partly caused by the 'switch of attention from teaching the language system to teaching the language as communication' (Howatt, 1984:277), as mentioned in Chapter 1. But it is also, as Ellis (1992:37) points out, the result of a shift in our approach to language teaching pedagogy: 'The starting point, which was once "What does the target language consist of and how do I teach it?" has become "How do learners acquire a second language and what do I have to do to facilitate it?" ' Ellis quotes Corder's explicit summary of this change in perspective: 'Efficient foreign language teaching must work with rather than against natural processes, facilitate rather than impede learning. Teachers and teaching materials must adapt to the learner rather than vice-versa' (Corder, 1976, quoted in Ellis, 1992:37). The effect of statements like Corder's has been to encourage a great deal of thinking about and research into the role of the classroom as a setting within which opportunities for learning are provided rather than as a place where language (grammar) is formally taught.

However, it would be misleading to imply that there has been a consistent view of the role of form-focused instruction among those claiming to espouse a Communicative Approach to language teaching, or that grammar has been sidelined by the majority of L2 teachers since the 1970s. While teachers adopting what Howatt (1984:286) characterises as the 'strong' interpretation of CLT (i.e. the 'focus-on-meaning' and 'focus-on-form' options outlined in Chapter 2) may have de-emphasised the importance of grammar in their classrooms, form-focused instruction has certainly retained a role in the classrooms of those teachers who use a 'weak' form of CLT. According to Littlewood (1981:10), form-focused activities can be a starting-point for meaning-focused (i.e. communicative) activities: 'Structural practice may still be a useful tool, especially when the teacher wishes to focus attention sharply and unambiguously on an important feature of the structural system.' Even with somewhat more radical versions of the communicative approach, such as those advocating a 'deep-end' strategy (e.g., Brumfit, 1978; Johnson, 1980), where the teaching sequence begins rather than ends with communicative activity, there is still a place for form-focused presentation and practice of grammar features which the learners have demonstrably failed to master.

In fact, in many classrooms (probably the majority in EFL contexts), the prevailing approach corresponds to what Thornbury describes as a very weak form of CLT (1998:110). In such classrooms, a communicative element has been absorbed into the conventional P-P-P (Presentation-Practice-Production) model of teaching, so that (a) new language is presented to learners in order to make the form and meaning clear and memorable; (b) the learners engage in concentrated controlled (and often mechanical) practice of the new language (possibly involving an 'information gap') in order to 'transfer what they know from short-term to long-term memory' (Ur, 1988:7); and (c) the learners participate in simulated communication tasks 'set up to provide opportunities for the use of those forms which have been presented and practised in a controlled manner' (Ellis, 1992:102). Teaching manuals like Gower and Walters (1983) justify concentrated controlled practice on the following grounds: 'Repetition practice helps to develop habits . . . habit-formation is . . . a small, if essential, part of learning to communicate' (p. 83). The rationale for such a view is no longer derived from behaviourist learning theory, as was asserted by some proponents of audio-lingualism. Indeed, according to Skehan (1996:18), 'The underlying theory for a P-P-P approach has now been discredited. The belief that a precise focus on a particular form leads to learning and automatisation (that learners will learn what is taught in the order in which it is taught) no longer carries much credibility in linguistics or psychology.' However, as noted in 1.4, alternative theoretical support for a P-P-P approach has now been offered (e.g., by Johnson, 1996; DeKeyser, 1998), drawing on skill-learning theory. Certainly, whatever the justification, the P-P-P approach remains very popular with many teachers, pedagogical texts such as Thornbury (1999) continue to advocate its inclusion among the range of grammar teaching strategies available to the L2 teacher, and major textbook series (see, for instance, Soars and Soars, 2006) are still based to some extent on P-P-P.

Some of these variations in the classroom implementation of CLT reflect the differences between the ESL and EFL contexts, and the role

TLA and the 'grammar debate'

that form-focused instruction so frequently plays in the latter. The constraints on adopting a 'strong' form of CLT in EFL settings, alluded to by Celce-Murcia, Dörnyei and Thurrell (1997; 1998) and Thornbury (1998), are clearly outlined by Fotos (2002). In the same paper, Fotos presents a case for the use of what she calls 'structure-based communicative tasks', which require learners to solve grammar problems through meaning-focused interaction about the grammar structure. The value she attributes to such tasks highlights the contrast between ESL and EFL settings: in ESL settings, structure-based communication tasks enable grammar instruction to be added to the communicative approach typically employed, while in EFL settings, they add meaning-focused language use to the form-focused pedagogic activities characteristic of such settings (Fotos, 2002:142–3).

3.3 The challenges to form-focused instruction

As pointed out in Chapter 1, it is important to separate discussion of the explicit/implicit knowledge distinction from the debate over the merits of form-focused approaches to L2 pedagogy (i.e. explicit/deductive grammar teaching) as opposed to more indirect (i.e. implicit/inductive) approaches. The former tends to focus upon the nature of explicit and implicit knowledge, the relationship between them and the significance of each in relation to language acquisition and language performance. The latter, meanwhile, centres on which pedagogical approach is most likely to promote the development of the type(s) of knowledge considered desirable.

As 3.2 makes clear, 'the major issue historically has been whether grammar should be taught *deductively* or *inductively*' (Roberts, 1998:146). Since the 1960s, however, the focus of the debate has undergone a subtle but significant change, largely as a consequence of Chomsky's suggestion that grammar is a property of mind rather than of language, and his hypothesis that the child's acquisition of its L1 is largely the result of an innate language acquisition device (see, e.g., Chomsky 1968). This innateness hypothesis 'holds that all normal newborn humans are hard-wired for Universal Grammar and predisposed to learn whatever natural language(s) they are exposed to in the course of their cognitive development' (Celce-Murcia, 2002:120). Chomsky's theories caused both linguists and psychologists to focus attention on the mental properties involved in language use and language learning. This in turn led to intense interest among applied linguists in investigating how learners acquire a second language and gave rise to the first serious research into second language acquisition (SLA). Growing acceptance of the role of innate heuristics in L1 acquisition also led to a variety of pedagogical approaches which, in different ways, sought to 'work with rather than against natural processes' (Corder, 1976; see 3.2 above) and in particular to replicate aspects of naturalistic language learning in young children. As a result of such developments, the focus of the debate has widened to incorporate such issues as the role of explicit knowledge in second language acquisition and language performance, and whether there is an interface between implicit and explicit knowledge (see 1.3).

In the latter part of the twentieth century, various opponents of form-focused L2 instruction emerged. The first was probably Newmark, who, in his 1966 paper 'How not to interfere in language learning' asserted that classroom L2 learning would be much more effective if teachers would stop 'interfering' in the learning process. In the early seventies, Dulay and Burt developed the argument further, in a paper entitled 'Should we teach children syntax?' (1973), a question which they answered in the negative. Dulay and Burt's proposal was that 'If children were exposed to a natural communication situation, the "natural processes" responsible for second language (L2) acquisition would be activated and a resulting "natural order" of development occur' (Ellis, 1992:53). The ideas of Corder (1976), referred to in 3.2 above, were also a strong influence upon those who advocated abandoning formal instruction.

In the eighties, the main opponents of form-focused instruction were Krashen (1981; 1982) and Prabhu (1987). Krashen's represents the more extreme view. As discussed in Chapter 1, his so-called 'non-interface' position is that learning does not become acquisition. He therefore rejects form-focused instruction 'because it does not contribute to the development of the kind of implicit knowledge needed for normal communication' (Ellis, 1994:653). According to Krashen, explicit knowledge cannot be converted into implicit knowledge, however much form-focused instruction is provided, and although such instruction may promote the learning of explicit knowledge, the latter is seen as having very limited use, for purposes of monitoring, and then only when the learner has time to monitor his or her output. Krashen and Terrell's 'Natural Approach' (1983) takes Krashen's ideas as its theoretical rationale. According to Richards and Rodgers (2001), the Natural Approach aims to conform to the naturalistic principles of successful acquisition of the L2 rather than the Ll. There is therefore 'an emphasis on exposure, or *input*, rather than practice; optimising emotional preparedness for learning; a prolonged period of attention to what the language learners hear before they try to produce language; and a willingness to use written and other materials as a source of comprehensible input' (Richards and Rodgers, 2001:179).

Krashen's view that 'grammatical competence cannot be taught' (Ellis, 1994:652) is not entirely shared by Prabhu (1987): according to Roberts (1998), Prabhu's position is rather more that 'teaching formal grammar, or teaching grammar formally, is neither necessary nor useful' (Roberts, 1998:150). Prabhu's Communicational Teaching Project in Bangalore was set up to test the hypothesis that grammatical competence is acquired most efficiently when learners are actively engaged in tasks focused on meaning. In his 1987 book, Prabhu claims that 'the development of competence in a second language requires not systematisation of language inputs or maximisation of planned practice, but rather the creation of conditions in which learners engage in an effort to cope with communication' (p. 1). Systematising input and maximising form-focused practice were therefore rejected because they 'were regarded as being unhelpful to the development of grammatical competence and detrimental to the desired preoccupation with meaning in the classroom' (ibid.). Not only do Krashen and Prabhu dismiss the value of planned interventions by the teacher in the form of grammar-focused presentation and practice activities, but they also reject the role of unplanned interventions through error correction. Meaning-focused feedback is permissible, but language-focused error correction is seen as being detrimental (Krashen, 1982).

As noted above, Prabhu's approach is based upon the argument that focusing learners' attention on the meaning or content of a message rather than its form is the best way of promoting the development of grammatical competence. A similar principle underpinned the range of content-based approaches to L2 education, which have had a considerable impact since they first emerged in the 1970s. These approaches, which are, as Richards and Rodgers (2001) observe, commonly used nowadays in many EFL and ESL settings, began with immersion programmes in Canada designed to enable English-speaking students to acquire French. Since then they have been adopted extensively in different forms in North America and Australia, and (arguably) in the English-medium (EMI) schools in Hong Kong. In Immersion Education, the regular school subjects are taught through the medium of the L2 rather than the L1, in the belief that this will facilitate learning of the L2 without having a negative effect on either the development of the L1 or the acquisition of the content (i.e. the skills and knowledge) of the other subjects. The most salient characteristic of Immersion Education in relation to the present discussion is that, as Johnson (2001:179) observes, 'the main focus of attention in the teaching is not on language but on the other subjects in the curricula that are being taught *through* the FL'.

Underlying naturalistic approaches like Krashen and Terrell's is the belief that learners will develop grammatical competence if they are given enough exposure to it and experience with it. Therefore, it is argued, form-focused instruction is not necessary: the learners' innate heuristics will do the job. Prabhu's argument bears similarities: if learners are actively engaged in meaning-focused tasks, then the language used in those tasks will be unconsciously absorbed, and grammatical competence will result. In such approaches, there is no place for explicit grammar teaching.

Although the evaluation of Prabhu's project (Beretta and Davies, 1985) suggested that the approach had some benefits, naturalistic pedagogies nevertheless have their limitations. Approaches such as Krashen and Terrell's, for example, which depend on the right kinds of comprehensible input, have limited application in EFL settings, where it may be difficult to guarantee a consistently high quality and large amount of in-class input, and where opportunities for exposure to the target language outside the classroom may be minimal. Krashen and Terrell's 'Natural Approach' is also targeted at beginners, aiming to bring them up to intermediate level: another limitation of such approaches noted in the literature is that it is difficult for 'naturalistic' learners to attain the high levels of grammatical competence required, for instance, in academic and professional speaking and writing (Hinkel and Fotos, 2002).

Widdowson (1990:162) talks about the inefficiency of relying on naturalistic processes, arguing that 'the whole point of language pedagogy is that it is a way of short-circuiting the slow process of natural discovery and can make arrangements for learning to happen more easily and more efficiently than it does in natural surroundings'. Meanwhile, in relation to Immersion Education, Swain (1985) notes the inadequacies of relying on comprehensible input to produce adequate development of the L2, pointing out that the language ability of immersion students in Canada, even after prolonged exposure to comprehensible input, was far below that of their native-speaker counterparts. This led Swain and others to argue that, in addition to input, output (i.e. the production of language) is also essential to L2 acquisition (the so-called 'output hypothesis').

As for approaches like Prabhu's, it has been suggested they may result in fossilisation and the development of classroom pidgins. Skehan (1996), for example, observes that learners experiencing task-based approaches of this kind may indeed develop fluency and strategies enabling them to make the best use of the language they already know. However, according to Skehan (1996:21), the deployment of such strategies does not 'provide an incentive for structural change towards an interlanguage system with greater complexity' and therefore does not result in 'continued language growth and interlanguage development'.

3.4 The value and role of form-focused instruction

In relation to the question **What is the value of form-focused instruction?**, there is an ever-growing body of relevant research evidence from SLA. Although the results of some studies are inconclusive or contradict the results of others, a consensus nevertheless seems to have emerged, based on SLA research, that form-focused instruction is of value. Long, for instance, in his 1983 paper 'Does second language instruction make a difference?', surveyed a range of early research studies in SLA and concluded that, '[p]ut rather crudely, instruction is good for you, regardless of your proficiency level, of the wider linguistic environment in which you receive it, and of the type of test you are going to perform on' (p. 379). Much more recently, a detailed statistical comparison of a large number of studies of form-focused instruction reported broadly similar findings (Norris and Ortega, 2001).

A decade on from Long's initial survey of research on form-focused instruction, Ellis, in his comprehensive review of SLA research (1994), posed the similar question 'Does formal instruction work?' In attempting to shed light on this question (in which 'formal' can be taken as a synonym for 'form-focused'), Ellis distinguished four specific issues which had been addressed by SLA researchers:

(a) whether learners receiving formal instruction achieve higher levels of L2 proficiency than those who do not receive such instruction;
(b) whether formal instruction affects the accuracy with which learners use specific language items/rules;
(c) whether formal instruction affects the order or sequence of acquisition; and
(d) whether the effects of formal instruction are lasting.

With regard to (a), Ellis concluded from his review of the relevant research that there is fairly convincing evidence that L2 learners do indeed progress most rapidly when they experience form-focused instruction, provided that it is combined with communicative exposure (see, e.g., Spada, 1986): foreign-language learners benefit by developing greater communicative skills, and second language learners by developing greater linguistic accuracy (Ellis, 1994:616–17).

In relation to issue (b), Ellis (1994:623) concluded that there is enough evidence to suggest that formal instruction can promote definite gains in accuracy, provided that the structure is 'simple' (in that it does not require mastery of complex processing operations), clearly related to a specific function, and provided also that the formal instruction is extensive and well planned (see, e.g., Pica, 1983, and Pienemann, 1984). However, a key factor may be the learner's stage of development: if the

57

learner is not yet developmentally ready to learn a particular structure, formal instruction may not have an immediate effect (Pienemann, 1984). It may, nevertheless, have a delayed effect, acting as an 'acquisition facilitator' (Seliger, 1979), or 'Advance Organiser' (Ausubel, Novak and Hanesian, 1978), by 'in some ways [priming] the learner so that acquisition becomes easier when she [*sic*] is ready to assimilate the new material' (Ellis, 1990:169).

Research relating to issue (c), and whether formal instruction can affect the 'natural order' of acquisition, has indicated, for example, that instructed learners progress along the sequence much faster than naturalistic learners (see Ellis, 1989). There is also evidence that grammatical features not subject to developmental constraints may be amenable to instruction (Pienemann, 1984). In summarising the findings of these and a number of other studies, Ellis points out that, as all the related research has focused on implicit knowledge, it may be that explicit knowledge of grammar rules is not acquired in a fixed order or sequence: 'If . . . the goal of grammar teaching is explicit knowledge rather than implicit knowledge, it may not be necessary to take account of the learner's stage of development.' Pienemann's 'teachability hypothesis', which predicts that 'instruction can only promote language acquisition if the interlanguage is close to the point when the structure to be taught is acquired in the natural setting' (Pienemann, 1985:37) may, according to Ellis (1994:635–6), be relevant only for grammar instruction targeted at the development of implicit knowledge.

As for (d), and the durability of the effects of formal instruction, the evidence appears inconclusive. As Doughty and Williams (1998:252) point out, 'The studies that have thus far demonstrated long-term effects have generally had two characteristics: (1) They have integrated attention to meaning and attention to form, and (2) focus on form continues beyond a short, isolated treatment period.' Ellis concludes from his own review of such studies that 'for the effects of the instruction to be lasting, learners need subsequent and possibly continuous access to communication that utilises the features that have been taught' (1994:637).

At the moment, therefore, the consensus seems to be that formal instruction does work. The question which then arises is which kind of formal instruction works best, i.e. **What role should form-focused instruction play in L2 pedagogy?** Long (1991:47) distinguishes between two possible roles: focusing on forms (isolating language forms to teach and test one at a time) and focusing on form. The latter refers to teaching that alternates 'in some principled way between a focus on meaning and a focus on form', as where, for example, teaching follows a task-based syllabus, but learners focus on specific formal features while carrying out communicative activities (see the discussion of 'focus on formS' and 'focus on form' in 2.4). Studies such as Doughty (1991) suggest that there are distinct learning advantages in a 'focus-on-form' approach, while Lightbown and Spada (1990) reveal the role that corrective feedback can play in promoting L2 acquisition as part of a 'focus-on-form' approach, provided that it occurs in response to naturally occurring errors or in the context of the learners' attempts to communicate.

Ellis (2002b) presents a persuasive argument in support of form-focused instruction of some kind. His case is based in part on SLA research evidence such as that summarised above. Unlike Long, however, he sees potential value in a 'focus-on-formS' dimension in L2 pedagogy, provided that it is understood that the objective of such teaching is explicit knowledge, and with no expectation of accurate production of the forms taught. Ellis claims that there are strong grounds for support-ing form-focused instruction from both a learner and a pedagogical per-spective: many learners, particularly those above a certain age, expect grammar to be part of the curriculum, while, from a pedagogical point of view, incorporating a structural syllabus within a L2 curriculum helps to ensure systematic coverage of the grammar of the language in a way which is not possible within a purely task-based or theme-based syllabus. At the same time, however, Ellis suggests that the cognitive view under-lying much current SLA theory requires us, as noted above, to modify the goals of form-focused instruction, which should aim at promoting learner awareness of the target grammar rule rather than the ability to produce the target language with total accuracy. This awareness ('notic-ing') should also include the learner noticing the difference between his/her current interlanguage rule and the target language rule (see, e.g., Schmidt, 1990).

Ellis (2002b; 2003) outlines alternative options for relating the two essential components of the L2 curriculum: the 'message' (i.e. meaning) focus and the 'code' (i.e. form) focus.[1] Ellis (2002b) labels his two options the 'integrated option' – essentially Long's 'focus on form' – and the 'parallel' option (Ellis, 2003, talks of an 'integrated approach' and a 'modular approach'). The 'parallel' or 'modular' approach proposes a language curriculum with two components: the main one, a syllabus con-sisting of communicative tasks, and a smaller component consisting of a systematically organised structural syllabus. Ellis suggests that these two components do not need to be integrated within the curriculum: inte-gration is something that needs to be achieved internally by the individ-ual learner in relation to his/her own internal syllabus. He proposes that the proportion of time spent on each component would change as the

---

[1] It should be noted that Ellis intends 'code' to include pronunciation and discourse, as well as grammar.

learners' proficiency develops: elementary students would spend all their time on communicative tasks (mainly receptive at first); form-focused tasks would begin at the intermediate stage and assume increasing importance, finally taking up roughly half the time at an advanced level.

Meanwhile, within Task-based Language Teaching (TBLT), which has been increasingly adopted (in name at least) as the model upon which educational institutions/systems and publishers base the planning of their L2 English courses, the place of a 'focus on form' remains controversial (Nunan, 2004). As we saw earlier, there have been those (such as Prabhu) who have advocated a 'strong' version of TBLT, in which focusing on form is seen as unnecessary. But there are a number of different versions of TBLT, and, as Johnson (2001:194) notes, 'Some differ substantially from Prabhu's, often not being based so centrally on a parallel with L1 acquisition.' Increasingly, it seems that the consensus view of those working within a TBLT paradigm favours some sort of 'focus on form'. This is the view expressed, for example, by Nunan (2004:111), who presents the case for a 'weak' interpretation of TBLT, in which focus-on-form activities, while not constituting tasks in their own right, 'do have a place in any task-based instructional cycle'. From this perspective, the major challenge facing the designer of task-based syllabuses or materials is not whether there is a place for a focus on form, but rather where in the instructional cycle that focus should come: pre-task, post-task or somewhere in the middle of the cycle (Richards, 2002; Nunan, 2004).

These then are some of the views of the role that form-focused instruction might play in L2 pedagogy. As section 3.6 argues, it is the task of the language-aware teacher to try to select the most appropriate way to focus on form, given the nature of the learners, the context of teaching and learning and the constraints affecting teaching within that context. The choices made by the language-aware teacher should take account of SLA theory and research. However, SLA theory and research represents only one source of the subject-matter cognitions upon which pedagogical judgements are based: the thinking L2 teacher should always treat the hypotheses and findings that emerge with a healthy mixture of interest and scepticism.

3.5 What is grammar?

The discussion so far in this chapter has focused upon changing perspectives on the role of form-focused instruction, with particular reference to the teaching and learning of grammar. However, this is not the only direction that the 'grammar debate' has taken in recent years: there has also been considerable discussion of the scope of grammar, and what should be included in any description of the grammar of a language. This area of the 'grammar debate' also has potentially significant implications for the TLA of the individual teacher.

Traditionally, descriptive grammar has focused specifically on the rules that govern word formation (**morphology**) and sentence structure (**syntax**) in a particular language. Such rules concern those changes in word form that have grammatical significance (**inflections**) – such as the *-s* and *-ed* word endings in *She has arrived* – and the way in which the elements of any sentence (words, phrases and clauses) are assembled and arranged, with, for instance, the rules of English syntax allowing the sequence *Has she arrived* to indicate (depending on the punctuation) a question or an exclamation, but not allowing the sequence *Has arrived she. Because of this primary concern with the sentence (an element of written language, identified by its punctuation), grammarians have conventionally concentrated on describing the forms and structures of the written language, rather than of speech. The teaching of language has also generally followed this lead, with textbooks and teachers tending to place an emphasis on helping students to produce well-formed sentences, often to the extent of requiring oral responses to be in complete sentences rather than in a form more characteristic of natural conversation.

In the past few years, however, these traditional views of grammar have been challenged and broadened in a variety of ways, many of them resulting from advances in technology which have made it possible to record and analyse large collections (**corpora**) of naturally occurring texts, spoken as well as written. One such challenge to our traditional conceptualisation of grammar, and of what should be included in a description of the grammar of a language, concerns the relationship between grammar and other levels of language, particularly lexis and discourse. The analysis of **discourse** – 'the patterns of language used beyond the level of the sentence or beyond the individual speaking turn' (Carter and McCarthy, 2006:8) – has received considerable attention in recent years, posing a major challenge to our conventional grammar-based view of language. Nunan (1999), for example, goes so far as to suggest that we need to reverse the way in which we normally view the relationship between grammar and discourse, by giving priority to discourse, and looking at grammatical features within their context of occurrence: 'Grammar and discourse are tied together in a fundamentally hierarchical relationship with lower-order grammatical choices being driven by higher-order discoursal ones' (p. 99).

This discourse-driven view of language has specifically drawn our attention to the way in which grammatical choices are influenced by knowledge of **context** (the situation in which a sentence or utterance is

61

produced, including the participants and topic) and **co-text** (the text that precedes and is likely to follow a sentence or utterance) rather than being the result of sentence-internal considerations (see, e.g., Celce-Murcia, 2002, for further discussion). For instance, the use of articles (i.e. making the choice between *a(n)*, *the* and zero article) is often determined by considerations beyond the sentence. Similarly, the decision to use passive rather than active voice in a particular sentence is not arbitrary, nor is it generally the result of factors internal to that sentence: it is much more likely to be motivated by discourse considerations such as the tendency in English to put given information (information treated by the speaker as if it is already known to the hearer) at the beginning of a sentence and new information at the end. The latter is the sort of insight of which Rose and her colleagues (Chapter 2, Snapshot 3) were apparently unaware.

Among the potential implications for L2 pedagogy emerging from discourse analysis is the need to incorporate a focus on cohesion and coherence. **Cohesion** is a property of the text itself, and refers to the ways in which grammatical (and lexical) links across sentences or utterances create connected text. Examples of grammatical linking devices in English include pronoun reference, substitution, ellipsis and linking adjuncts. **Coherence**, on the other hand, is not so much a property of the text, but rather 'of the relation between the text and its context, and between the writer and reader (or speaker and listener)' (Thornbury, 2006:32). A text is coherent when it 'hangs together' and makes sense (McCarthy, 1991), because it exhibits such features as a consistent topic, a logical relation between the sentences and relevance to context.

The reconceptualisation of the relationship between grammar and **lexis** can be attributed in part to the insights of linguists such as Halliday (see, e.g., Halliday, 2004), who argue that the vocabulary of any language forms one part of that language's grammar or, to use Halliday's term, its 'lexicogrammar'. According to Halliday (2004:2), 'The lexicogrammar of a language consists of a vast network of choices, through which the language construes its meanings.' Some of these choices, as Halliday points out, are very general (for instance, 'singular' or 'plural') and are linked to the selection of particular grammatical forms. Others are more specific, associated with particular domains of meaning and typically expressed lexically – such as the choice between 'lecture', 'seminar', 'tutorial' and 'workshop' to describe an interaction in the academic context.

Technology has played a significant role in this reconceptualisation, in that it has shed light on the patterned relationship between lexis and grammar and highlighted hitherto unrecorded instances of that relationship. **Corpus linguistics**, involving the use of computers to analyse corpora of texts, has helped to reveal not only the most frequent collocations of a word, but also how words entail grammatical choices and vice versa. As Biber et al. (1999:13) note, 'Analysis of real texts shows . . . that most syntactic structures tend to have an associated set of words or phrases that are frequently used with them.' Carter and McCarthy (2006), for example, describe how computer-assisted research has shown that the pattern of about twenty verbs in English involves the verb being followed by the preposition *by* and an *-ing* clause, and that most of these verbs fall into two groups: one meaning 'start' or 'finish' and the other 'respond to' or 'compensate for' something. Carter and McCarthy (2006:8) note that 'Experienced users of English recognize such patterns intuitively but it is often only when computer analysis demonstrates the patterns across many examples of use that they are fully acknowledged.'

Another aspect of our changed understanding of the grammar/lexis relationship, supported by insights from corpus linguistics, and again raising issues regarding what to include in a description of grammar, is the growing recognition of the importance, in language acquisition and language use, of prefabricated or formulaic multi-word units. Lewis (1993), for example, refers to polywords (short phrases recurring frequently without variation), collocations and what he labels 'institutionalised expressions' (such as sentence heads, or even complete sentences), with the last of these performing a primarily pragmatic function. It has been pointed out (by, e.g., Pawley and Syder, 1983; Nattinger and DeCarrico, 1992) that prefabricated patterns of different sorts form a major part of everyday conversation. The use of such patterns promotes the fluency of spoken communication by removing the need to generate each utterance from scratch, thereby saving on the time required for planning.

Corpus linguistics has played an especially important role in revealing characteristics of spoken language. The analysis of spoken texts has revealed a number of distinctive features of the grammar of everyday conversation. Leech (2000), for example, notes the following characteristics of **spoken grammar**:

(a) loose, relatively unintegrated structure with a very wide-ranging use of independent non-clausal ('fragmentary') units;
(b) the inappropriateness of the *sentence* to the analysis of spoken grammar;
(c) simplicity of phrase structure (particularly of noun phrases);
(d) repetitive use of a restricted lexicogrammatical repertoire;
(e) grammatical features reflecting interactiveness and on-line processing constraints'

(Leech, 2000:676)

63

Carter and McCarthy (2006), discussing certain specific features of spoken grammar, argue that for some there is no appropriate metalanguage. For instance, they point to the role in spoken language of what they label 'headers' and 'tails': 'headers' referring to the fronting of a clause element in order to highlight or thematise it (*The white house on the corner, is that where she lives?*), and 'tails' referring to an element following the clause, often a full noun phrase clarifying the reference of a pronoun in the preceding clause (*He's amazingly clever, **that dog of theirs***) (Carter and McCarthy, 2006:193–4). Existing labels for such grammatical phenomena, which also occur in written English, are inappropriate for spoken grammar, according to Carter and McCarthy, because they use terms like 'left-' and 'right-dislocation': such terms 'are metaphors of the space on a typically western, written page. Spoken language exists in time, not space' (2006:193).

Insights into the spoken grammar of English are greatly enriching our understanding of the language and how it is actually used in spoken communication. At the same time, however, they have provoked debate among linguists, in particular regarding 'the differentness and sameness of spoken versus written grammar' (Leech, 2000:687). Some writers, according to Leech (2000), emphasise the differentness of spoken grammar, and the need for a totally different grammatical model from those traditionally applied to written language, while others (albeit acknowledging the marked differences of frequency in the way grammar is used in speech and writing) argue for the underlying sameness of spoken and written grammar. Insights from corpus linguistics also provoke debate among applied linguists, particularly about the extent to which such insights are of direct relevance to the teaching of language. The relevance of the findings from corpus-based research is clearly an issue with potential implications for L2 teachers. This will be discussed in the following section.

3.6 The implications for TLA

Given our present level of understanding of the processes of SLA, in particular as they relate to grammar, and of the nature and scope of grammar, what are the implications for the individual teacher's language awareness? Larsen-Freeman (2002:104) observes that 'teachers teach subject matter the way that they conceptualise it': as far as SLA theory and research are concerned, one of the main impacts upon the individual L2 teacher should therefore presumably be upon that teacher's subject-matter cognitions, prompting in particular a reconceptualisation of the objectives of form-focused instruction in light of what we now

know to be achievable in language pedagogy. It may be wise to be sceptical, but as teachers we need to be aware, and to adjust our views if the
evidence demands it. In the research referred to earlier, there is plenty of
evidence, for example, that learners do not acquire grammar in a simple
linear sequence, learning each grammatical feature perfectly, one at a
time. Instead, they learn numerous features imperfectly all at once.
Language acquisition, according to Nunan (1996:83), is an inherently
unstable, 'organic' process, 'characterised by backsliding and plateaux,
as well as by progressions'. Therefore, the inclusion of a systematically
organised structural component in a language curriculum (as in Ellis's
'parallel option' discussed above, for instance) can no longer be justified
in terms of enabling learners to achieve full and immediate control of the
targeted structure.

As Hinkel and Fotos (2002:6) note, 'Many teachers and researchers
currently regard grammar instruction as "consciousness raising".' The
implications for teachers subscribing to such a view are that form-
focused pedagogy is not employed in anticipation of instantly accurate
production of the linguistic features taught. As teachers, we know that,
with some learners and some features of form, immediately successful
learning of that kind may seem to happen some of the time. But as a
general aim it represents an unrealistic expectation. A more realistic goal,
in the view of many, is to ensure that learners are fully aware of the target
linguistic features in the input. Such awareness is seen as setting up the
potential for each learner to notice the gap between his/her own language
use and target-like forms, thereby promoting the restructuring of each
learner's internal grammar (or interlanguage) at a point when it is developmentally ready. Recognition that one of the main objectives of form-
focused instruction is raising learners' awareness of a particular
linguistic feature by means of 'input enhancement' (Sharwood Smith,
1991) implies a key role for the teacher: both the selection of appropriate ways to enhance input and the effectiveness with which the teacher
sets about the task of input enhancement will depend greatly on that
teacher's language awareness (see 2.3).

SLA research has also helped to clarify some of the processes that are
said to be involved in the acquisition of new language, such as restructuring (Richards, 2002). **Restructuring** is the term used by SLA
researchers to describe the process by which the reorganisation of each
learner's underlying and developing language system occurs. According
to Richards (2002:43), 'Restructuring is currently viewed as central to
the process of interlanguage development, accounting for the way in
which learners' grammatical systems show evidence of ongoing revision
and expansion rather than progression in a simple linear order.' As part
of an overall reconceptualisation of grammar as process rather than

65

product (or, more accurately, as process *and* product), the language-aware teacher needs to understand the nature of restructuring, to appreciate its importance and to be sensitive to the ways in which the process can be promoted (see Larsen-Freeman, 2003, for discussion of grammar as process and of 'grammaring'; see Thornbury, 2001a, for discussion of restructuring and suggested pedagogical strategies to promote it).

Another implication for TLA to be drawn from the discussion in this chapter is that thinking professional L2 teachers need to keep re-evaluating their conceptualisations of subject-matter knowledge itself. As we noted in 3.5, in relation to grammar, the present-day language-aware teacher needs to take account of insights regarding, for instance, the interrelationship between grammar, lexis and discourse, and information about language use emerging from work in corpus linguistics. However, insights such as those to be found in corpus-based descriptions of language should not be absorbed uncritically into pedagogic practice. As Widdowson (1991:20–1) observes: 'Language prescriptions for the inducement of learning cannot be based on a database. They cannot be modeled on the description of externalised language, the frequency profiles of text analysis. Such analysis provides us with facts, hitherto unknown, or ignored, but they do not of themselves carry any guarantee of pedagogic relevance.'

The new thinking on grammar arising as a result of corpus-based research in fact raises major issues of debate for teachers of language. For instance, in relation to spoken grammar and L2 English:

- Does the spoken grammar of English need to be taught as a separate topic, in addition to the written grammar?
- To what extent is it useful or feasible to try to teach learners of L2 English to use 'headers' and 'tails', or other common features of speech such as 'vague language' (for instance, *sort of, stuff, thing, whatsit*) and fillers (such as *er* and *erm*)?
- To what extent are features typical of English spoken grammar found in the spoken variety of other languages, particularly the L1 of the learner(s)? If they are found across languages, is it necessary to teach such features of spoken English?

These and related issues all need to be considered very carefully by the language-aware teacher. The form-focused pedagogical interventions, both planned and spontaneous, of each L2 teacher will be influenced by the extent to which that teacher has a critical awareness and an understanding of insights and issues concerning language(s) in general, the target language in particular and the ways in which language is acquired, and by the stance which the teacher adopts as a result of that (lack of) awareness and understanding.

If the teacher is language-aware, then (as suggested above) these understandings and stances will regularly evolve as a result of on-going reflection and re-evaluation. The quality of each teacher's pedagogical interventions will be heavily dependent on the nature of that teacher's cognitions about subject matter (including those just mentioned), as well as on the factors of teacher attitude outlined in 2.6. In practice, however, as noted previously, the way in which any teacher responds to these issues may be significantly constrained by the contextual factors outlined in 2.6 (Figure 3), including the textbook(s) available for the teacher's use. The impact of textbooks and teaching materials upon the procedural dimension of TLA is among the issues discussed in Chapter 5.

3.7 Conclusion

The present chapter has endeavoured to outline some of the major issues relating to grammar and its role in L2 pedagogy. In the course of the discussion, we have noted the following:

- The debate about the importance of grammar in language teaching and the role of form-focused instruction has a long history; although the nature of the arguments has evolved over the centuries, the debate has gone on;
- In recent years, that debate has been informed by the evidence from an ever-increasing number of SLA research studies;
- The findings of those studies seem to confirm that form-focused instruction is of value; however, it has been widely acknowledged that the nature and the purpose of that form-focused instruction need to be re-evaluated in the light of SLA theory and research;
- Traditional views about the scope of grammar have been challenged by the findings of research that has enhanced our understanding both of the interrelationship between lexis, grammar and discourse, and of the differences and similarities between spoken and written grammar;
- Although SLA theory and research represent only one source of insights for the L2 teacher, thinking professional teachers need to be aware of developments in that area, since their understandings of these developments will affect their cognitions about subject matter, which form a central part of their TLA, potentially exerting a significant influence upon the quality of teachers' form-focused pedagogical interventions (e.g., when mediating input);
- Language-aware teachers need to re-evaluate, and to keep re-evaluating, their personal conceptualisations of subject-matter knowledge to take account of new developments and new insights;

in the case of grammar, these include advances in our understanding of spoken grammar, and of the relationship between lexis, grammar and discourse.

The next chapter focuses on TLA and teachers' subject-matter cognitions.

Questions for discussion and reflection

1) What is your (a) personal experience and (b) opinion of P-P-P as a model of language teaching? Do you ever employ a P-P-P approach in your own classroom? If so, what is your rationale for doing so?
2) What do you understand by the terms 'communicative' and 'task-based'? Would you use either term to describe the approach you are expected to employ in your institution? If so, would you describe that approach as a 'weak' or a 'strong' form of CLT/TBLT? Why? Does your personal approach in the classroom conform to the expectations of your institution? If not, why not?
3) What, in your view, are the potential benefits and drawbacks *for the learner* of naturalistic approaches to language learning (such as immersion)? How feasible are such approaches in your own teaching context?
4) Ellis (2002; 2003) proposes a language curriculum with two components: one consisting of communicative tasks, and the other of form-focused tasks (see pp. 59–60). He suggests that elementary students should focus entirely on communicative tasks, with form-focused tasks being introduced only at intermediate level. What is your opinion of (a) Ellis's overall model, and (b) his proposal that form-focused tasks should not be introduced until the intermediate stage?
5) What do you think are the pedagogical implications of our increased understanding of spoken grammar?
   - Should spoken grammar be taught at all?
   - If spoken grammar is taught, should it be dealt with separately? Or should it be treated as an integral part of the grammar of the language?
   - To what extent is it useful or feasible to try to teach learners of L2 English to use 'headers' and 'tails', or other common features of speech such as 'vague language' and fillers?

- Are such features of English spoken grammar found in the spoken variety of the L1(s) of your student(s)? If so, do such features of spoken English need to be taught in the classroom?

6) 'There is plenty of evidence . . . that learners do not acquire grammar in a simple linear sequence' (p. 65). How far does this statement reflect experiences you may have had as a language teacher and/or learner?

4 TLA and teachers' subject-matter cognitions

4.1 Introduction

This chapter and the next return to issues initially raised in Chapter 2. In that chapter, I outlined a model of TLA (Figure 1), which underpins the discussion in the rest of the book. The selection of the terminology used in that model and defined in Chapter 2 was intended to make some specific points, as, for example, in the use of the phrase 'subject-matter **cognitions**' instead of just 'subject-matter **knowledge**'. In Chapter 2, the use of 'cognitions' in preference to 'knowledge' was explained as an attempt to convey the closeness of the relationship between teacher knowledge and teacher beliefs. In other words, while subject-matter knowledge may constitute the core of TLA, any teacher's knowledge is inevitably bound up with beliefs about that subject matter and, for example, how it should or can be taught and learned in a given context.

The present chapter focuses on L2 teachers' subject-matter cognitions, and in particular their feelings, beliefs and understandings about subject matter. It begins by examining teacher cognitions, and the relationship between knowledge and beliefs. This is followed by a brief review of research on L2 teacher cognitions. The discussion then moves on to consider the relationship between teachers' subject-matter cognitions and their pedagogical practice. Finally, in what constitutes the major part of the chapter, the nature of such associations is explored further via a case study of a particular group of teachers, their content-related beliefs, feelings and understandings with specific reference to grammar, and the evolution of their subject-matter cognitions. According to the argument in Chapter 2, the quality, extent and sophistication of a teacher's cognitions about subject matter are perhaps the most significant of the professional factors influencing the operation of TLA in pedagogical practice. The present chapter therefore presents essential background to the discussion of TLA and pedagogical practice in the following chapter.

4.2 Teacher cognitions: beliefs and knowledge

When talking about teacher cognitions, the focus is on teachers' 'mental lives', or what Freeman (2002) describes as the 'hidden side' of teaching. Freeman speaks of the critical importance of teacher thinking and of teachers' 'mental lives' in shaping effective teaching and learning (2002:2). Tsui (2003:61), acknowledging the overlap between beliefs and knowledge, speaks of the powerful influence on pedagogical practice of 'conceptions of learning and teaching'. Tsui subsumes under that heading teachers' metaphors, images, beliefs, assumptions and values. Conceptions of subject matter itself might usefully be added to that list, given that teacher cognitions relevant to TLA include beliefs and assumptions about the language itself (e.g., whether the Present Progressive is regarded as a tense or as a combination of tense and aspect), as well as how it is taught and learned.

Teacher thinking has been a major research area in general education for nearly three decades (see, e.g., the review articles by Shavelson and Stern, 1981; Clark and Peterson, 1986; and more recently Freeman, 2002; as well as such works as Elbaz, 1983; Calderhead, 1987; Lowyck and Clark, 1989; Kagan, 1992; Pajares, 1992; and Fang, 1996). It has only been in the past ten years or so, however, that teacher thinking has become an area of interest to researchers in language education (see, e.g., Palfreyman, 1993; Johnson, 1994; Richards, 1996; Woods, 1996; Golombek, 1998; Borg, 1998; 1999a; 1999b; Breen et al., 2001; and Tsui, 2003. See also the overviews of such research in Borg, 2003a; 2003b; 2006; and the papers in Bartels, 2005a).

In the late seventies, Fenstermacher (1979) predicted that teacher beliefs would become a major focus of research into teacher effectiveness, and indeed much of the research on teacher thinking has set out to examine the influence of teachers' beliefs on their pedagogical practice. However, as Pajares (1992) has pointed out, teachers' beliefs do not lend themselves easily to empirical investigation, partly because of problems of definition. One of the sources of difficulty for researchers has been the distinction between beliefs and knowledge. Although beliefs are based on evaluation and judgement, and knowledge on objective fact, the two are intertwined: beliefs underlie both declarative and procedural knowledge (Pajares, 1992:312–13).

Several researchers have drawn attention to the close interrelationship of beliefs, knowledge and also experience in influencing pedagogical practice. Elbaz (1983:134), for example, in outlining her conception of a teacher's practical knowledge, emphasises the role of 'the teacher's feelings, values, needs and beliefs' in helping the teacher to integrate experiential and theoretical knowledge and orient these to his/her practical situation. Connelly and Clandinin (1985) develop this concept of practical knowledge by coining the term 'personal practical knowledge'. Clandinin's (1992) definition of personal practical knowledge is illustrative of the extent to which belief, knowledge, experience, context and reflection are seen to be interrelated: 'It is knowledge that reflects the individual's prior knowledge and acknowledges the contextual nature of that teacher's knowledge. It is a kind of knowledge carved out of, and shaped by, situations; knowledge that is constructed and reconstructed as we live out our stories and retell and relive them through processes of reflection' (Clandinin, 1992:125).

4.3 L2 teacher cognitions

In L2 teaching, the importance of teacher beliefs has been discussed by a number of researchers (see, e.g., Richards, 1996; Woods, 1996; Borg, 1998; 1999a; 1999b; Breen et al., 2001; Tsui, 2003). Woods's case studies illustrate both the powerful effects of teacher beliefs upon practice, and also the close interrelationship of beliefs and knowledge. The closeness of this relationship leads Woods (1996:184–212) to talk of an *integrated* network of beliefs, assumptions and knowledge, which he labels BAK.

Richards (see, e.g., Richards, 1996) develops the concept of teacher maxims: rational principles for professional behaviour. According to Richards (1996:284), these maxims derive from teachers' belief systems 'founded on the goals, values, and beliefs teachers hold in relation to the content and process of teaching and their understanding of the system in which they work and their roles within it. These beliefs and values serve as the background to much of the teachers' decision making and action and hence constitute what has been termed the *culture of teaching*.' Breen et al. (2001) also focus on L2 teachers' guiding principles and examine the link between those principles and pedagogical practice. Their study reveals diversity in principle and practice among a group of 18 teachers, while suggesting a pattern in the links between principles and practices.

Meanwhile, Borg's work (e.g., 1998; 1999a; 1999b) relates specifically to the linguistic dimension of the L2 teacher's belief system, showing the extent to which teachers' decisions about grammar teaching may be shaped by their cognitions and experiences and the context in which they work. Borg (2005) examines the subject-matter cognitions of two teachers, the influences on the development of those cognitions and the contrasting ways in which each teacher's cognitions impact on that teacher's grammar teaching practices. Borg's 2003 papers (2003a; 2003b) and his 2006 book survey the work of others in the field. Borg (2003a) reviews research on teacher cognition in L2 teaching, the vast majority of which has been published since 1996. Borg (2003b) focuses specifically on teacher cognition in grammar teaching, in the L1 as well as L2 contexts. Borg (2006) provides a comprehensive discussion of research on language/teacher cognition, focusing specifically on teachers' cognitions in teaching grammar, reading and writing.

Tsui (2003) explores the nature of expertise in teaching, via case studies of four Hong Kong teachers of secondary English, undertaken over a one-year period. Each of the four case studies provides a detailed analysis of how the teacher's personal theories, knowledge, experience and goals have shaped her classroom practices and influenced her development towards expertise. Tsui also lays emphasis on the 'situated' nature of teacher cognitions, and the fact that such cognitions are jointly constituted by the teacher's specific context of work and how that teacher understands and responds to the work context. Tsui refers to Benner, Tanner and Chesla's (1996) argument that contexts present 'situated possibilities' rather than totally determining or constraining what one can do. For Tsui, therein lies the critical difference between the expert teacher and the non-expert teachers in her study: 'how they interact with their specific contexts of work, of which they are a part, and how they see the possibilities that can be opened up for the effective achievement of instructional objectives' (2003:254).

4.4 TLA, subject-matter cognitions and pedagogical practice

One domain of teacher thinking which has been the focus of much attention in recent years is subject-matter knowledge, and its link with pedagogy. As discussed in Chapter 2, the concept of pedagogical content knowledge (PCK) was coined by Shulman to account for the uniqueness of the professional understanding of teachers which informs their pedagogical practice, 'that special amalgam of content and pedagogy that is uniquely the province of teachers, their own special form of professional understanding' (1987:8), and it has become 'a commonly accepted construct in the educational lexicon' (Gess-Newsome, 1999:4). More recently, Turner-Bisset (1999; 2001) has proposed a model of PCK as an amalgam of all the interacting knowledge bases that underpin expert teaching, including beliefs about the subject. As noted previously, my own conceptualisation of TLA sees it as one of the key knowledge bases of the L2 teacher, which interacts with the other knowledge bases and blends with them in acts of expert teaching.

Subject-matter cognitions are seen as being at the core of that model of TLA. These subject-matter cognitions interrelate with each other to influence the L2 teacher's handling of grammar. Knowledge of subject matter (or the limitations of that knowledge) will, of course, play a central role in the teacher's thinking and decision-making, as noted in Chapter 2. However, that knowledge and the way it is deployed will be bound up with a number of closely related cognitions, such as that teacher's personal feelings about grammar and grammar pedagogy (e.g., interest and confidence); perceptions of students' feelings about grammar; understandings of the role of grammar in communication, and of its significance in L2 acquisition and formal instruction; awareness of options in the handling of grammar in formal instruction; understandings of the expectations of stakeholders (for instance, the school, students, parents) in relation to grammar and grammar pedagogy; and the teacher's personal response to those expectations. A number of these cognitions are clearly linked to some of the broader aspects of PCK as shown in Chapter 2, Figure 1, such as knowledge of contexts, curriculum and knowledge of pedagogy. At the same time, however, they are all intimately concerned with subject matter, and they have therefore been assigned a central place in my conceptualisation of TLA under the single heading 'subject-matter cognitions'.

In the present discussion, knowledge, beliefs, feelings and understandings are therefore seen as a single entity: knowledge and beliefs refer to cognitive responses (i.e. factual knowledge, and views both of how things are and how they should be), feelings refer to affective responses, while content-related understandings of, for instance, contextual and learner factors are seen as interacting with and informing both sets of responses. In highlighting the importance of these cognitions to an understanding of TLA and how it operates in teachers' professional lives, my position is not a deterministic one, where teachers' beliefs might be seen as causing them to behave in particular ways in the classroom. Research has shown (see, e.g., Basturkmen, Loewen and Ellis, 2004) that teachers' classroom behaviour does not necessarily reflect their stated beliefs, particularly as they react spontaneously to unanticipated incidents in a lesson. However, it seems logical to assume that there is potentially some kind of association between teachers' cognitions and what those teachers cause to happen in their classrooms. My view therefore is that, in order to understand teachers' pedagogical practice, it is necessary to have a sense of their beliefs, feelings and understandings, since these form part of teacher awareness, or awarenesses (see Marton, 1994), shedding light on how teachers experience their professional world.

4.5 TLA and subject-matter cognitions: a case study

In this section, the subject-matter cognitions of a specific group of teachers are discussed. I begin by outlining the context in which these teachers are working. I then comment briefly on the subject-matter knowledge of those teachers, before focusing on their beliefs, feelings and understandings about subject matter, as revealed in interviews, in their writing and in their actual classroom practice. Their beliefs, feelings and understandings are explored in relation to four themes: feelings about grammar (both the teachers' feelings, and also their perceptions of their students' feelings); the teachers' views about the kind of grammar knowledge needed by Hong Kong secondary school students; their approaches to grammar pedagogy; and the extent to which they believed their pedagogical practice had been influenced by Communicative Language Teaching (CLT). I then discuss the relationship between these cognitions and pedagogical practice, before reporting on the evolution (over a seven-year period) of the subject-matter cognitions of a small sub-group of these teachers.

4.5.1 The context

The context framing these teacher cognitions is the Hong Kong secondary school classroom. The 17 teachers were all non-native speakers of English, teaching English to secondary-age students in Hong Kong. They were graduates (not necessarily of English), with an average of three years' full-time teaching experience. When these data were gathered, they were at or near the beginning of a two-year part-time course of initial professional training, the Postgraduate Certificate in Education (PCEd) at the University of Hong Kong, as English Majors. Post-experience initial teacher education has been a common phenomenon for a long time in Hong Kong across all subjects of the curriculum, but especially for English, with many secondary school teachers of the subject having entered the profession without a teaching qualification, or even a relevant first degree.

The English Language curriculum for Hong Kong secondary schools has been designed in accordance with CLT principles for more than 20 years. The 1983 curriculum document (Curriculum Development Committee, 1983) was the first to shift from a structural towards a more communicative focus. Since 1999 the English Language curriculum has espoused task-based learning (see, e.g., CDC, 1999). Although practices vary, most secondary schools have ended up adopting a 'very weak' version of CLT/TBLT, in which the explicit teaching of grammar continues to play a significant role, as confirmed by the 17 teachers in this case study. Evans (1996) examines the implementation of CLT in Hong Kong's English Language classrooms.

4.5.2 Knowledge of subject matter

The subject-matter knowledge of these teachers was measured by means of two tests: one consisting of 50 multiple-choice (M/C) items focusing on vocabulary and usage, the other a 60-item test of explicit knowledge of grammar and grammatical terminology (the 'Language Awareness' or LA test). The Appendix contains further information about the second of these two tests.

Among the 17 teachers, there was a very wide range of levels: from 50% to 94% on the M/C test, and from 51% to 90% on the LA test. The mean score of 68% on the M/C test might be considered reasonably good: it compares, for example, with a mean of 53.5% for a group of 187 teachers with similar profiles of qualifications, experience and teaching context (see Andrews, 1999b). There were, however, a number of the group with M/C percentage scores in the fifties who also performed less than satisfactorily on a pedagogically related test of writing, seeming to confirm that there might be serious limitations to the language competence underpinning their communicative language ability. Although most of these teachers achieved similar levels of performance on the two tests, there were four cases in which the gap was over 20 percentage points (two teachers scoring higher on the M/C test and two on the LA test).

As for these teachers' explicit knowledge of grammar and grammatical terminology, their overall mean score on the LA test was 71.1%. Again this might be considered quite good, if compared with the mean for the group of 187 teachers referred to above (see Andrews, 1999b), which was 65%, and even more so if compared with the performance of a group of prospective teachers (all English native speakers) with a background of English Studies, who achieved a mean of 43.2% (see Andrews, 1999c). However, the performance of the 17 Hong Kong teachers on the cognitively most demanding part of the LA test, a task in which they had to explain their correction of 15 sentences containing grammatical errors, was generally poor, with a mean of only 43.1%. Given that the task did not involve any complex or obscure rules of grammar, and that explanation typically forms part of classroom practice in Hong Kong secondary schools, such a level of performance among serving teachers has to be a cause for concern.

In the discussion of these teachers' pedagogical practice, and the procedural dimension of their TLA, in this chapter and the next, the potential influence of their knowledge of language and their knowledge about language should be borne in mind.

4.5.3 Feelings about grammar

According to most of these teachers, the vast majority of their students have a strongly negative view of grammar. To quote one of them: 'Grammar has always been a nightmare for Chinese students, especially when they think of those technical terms and the thickness of their grammar textbook' (Maggie). Maggie's dislike of grammar may run unusually deep, but 13 of the 17 teachers reported strongly negative reactions to grammar among their students. The majority of the teachers (9 out of 17) appeared to feel as unenthusiastic about teaching grammar as their students did about studying it.

These feelings of boredom (among student and teacher alike) seemed to be associated with an approach to grammar teaching typically consisting of deductive presentation followed by mechanical practice exercises. Clara, for example, described her students' response to this style of presentation as follows: 'if we just follow the books . . . and then tell them the rules that they have to follow it's very boring, and the students won't want to listen to you', while Flora confirmed the unpopularity of the exercises: 'they said they actually detest these grammar exercises, and I must say I find them very boring, tedious as well'.

More than a quarter of these teachers revealed a marked lack of confidence in their ability to handle grammar adequately. Rose, for example, whose difficulties we encountered in Chapter 2, admitted: 'Actually I am very afraid of grammar. I think . . . it was influenced by the secondary school. So I am afraid to teach grammar to my students, too.' Maggie, too, confessed that 'I'm not much of a grammar person' and gave a graphic description of her fears of teaching the infinitive again after her previous experience two years earlier:

> I can foresee when I get into infinitive, that's where I got a
> trouble . . . because two years ago, also Form 4, when we get to
> infinitive, we're dragging on for the whole two weeks, and we
> don't know what we're doing . . . I've no idea what, how to teach
> them, and they've no idea what infinitive is. But . . . when I get
> into infinitive I get so nervous. They don't understand it, I don't
> understand it, and I don't know how to teach it . . . we just don't
> have any way of connecting to each other at all. So . . . that's
> my fear.

In some cases, this lack of confidence appeared to be reinforced by a sense of inadequacy in dealing with something as important as grammar: 'I'm always afraid that my students don't understand grammar . . . I think it's very challenging teaching grammar . . . sometimes I'm afraid that they feel bored, and I know that they must know that grammar, otherwise they don't know that language' (Agnes). In Agnes's case, when her students continued to make mistakes with grammar items she had taught, her lack of confidence led her to blame her own teaching, rather than accepting (as proponents of CLT, for instance, would assert) that error is an inevitable part of L2 acquisition: 'when I mark their compositions, that mistake appear again. I've taught this grammar, so how can the mistake come again? So I blame myself . . . That lesson is not effective, they make the same mistakes in the composition.'

4.5.4 Beliefs about the grammar knowledge needed by Hong Kong students

One reason why a number of these teachers were so worried about their competence in handling grammar was that the great majority of them saw grammar as playing a highly important role for Hong Kong students. Diana, for example, suggested that grammar underpins communicative ability in all four language skills: 'If one wants to communicate well with others, one must be able to master the four skills: writing, reading, listening and speaking. All these four skills require knowledge of grammar.'

Shirley spoke for the small number of the 17 teachers with a relatively sophisticated understanding of CLT when she advocated a change of approach to grammar rather than a drastic diminution of its role: 'Grammar definitely has a role to play in teaching and learning English. But . . . I think we should kind of teach grammar in a communicative setting . . . Instead of teaching grammatical items in isolation . . . we should treat the grammatical items in meaningful contexts.'

Not all the teachers were wholeheartedly committed to the importance of grammar in L2 teaching. However, even Maggie acknowledged a supporting role for grammar: 'if you think of language as a way of communicating . . . the only important point will be for people to understand you and you to understand people. Grammar helps you. But it's not necessarily the main focus, and should not be the main focus of . . . the learning part.'

When considering whether their students' primary need was for implicit or explicit knowledge of grammar, all 17 of these teachers seemed to agree that the former – practical control of grammar for communicative purposes – is of greater importance. According to Flora, for instance: 'To be able to use the language is more important than being a hundred percent grammatically correct all the time . . . to be able to communicate . . . as long as they're expressing themselves, and I understand what they're trying to say . . .', although, in common with one or two others, she expressed a somewhat wistful longing for accuracy as well as fluency: '. . . but obviously it would be nicer if they were a hundred percent accurate as well'.

There was rather more disagreement about the usefulness of explicit grammar knowledge for L2 learners, particularly about its impact upon the development of the implicit knowledge which underpins effective communication (the so-called 'interface' issue referred to in Chapters 1 and 3). Seven of the teachers expressed the belief that explicit knowledge has a direct impact on the development of practical control of grammar. For example, Karen reported: 'I remember some days ago I told my students . . . OK you're learning the item . . . but I hope that later, when you understand this, when you can handle this, then . . . the usage of this item . . . can become your instinct and you can use it naturally.'

Another seven (including Maggie) saw a more limited role for explicit knowledge, with students needing only what one of the teachers, Tony, referred to as 'the basics'. According to Tony, 'they need [explicit knowledge] but not that deep. You know, like they don't need so difficult ones like . . . past perfect continuous tense. . . They need the basics.'

Of the other three teachers, one expressed doubts about the value of explicit knowledge of grammar: 'of course they need to have a practical control of it . . . the implicit knowledge . . . "know" in that sense, yes. But whether they need to have . . . explicit knowledge, conscious knowledge . . . maybe that helps to a certain extent, I'm not sure . . . but maybe they don't really need that' (Shirley). One of the two remaining teachers saw the primary purpose of supplying explicit knowledge of grammar as being to serve learners' needs for reassurance that their English lessons actually had some serious content: 'just the purpose of reassuring that . . . they have learned something about English' (Eva), while the other linked students' need for explicit grammar knowledge with the specific demands of written exams: 'the student here in Hong Kong . . . they have to prepare for the compo examination so they need to know grammar well. They know to write good sentences' (Hilda).

4.5.5 Approaches to grammar pedagogy

As suggested by their previous responses, the predominant approach to grammar pedagogy adopted by these teachers was deductive. Ten of the 17 described their accustomed style of teaching in similar ways. Pearl, for instance, said that in a typical grammar lesson with her Secondary 1 students (11- to 12-year-olds) she would: 'explain the structure and then ask them to do exercise. And I will ask them questions to see whether they understand me or not', while Diana said that with her Secondary 3 class (13- to 14-year-olds) she would usually: 'spend say ten minutes explaining the rules . . . the form or the use of that special grammar item . . . and then after that maybe I give them some exercise to do, or if possible I will give them some games to play . . . Of course the games have . . . to be related . . . to the grammar items they learn.'

Not all of these teachers espoused a deductive style of grammar teaching, however. Seven out of the 17 described approaches to grammar pedagogy that were rather more inductive in style (inductive referring here to an approach favouring, for example, discovery learning). Wendy, for example, spoke of her handling of comparative adjectives in the previous day's Secondary 1 class as follows:

> I drew two boxes on the board, one big one small . . . I just
> told them well, this is box A and this is box B, and then I asked them
> . . . in a sentence describe their sizes, and compare the sizes. They
> did it very well . . . so then I put the price on the boxes and they also
> did it very well. And then I asked them 'Why would you put "-er"
> after "big", and why wouldn't you put "-er" after "expensive"?'
> And then they were able to tell me the explanation too.

Among the seven more inductive teachers (according to their interview descriptions) there were two who had recently moved out of mainstream secondary school teaching and into a sixth-form technical institute (with students normally ranging between 16 and 19 years old), where the prevailing culture appeared to favour a more communicative (or 'task-based') approach to teaching and learning. Joanna, for example, contrasted her former secondary school approach: 'Just explain the rules, and then get them to do the exercises. No games, no interaction' with her more inductive technical institute approach: 'I will get my students to look at a passage which was written in passives . . . and then ask them to explain to me why the passive has to be used, why not active. What's the purpose, or what are the advantages . . . what are the good reasons for using passive?' When asked to explain her change of approach, she answered as follows: 'For what reason? I don't know . . . just something automatic. I think now I don't believe in explanation . . . I may have changed my view towards language teaching, or grammar teaching. Or . . . just because of the fact that I'm now in a different situation.'

Joanna's comments illustrate the dynamic and situated nature of teacher cognitions. Although teachers' beliefs and attitudes may at times appear resistant to change, for instance in response to curricular innovations, their beliefs at any given time have been moulded by a lifetime's experience of learning and teaching and have at least the potential for being restructured as a result of new experiences. This is evidently the case with Joanna, who was able to recognise the influence of context on the evolution of her cognitions.

Whatever the preferred style of presentation, inductive or deductive, grammar learning was treated by all 15 mainstream secondary school teachers as a linear process of accumulating grammatical entities. For instance, Karen, the member of this group with probably the strongest preference for a deductive approach, described as follows her application of this step-by-step approach to the teaching of tenses with her Secondary

4 class (14- to 15-year-olds): 'for example, for tenses . . . I split it into some parts . . . into two to three weeks . . . and then maybe one day for present, present perfect, present perfect continuous. And then I went to passive form . . . And next week again OK we go to past tense.'

The two teachers now working in technical institutes, Shirley and Joanna, reported a rather different approach: 'We will teach grammar . . . only if a particular grammar point is, or can be, incorporated into a certain function . . . which is trade related' (Shirley). According to Shirley, this was the approach embodied in the technical institute syllabus: 'in our syllabus . . . it is stated that a grammar point should not be dealt with . . . in isolation. It has to be incorporated in meaningful context.'

Several of the mainstream secondary school teachers indicated that they would also prefer to be able to adopt a different approach to grammar pedagogy. Benjamin, for example, having described his approach to grammar teaching as 'just like instant noodles . . . just feed them, and then have the response and do some evaluation', revealed that he would much prefer to deal with grammar more flexibly, as it arose, in response to students' needs: 'I would like to do it really more freely . . . when it is needed . . . when the student have inquiries and they're curious to learn something and then I can teach them all right, but it is not necessary to be fixed.'

A number of the teachers mentioned factors which constrained the ways in which they could handle grammar. Eleven of the 15 mainstream secondary teachers referred to the impact of the public examinations, particularly in Secondary 4 and 5 (leading to the Hong Kong Certificate of Education in English exam, taken at the end of Secondary 5) and Secondary 6 and 7 (in preparation for the Use of English Advanced Supplementary level exam taken at the end of Secondary 7). Hilda, for example, said that she could not teach in the way she would wish with either Secondary 5 or Secondary 6, partly because of student expectations: 'So for Form 5 I have to follow the syllabus, give them exam practice paper . . . and Form 6 too . . . cos you have to prepare them for the examination. And they like to do exam practice paper. You know, if you tell them to do something else, they think it's meaningless. So you have to cater for their needs.'

These teachers discussed several other constraints. The demands of a rigid and overcrowded syllabus, for example, were mentioned by 9 of the 15 mainstream secondary teachers. Flora described the limits placed on her teaching at Secondary 3: 'we have to . . . follow our teaching schedule, and we have to have so many dictations . . . and per chapter we cover so many grammar exercises'. In a number of cases, the inflexible syllabus appeared to be enforced by an equally inflexible Panel Chairperson (Head of Department): 'I don't have much choice in doing what kind of things that we have to do in class because the Panel Chairman force us to do grammar' (Maggie).

4.5.6 CLT and pedagogical practice

Since the early 1980s, as noted earlier, the official primary and secondary English syllabuses in Hong Kong have been designed in accordance with CLT principles. However, the analysis of what the 17 interviewees said about their teaching suggests that the impact of CLT has been fairly superficial, although certain communicative principles and practices might have been absorbed into the pedagogical styles and repertoires of a sizeable minority.

Several of these teachers seemed to have a very narrow view of CLT, perceiving it as being related primarily to oral activity. Hilda, for example, equated a communicative approach with teacher–student oral interaction: 'communicative approach . . . usually I consider it as an oral practice, you know . . . ask and answer'. Others appeared to have a somewhat broader conception of CLT. Of the 17, however, only Agnes seemed to recognise the application of 'communicative' to both productive and receptive skills: 'I think all sorts of skills . . . like speaking, listening . . . writing . . . all sorts of activities are communicative', although her responses did not make clear exactly what she understood by the term communicative.

About a third of the teachers discussed their practices in ways suggesting that they had, at least in part, adopted a communicative approach in their general teaching. Wendy, for example, described her 'task-based' approach, although it is noteworthy that she seemed to apply it only to the productive skills: 'Certainly communicative work is emphasised these days . . . we do a lot of tasks . . . activity with a purpose . . . artificial and natural . . . in which they get to do a lot of work, they need to produce . . . Interesting tasks because students . . . need to see what's in it for them . . . and they get their first-hand experience . . . they get to speak, write, or produce in whatever way . . . sentences.'

Johnson and Johnson (1998:69–72) describe five ways in which the standard form of communicative methodology represents an enrichment of its predecessors: the teaching of appropriateness; the central importance of message focus; the replication of psycholinguistic processes used in communication (such as top-down processing); the emphasis on risk-taking skills (in both production and reception); and the development of free practice techniques. In order to estimate the degree to which CLT principles had been absorbed by these teachers, it may be helpful to consider the extent to which each of these five characteristics was apparent in their descriptions of their pedagogical practices.

Partly, no doubt, through the influence of Hong Kong secondary school coursebooks (all of which in recent years have incorporated a functional-notional dimension within their multifaceted, now 'task-based'[1], syllabus framework), the teaching of appropriateness seemed to have taken root, at least to some extent. Diana, for example, noted the way in which textbooks encourage a focus on speech acts as well as grammatical structure: 'Nowadays . . . the grammar exercises in the textbooks, they try to be communicative . . . They will set a context . . . a situation for that exercise . . . and also some function . . . is it for greeting, or for what purpose?'

Message focus also seemed to have become part of the approach of at least some of the teachers. Eva, for instance, reported having made use of such activities, although her attempts to give tasks a personal message focus appeared to have been a source of considerable frustration: 'I'm discouraged to use activities in grammar lessons . . . because they're not sincere in the way they . . . make answers . . . they won't tell the truth . . . Maybe they don't want to share in this way . . . they find it's not natural to use English . . . to talk about something they find is quite personal.'

For the majority of the 17 teachers, however, there was a tendency for both message focus and risk-taking activities to be confined to those lessons set aside for exam-related oral practice. The addition of an oral component to the public exam taken in Hong Kong at the end of Secondary 7 (the Use of English, or UE) and the enhanced importance of the Secondary 5 oral exam (the HKCEE English exam) appeared to have had an impact on the attitudes and practices of all those with classes at Secondary 4 and above. As a result of these exam changes, all those working with upper forms had on their teaching schedule designated oral lessons in which (at least part of the time) they conducted free practice activities with a message focus, i.e. activities targeted at fluency rather than accuracy, where risk-taking was encouraged. For that reason, in such lessons the teachers all adopted a non-interventionist strategy in relation to grammatical errors: 'if you interfere into a group discussion, they get more conscious about the grammar rather than the content. But when you're doing the UE oral level, I think what the marker's more aware of is the content – are you discussing what you're asked to? – rather than every grammatical mistake you've made' (Maggie). As Maggie's comment makes clear, however, the adoption of communicative principles in these oral lessons tended to be motivated primarily by exam considerations rather than as part of any coherent overall pedagogical approach. This is confirmed by observation of several such

---

[1] Most of these coursebooks reflect what Ellis (2003) describes as 'task-supported' rather than 'task-based' language teaching.

lessons, where the communicative oral activities were all precise imitations of the public examination format.

Of Johnson and Johnson's five characteristics of 'standard' communicative methodology, the one least affecting the pedagogical practices of these teachers seemed to be replication of the psychological processes involved in communication. This was particularly the case with the receptive skills. Indeed, only one of the 17 (Agnes) made any overt connections between CLT and listening and reading.

4.5.7 Feelings, beliefs, understandings: the relationship with pedagogical practice

From the summaries and comments above, there seem to be discernible general patterns in the cognitions about subject matter of these 17 teachers. For instance, grammar teaching is seen as a boring necessity by all of them, a view apparently shared by their students. The feelings of boredom may be related at least in part to the conservative classroom practices employed by most of the teachers in their grammar teaching. Observation of at least two grammar-based classes conducted by each respondent showed that all of the mainstream secondary teachers in the group adopted an 'accumulated entities' approach to grammar pedagogy, following a conventional 'P-P-P' pattern. Typically (though not exclusively), their style of presentation was deductive, their practice activities were mechanical and form-focused, and production took the form of written composition. Many of them seemed to feel constrained to follow such a pattern because of rigid and overcrowded teaching syllabuses, the demands of the examinations and the characteristics of their students.

At the same time, some features of CLT did nevertheless seem to have been absorbed, into the belief system if not necessarily into pedagogical practice. There was recognition among all 17 teachers, for instance, that students need grammar primarily for communicative purposes, and that such grammar knowledge should embrace both form/usage and meaning/use. The impact of other features of CLT, however, seemed generally to be limited to specific parts of the syllabus, especially the oral lesson, where (largely in response to examination changes) spoken free practice activities with a message focus had become part of the repertoire.

These teachers' feelings, beliefs and understandings about grammar and grammar teaching within their context combine to inform what they consider to be necessary, feasible and desirable in relation to grammar pedagogy. These awarenesses (Marton, 1994) therefore have a close relationship with the ways in which teachers engage with grammar-related issues in their pedagogical practice, and hence with their TLA. Table 3 summarises the main patterns of teacher cognition (feeling, belief and

Table 3: Hong Kong secondary school teachers of English – their cognitions about grammar and associated pedagogical practice

Cognitions about grammar and grammar pedagogy		Associated pedagogical practice
Feelings about grammar and the teaching and learning of grammar	• Students perceived to consider grammar as boring, but important for exams.	• Perseverance with grammar-based lessons seen as an unpleasant necessity.
	• For teachers, it is also important (for exams, but also because of its central role in communication).	• Limited expectations, despite teacher efforts, of student enjoyment or achievement.
	• Grammar teaching is a source of frustration for many teachers.	
	• For some teachers, grammar and grammar teaching are a source of anxiety.	• Tendency to abdicate grammar responsibilities to textbooks or materials supplied by others.
Beliefs about grammar and the teaching and learning of grammar	• Students' primary need perceived as practical control of grammar for communication.	• Explicit, form-focused teaching, often involving deductive presentation and mechanical practice.
	• Students also thought to need explicit grammar knowledge to support the development of their implicit knowledge and to help them cope with exam demands.	
	• Grammar learning is a process of 'accumulating entities' (Rutherford, 1987).	
	• Grammar teaching needs to be 'active'/ 'creative'.	• Constraints limit scope for teachers' own contributions.
	BUT	
	• Teachers are constrained by the need to complete syllabus, prepare students for	• Students are 'spoon-fed' explicit grammar information in 'digestible' form, accompanied by

Table 3: (cont.)

Cognitions about grammar and grammar pedagogy		Associated pedagogical practice
	exams and cater for their limited ability/interest.	undemanding practice activities.
Under-standings about grammar and the teaching and learning of grammar	• Acceptance of students' need to know the function(s) associated with a grammar item, not just the form(s).	• Presentation generally focuses on meaning/use, as well as features of form.
	• Limited understanding of ways in which grammar might be practised.	• Practice activities are form-focused, rather than message-focused.
	• Limited familiarity with communicative tasks, which are generally not seen as linked to the acquisition of grammar.	• Task-related oral activity (with message focus and risk-taking) takes place only in the context of preparation for public oral exams.

understanding) reported above. It shows the associations between those cognitions about subject matter and pedagogical practices and highlights how the feelings, beliefs and understandings of these 17 teachers tend (with a certain degree of variation) to be associated with a narrowly form-focused style of L2 teaching.

One of the most striking aspects of these snapshots of teacher cognition is their contextually developed nature. Clandinin (1992) emphasises the importance of context and experience in shaping the development of the teacher's personal practical knowledge. The cognitions just described are the result of each teacher's accumulated experience of a variety of learning and teaching contexts: up to 13 years as a learner in primary and secondary classrooms; study at tertiary level and on professional development courses of various types and durations; and practical experience of the institutional and classroom contexts in which that individual has worked.

As the discussion above has indicated, among these 17 teachers there are patterns of response to context and experience, and there is also individuality of response. The summary in Table 3 provides examples of the former, with patterns of cognition and pedagogical practice seeming to be strongly influenced by the experience of teaching within the context of the Hong Kong secondary school. The discussion has shown how teachers are influenced by 'their understanding of the system in which they work and their roles within it' (Richards, 1996:284). The strength of those influences is perhaps most notable in the case of Maggie. Although in many ways the most individual and rebellious of the subjects, Maggie revealed, in both her comments and her practices, a large degree of conformity, albeit grudging, to the prevailing culture.

At the same time, there is individuality of response. Each teacher's beliefs and practices are influenced not only by the macro-culture of society (and such factors as the syllabus, the textbooks, the examination system, the expectations of parents and student characteristics), but also by the micro-culture of their particular institution. Many of the individual variations noted in the discussion above may be associated at least in part with differences in teaching conditions between schools. The strength of these macro- and micro-cultural influences is especially noteworthy in the case of Joanna, whose cognitions and practices regarding subject matter have undergone a marked change as a result of her move from a very traditional secondary school to a technical college and her recognition that the new working environment presents a different set of 'situated possibilities' (Benner, Tanner and Chesla, 1996).

The relationship between cognitions and practice noted in this case study in many ways reflects the findings reported in Breen et al. (2001). In their analysis of teachers' principles and classroom practices, Breen et al. (pp. 495–6) identify complex relationships between principles and practices: for instance, that a shared principle might be implemented through a diverse range of practices, while a common practice may be justified by a variety of principles. Similarly, among these 17 teachers, it was evident that a shared principle, such as that grammar learning is a process of 'accumulating entities', might be associated with a different set of practices for each teacher: the majority adopting a primarily deductive approach, others preferring to employ a more inductive approach, and each doing so in individual ways. It was also noted that a common practice, for example explicit form-focused presentation and practice of grammar, was justified by a range of principles: explicit knowledge of grammar supports the development of implicit knowledge; students need to be adequately prepared for their written examinations; students need to feel that they have learned something specific in a lesson. At the same time, it seemed that, as with Breen et al.'s subjects, 'despite individual diversity in the teachers' enacting of their role, *as a collective* there is an underlying and consistent pattern between the ways they think about their work and the ways in which they act in the language class' (2001:496).

4.5.8 *The evolution of subject-matter cognitions*

Further data were gathered about the subject-matter cognitions of three of these teachers seven years after the first data-collection exercise. All three teachers who took part in the follow-up study (Eva, Maggie and Tony) were among those who were less convinced about the value of explicit grammar knowledge for L2 learners. The aim of the study was to find out to what extent and in what ways L2 teachers' subject-matter cognitions develop over an extended period of time (see Andrews, 2006, for details of the study). The data from this follow-up study suggested that the grammar-related cognitions of these three teachers had actually altered very little. Their underlying beliefs about grammar pedagogy and the role of explicit grammar teaching seemed to be largely unchanged. The same was true of their explicit knowledge of grammar and grammar terminology, as measured by the 60-item LA test referred to in 4.5.2.

There were certain aspects of the subject-matter cognitions of these three teachers which had evolved in some ways. Both Maggie and Tony, for instance, now have less compartmentalised views of grammar, and an enhanced awareness of the role of grammar in discourse, while Eva and Tony seem to have a broader understanding of the methodological options for dealing with grammar. However, the evolution of their subject-matter cognitions appeared to have been uneven and rather limited, possibly because they had not actively sought to develop this aspect of their professional competence through further study, formal or informal. All three teachers have engaged in various forms of professional development in recent years (at the time of writing, Eva and Maggie are both enrolled on doctoral programmes), but none of them has opted to focus significantly on grammar in any of the courses they have taken. Such findings are consistent with those in other studies: that teacher learning in an area is dependent on a teacher investing time and effort in that specific area and actively seeking out related professional challenges (Tsui, 2003), and that those teachers who do not actively seek knowledge do not get it (Borg, 2005).

Perhaps the most noteworthy feature of the evolution of these teachers' subject-matter cognitions as revealed by the follow-up study is the importance of the teachers' interaction with context. Huberman (1993), among others, emphasises that context does not impact upon teacher development in a deterministic way. Instead, as Huberman (1993) points out, the process is interactive: individuals act on as well as adapt to their social environment. As noted earlier, Tsui (2003) makes a similar point when talking about the 'situated' nature of teacher knowledge. The individual variability of this interactive process was strongly evident in the follow-up study (Andrews, 2006). All three of the teachers have had to adapt to some extent to the conditions and expectations of their working environment. However, each one has responded to the work context in different ways.

Maggie and Eva, for instance, have both been pro-active in shaping their situational response and in working towards the achievement of a satisfactory compromise between their beliefs about language pedagogy and the constraints of the context. Maggie has achieved this by moving to a more academic and genuinely English-medium (EMI) school, and then negotiating for herself a timetable that keeps the need to focus on grammar to a minimum. Meanwhile, Eva, who is the Panel Chair (Head of the English Department) in the school to which she has moved, is taking advantage of her position to assign herself classes only with the most senior forms, where she feels she has the best chance of being able to teach in accordance with her principles.

Of the three, Tony is the one who has compromised the most with the expectations of his working environment. However, Tony's story is a little different from Maggie's and Eva's, in that it illustrates how teachers' thinking and practice may be influenced by events in their personal lives at least as much as by professional considerations. We shall therefore examine the case of Tony in more detail in 4.5.9.

4.5.9 Subject-matter cognitions and the context of teaching: the case of Tony

Tony teaches in a Chinese-medium co-educational secondary school in an industrial area of the New Territories. He joined the school after gaining one year's experience in a similar school in the same district.

When Tony started teaching, he had limited subject-matter knowledge (his first degree is in Social Sciences) and no pedagogical training. At that stage his ideas about teaching grammar: 'mostly came from the way I was taught in secondary school. I was modelling my English teacher at that time.' His approach focused on the transmission of grammar rules, followed by mechanical practice exercises.

This approach was not entirely consistent with Tony's own views of the best way to acquire languages: 'if we teach grammar, we just teach grammar only, then . . . we can't help the students . . . to learn English'. He taught like this because he was following instructions: 'I just follow . . . what I was told to do . . . If I can decide what I can teach, I will give them passages to read and just let them recognise grammar items.' He also found that this formulaic rule-driven approach to the teaching of grammar was initially popular with students, even though he personally doubted its value: 'to them it's quite important, because there's something they can study . . . the grammar . . . To them it's quite . . . helpful cos they can study for their exams. But to me, I don't think it's enough to teach them so many grammar items.'

However, the deficiencies of this rule-driven approach became increasingly apparent to Tony, partly because of the response of the students: 'They found that grammar was very difficult. It's a very difficult thing and then it's very boring. And I found that it's quite difficult for me to teach them, too. It's kind of boring just to tell them the forms and ask them to do exercises. So I started to question whether teaching grammar is the right way to help students to learn English.' As a result of such reflections, as Tony's awareness of the available options increased, he modified his approach, trying to reduce the focus on explicit grammar teaching and instead introducing tasks, tailored to a level that would suit the students in the school: 'I tried to teach less grammar. I used the lessons to ask them to read newspapers . . . and I encouraged students to borrow books from the library, and read story-books when they have spare time. And I started to organise a lot of activities during the lessons and tried to make students use the language forms in a more meaningful way.'

These changes met with mixed success, however. There was initial interest among the students, but Tony found it very tiring to prepare suitable tasks, and he also found it difficult to implement a more holistic, task-based approach to language teaching in a school where the assessment system still emphasised discrete-point testing of language items and where the Principal took a particularly keen interest in the public examination results. He has therefore reverted to a more grammar-based approach: 'I was exhausted. And I had no time to prepare some more tasks. So I just went back to the textbook, the grammar textbook, doing exercises.' According to Tony, 'I've been forced to change. I have to teach grammar, otherwise my students will fail. I will lose my job. It's a pity, right?'

Tony's re-adoption of a more grammar-focused approach to teaching has also taken place in the aftermath of an event in his life that has had a particularly significant impact on his development as a teacher. In May 2003, he was diagnosed as suffering from depression, and was obliged to take a long period of sick leave:

> I think it [my depression] is related to how I see myself. I always demand myself to do a lot of things, to try to be idealistic all the time, but that's not the reality. So I don't think it's the frustrations that I face in teaching that make me have the depression. Of course, it had some contributions . . . I mean the workload, the kind of frustrations when I see the HKCEE results, and the pressure from the Principal . . . all these will contribute to the pressure. But the underlying most important thing is not all these factors . . . it's how I see myself.

Tony thought about moving to another school during his sick leave, and was tempted by an offer elsewhere. But worries about the salary and the likelihood that the pressures would be just as great led him to stay in his present job, and to reappraise his whole approach to teaching: 'I become more relaxed, and teach what I was told to do. I do what I was told to do, teaching grammar, and helping students to get a pass in tests.' Tony has modified his teaching approach for very pragmatic reasons: 'The school will evaluate me in terms of what I have taught to the students. OK, if their results are not good enough, they will look at what I have taught. If I try to make something not according to their syllabus and everything screws up, that will be my responsibility. But if I have done what I was told to do, and their results are not good, then it's probably not my responsibility. So I was forced to change.'

Tony's understandings of grammar have broadened considerably during the past eight years. He now pays attention in his teaching to aspects of what he calls 'genre grammar', and he has more fully formed views of where grammar might fit into a more 'meaning-focused' task-based approach. However, his underlying views of grammar and its role in teaching have not changed fundamentally: he still sees the need for students to know 'the basics', supported by as much exposure to the language as possible.

Although Tony has now reverted to an explicitly form-focused approach, his handling of grammar in the classroom has evolved to some extent since his first years of teaching. He still describes his approach as 'chalk and talk', but he now gives the students a chance to talk as well and pushes them to take responsibility for their learning: 'In the past I do all the talking all the time. I make sentences on the blackboard and write down the other things. But now I will talk, give them the forms plus examples, and then I will ask them to make sentences, ask them to stand up, and give the sentence orally. That's the main difference. They have their turn to participate. They can use the language forms. They can try it out.'

4.6 Conclusion

In this chapter, we have examined the relationship between teachers' language awareness and their cognitions about subject matter. In the course of the discussion, we have noted the following:

- the importance of recognising how different aspects of teachers' thinking, or cognitions (most notably their knowledge, feelings, beliefs and understandings), intermesh;

- the potentially crucial influence that feelings, beliefs and understandings about subject matter (together with declarative knowledge) can exert on the procedural dimension of TLA through their impact upon the decisions teachers make about content-related issues in their pedagogical practice;
- the contextually developed nature of subject-matter cognitions and TLA, which was examined in relation to a group of teachers all working within the specific macro-context of Hong Kong;
- the interactive nature of the process of development of teachers' grammar-related cognitions, with individuals acting on as well as adapting to their working environment, as seen from the experiences of a small sub-group of the Hong Kong teachers;
- the close relationship (as illustrated by Tony's story) between the individual teacher's subject-matter cognitions, and that teacher's work environment and life experiences which both frame and help to shape those cognitions.

The following chapter examines the relationship between TLA and pedagogical practice, both in general and also in context, focusing on the teachers discussed in the present chapter.

Questions for discussion and reflection

1) Do you have any 'maxims' or 'guiding principles' which sum up aspects of your approach to the teaching and learning of language? If so, what are they? How did you acquire them?
2) How do your own students feel about grammar? Why do you think they have such feelings? What are your own feelings and beliefs about grammar?
3) To what extent have your own knowledge, feelings, beliefs and understandings about grammar evolved since you started teaching? What is the most significant change that you are aware of? What prompted that change?
4) To what extent do you think that the <u>development</u> of your cognitions about subject matter has been influenced by the <u>context(s)</u> in which you have (a) taught language or (b) learned language? Can you recall specific individuals, incidents or experiences within those contexts that have influenced your thinking about subject matter? How have they influenced you?
5) In the institution where you work, who are the key stakeholders? What are those stakeholders' expectations in relation to grammar and grammar pedagogy? To what extent and in what

---

ways is your own teaching influenced by your understandings of stakeholder expectations?

6) Tony's story demonstrates the potential importance of life experience in the development of teachers' cognitions, including their subject-matter cognitions. Are there experiences in your own life (out of school) which have had an impact on your thinking about teaching in general, and your handling of language content (especially grammar) in particular?

5 TLA and pedagogical practice

5.1 Introduction

The present chapter focuses on TLA in pedagogical practice, examining how the L2 teacher's language awareness both influences and is influenced by that teacher's engagement with the content of learning. The chapter begins with snapshots of various teachers' TLA and engagement with the content of learning, before moving on to considering the relationship between TLA and materials: to what extent do materials influence, determine or constrain TLA in pedagogical practice, and how far does TLA affect teachers' handling of materials?

As we have noted at various points so far, there is a crucial distinction between the two dimensions of TLA: the declarative dimension (the possession of subject-matter knowledge) and the procedural dimension ('knowledge-in-action'). In order for the L2 teacher's handling of the content of learning to be 'language-aware', that teacher needs to possess not only a certain level of knowledge of the language systems of the target language, but also those qualities (i.e. the 'awareness') that will enable the subject-matter knowledge base to be accessed easily and drawn upon appropriately and effectively in the act of teaching.

The relationship between TLA and the way teachers engage with the content of learning in the act of teaching is a complex one. That complexity is partly a reflection of the different interpretations associated with the word 'engagement'. The two relevant meanings in this case are (i) its neutral application to the act of engaging in or with something (i.e. 'involvement'), and (ii) its use with attitudinal connotations (to convey 'commitment' as opposed to 'detachment', for example). The attitudinal interpretation of 'engagement' highlights the 'macro' level of the relationship with TLA, and the general stance that the teacher takes towards form- (or formS-) focused teaching. With this interpretation, engagement is seen as affecting TLA, in that the application of TLA in pedagogical practice may be significantly influenced by the extent to which the teacher seriously engages with content-related issues in the classroom at all, and by the relative importance the teacher gives to the language focus of the lesson rather than to questions of methodology, classroom organisation and student responsiveness. The neutral interpretation, on the

94

other hand, focuses attention on the 'micro' level of the teacher's handling of language at every stage of the act of teaching. With this neutral interpretation, the direction of the relationship is reversed: in so far as the teacher does engage with content-related issues, the quality of that engagement, in whatever form it takes, will potentially be affected to a large extent by the TLA of that teacher.

Table 4 illustrates some of the aspects of enactment of the curriculum that may be affected by this interplay between TLA and the teacher's

Table 4: Engagement with the content of learning and enactment of the curriculum

---

1. **General priorities and strategies**
    (a) *Priority given to language issues in planning*
        - What is the teacher's major focus in planning?
            - Methodology?
            - Classroom organisation?
            - Language?
        - Does the teacher give attention to language issues in, e.g., skills lessons?
    (b) *Strategies for dealing with challenges to subject-matter knowledge*
        - Does the teacher engage with such challenges, or seek to avoid them?
        - Does the teacher attempt to fill gaps in his/her own subject-matter knowledge? If so, how?

2. **Pre- and post-lesson thinking about language content**
    (a) *Pre-lesson*
        - How does the teacher approach the task of planning the handling of the language content of the lesson?
        - How far do the teacher's approaches take account of the learners?
    (b) *Post-lesson*
        - Do any of the teacher's post-lesson reflections focus on language content?
        - Do such reflections feed back into the subsequent handling of similar/related content?

3. **Dealing with 'input for learning' in the classroom**
    (a) *Teacher-produced input*
        - Does the teacher control his/her own language?
        - What use does the teacher make of metalanguage?
        - What explanations does the teacher provide?
        - How does the teacher respond to students' questions about language?
    (b) *Learner-produced input*
        - How does the teacher handle learner error?

---

engagement with the content of learning. This interplay will be explored further in the following sections.

5.2 TLA and engagement with the content of learning

Let us begin by looking at snapshots of two teachers, Shirley and Pearl, who have little in common, beyond the fact that they are both Hong Kong Chinese female teachers of L2 English who happen to be taking the same in-service programme of initial professional training. They teach in different types of institution and work with students of differ-

---

Snapshot 5: Shirley

Shirley teaches English in a technical institute in an industrial area of the New Territories. She previously taught in secondary schools for five years. Most of her technical institute students left school the previous year with minimal qualifications and are now taking vocational courses. The students' English is generally weak, but English is the medium of instruction in the majority of their technical subjects, and therefore English classes are a compulsory part of their study programme.

Shirley is teaching a group of twenty-four Computing Studies students. They are a mixed-gender group, containing more boys than girls. Most of the group are 17 years old. The theme of the lesson is 'Making enquiries'. The students have been given a task requiring them to find out about a laptop computer which they are thinking of buying. Having brainstormed items they want information about (such as price, speed, memory and functions), the students are working out how to make the appropriate direct wh-questions. In relation to the first item of information (price), one student produces the question: 'How much is the computer cost?'

Shirley handles the student's error as follows:

> It costs $20,000. So how's the question? Do you say
> *How much is the computer cost?* . . . But how much . . .
> It is a verb, right? [pointing to costs on her OHT] so *How
> much . . . ?* [student: *does*] Yes, right. The whole question
> again. *How much . . . ?* [students: *How much does the
> computer cost?*] Yes, right. *How much does the computer
> cost?* [writing] *Cost, -s* or no *-s?* No *-s*, right? Because you
> have *does* here [writing], so you have no *-s*.

Snapshot 6: Pearl

As noted in the Prologue, Pearl teaches in a co-educational secondary school on Hong Kong Island. The snapshot is from the same lesson as in the Prologue: the students are a group of twenty 11- to 12-year-olds. The entire 40-minute lesson is focused on the Present Simple and Present Progressive. The students have been taught these forms before, both at primary school and again earlier this year, but as they are 'remedial' students, the school thinks that they need further revision.

Pearl begins the lesson by taking the students through the uses of the two verb forms, as set out in the Secondary 1 textbook. The last half-hour of the lesson is spent on working through the grammar exercises in the accompanying workbook, each one involving multiple-choice, mechanical sentence transformation or blank-filling. While they are correcting a question-formation exercise orally, one of the students produces the question: 'How much it is cost?'

Pearl handles the student's error as follows:

> *Cost* is a verb, OK? When *cost* is a verb, what should we use? Yes? [inaudible student response] . . . *does it cost* . . . *does it cost*. When you have the verb, you do not use *is*. You use *does* or *do*. Here you say *How much does it cost?* Do you get it?

ent age groups. They also have contrasting educational and professional backgrounds. What brings Shirley and Pearl together in these snapshots is the fact that they are dealing with very similar student-produced errors.

If we look at the way the two teachers deal with these errors, what do we see? In Shirley's case, the error is dealt with clearly, efficiently and comprehensively. Shirley begins by focusing on the word *cost* to make sure that the student was trying to use it as a verb in his question (the way it is used in the example sentence on her overhead transparency) rather than as a noun. Having confirmed that *cost* is in this case a verb, she elicits the appropriate auxiliary *does* from one of the students before guiding the whole class to produce the full question. Finally she makes sure that the student's attention is drawn to the fact that there is no -*s* at the end of *cost*, because it is the auxiliary rather than the main verb in the wh-question that is inflected for tense/person. It is clear from the way Shirley handles this error that she is trying to view the problem from the learner/learning perspective. She realises that there are potentially two reasons for the error: confusion over whether *cost* is a verb or noun, and selection of an inappropriate auxiliary. She therefore systematically addresses both reasons, starting with the former, since the latter presupposes identification of *cost* as a verb. In doing so, she keeps her own language at an appropriate level of simplicity and non-technicality, and says or writes nothing that is potentially confusing. Instead, she makes briskly efficient use of both OHT and whiteboard to make salient the points she wants her students to notice.

In Pearl's treatment of the error, she also begins by emphasising that *cost* is a verb, before she supplies the correct version of the question with the appropriate auxiliary. It might therefore be argued that Pearl, like Shirley, is endeavouring to analyse the error from the point of view of the learner. Thereafter, however, the similarities between the two treatments end. Pearl's correction is neither clear nor comprehensive. First of all, she produces a generalisation ('When you have the verb, you do not use is') that could be very misleading in a lesson focusing on both Present Simple and Present Progressive verb forms, as well as the verb *to be*. Then, for whatever reason, she does nothing about the student's error of word order in a wh-question.

It is, of course, dangerous (and potentially unfair to the teacher involved) to jump to conclusions based on a snapshot that does not take account of the teacher's perspective on events. There could, for example, be a number of reasons for Pearl's non-treatment of the student's word-order error. She may simply not have heard it. Or she may have made a deliberate decision not to focus on it explicitly – regarding it as a performance slip, or perhaps feeling that her young and relatively weak students would not be able to cope with too many points to remember at once. It would also be wrong to generalise about the procedural dimension of a teacher's language awareness on the evidence of a single snapshot, which may be quite unrepresentative of a teacher's general behaviour. As we noted in Chapter 2, with any teacher there will be variation in the degree of skill with which language-related issues are handled in class, within a single lesson as well as across classes. However, these two teachers were observed teaching in their schools on at least three occasions. They were also videotaped performing various tasks that simulated aspects of pedagogical practice. On the basis of that evidence, I would claim that both snapshots are typical examples and fair representations of the way that Shirley and Pearl engage with grammar in their teaching.

In an earlier study (Andrews, 2001), I examined aspects of the complex interrelationship between TLA and teachers' engagement with the content of learning. This complexity is in part due, as noted above, to the different interpretations of the word 'engagement', but it is also linked to the nature of TLA, where awareness is dependent upon knowledge but is not synonymous with it. As we have seen from the snapshots so far, problems with language awareness take various forms. There are teachers who have knowledge, and whose declarative TLA is very sound, but who lack awareness. Such teachers possess the relevant knowledge base, but they lack the ability, for instance, to view the challenges of language content from the learner/learning perspective, and/or the ability to monitor aspects of their own language output. There are also teachers who have a degree of awareness, but who lack knowledge. These teachers may be capable of reflection, and of perceiving the needs and problems of their students, and they may well be aware of the importance of viewing what is to be taught from the learning perspective. They may, however, find that their attempts to engage with content-related issues are undermined by a lack of knowledge.

Whilst acknowledging this complexity, and the fact that both TLA and engagement (commitment) are matters of degree, the discussion in Andrews (2001) offers four possible profiles of teachers illustrating different combinations of awareness and engagement:

- *Teacher A* engages with content fully, in a principled manner. She possesses a sound language systems knowledge base, is well aware of issues of language content, confident about her ability to handle them and fully prepared to engage with them from a learner/ learning perspective.

- *Teacher B*, by contrast, adopts a position of principled, informed detachment from content issues. Like Teacher A, she too possesses a very solid language systems knowledge base, but she espouses a set of teacher beliefs which emphasise fluency/acquisition to the virtual exclusion of any explicit focus on grammar.

- *Teacher C* attempts to engage with issues of language content but does so in a naïve, ill-informed way. She appreciates the need to try to engage with such issues but lacks the knowledge base, the awareness and/or the confidence to do so effectively.

- *Teacher D* does not attempt to engage with issues of language content and lacks the language systems knowledge base which might enable her to do so effectively. She may be unaware of the desirability of engaging with the language-related aspects of her teaching, or she may simply be unsure how best to engage with content.   (Andrews, 2001:86)

Probably in the EFL context, the principled non-engagement of a Teacher B is a rarity. As Fotos has noted (see, e.g., Fotos, 2005), in many EFL (as opposed to ESL) situations, the L2 is being taught within a centrally controlled education system with a set curriculum, prescribed textbooks and highly competitive high-stakes public examinations which require the demonstration of grammar knowledge. Within such a context, most teachers are likely to feel that they have little alternative but to engage with form. However, the intensity and quality of such engagement may differ markedly.

In the case of the two EFL teachers we have just looked at in Snapshots 5 and 6 (Shirley and Pearl), Shirley is much the less influenced by the contextual factors referred to by Fotos (2005): she is teaching in a technical institute, where a more communicative ('task-based') approach is encouraged, she and a team of colleagues devise their own materials (because there is no textbook), and her students are not studying towards any high-stakes English examination. Pearl, by contrast, is in a school where she is obliged to focus on formS in her teaching. Although her Secondary 1 students are at least four years away from their first public examination, the internal tests and examinations throughout the school involve a substantial grammar component, and the students all have a grammar workbook which has been bought by the parents and which therefore needs to show signs of having been used. The Hong Kong English Language curriculum may have been conceptualised in accordance with communicative (and now 'task-based') principles, but the realisation in many secondary schools, including Pearl's, has been a very weak form of CLT/TBLT.

In spite of these contextual differences, both Shirley and Pearl engage with grammar in the sense of being committed to the importance of grammar in L2 teaching. According to Pearl, for instance: 'if you want to speak good English, I think you need to study grammar', while Shirley, as noted in the previous chapter, sees a clear role for grammar in L2 teaching and learning, within a communicative framework. There are, however, differences in the intensity of their engagement. Shirley is very interested in grammar, and this carries over into her teaching: 'actually I enjoy teaching grammar, particularly if I can see that the students are learning grammar to do something meaningful'. Pearl, on the other hand, gives the impression of being committed out of a sense of needing to conform to the expectations of the school, the students and their parents, and a feeling that grammar is a necessary part of learning L2 English. Pearl exhibits no great interest in grammar, and in both her observed lessons and in interviews she seems unsure of herself when handling grammar or discussing grammar-related issues.

The differences between Shirley and Pearl in the intensity of their engagement with grammar, and also in the quality of any such engagement, may well be linked to their backgrounds. Shirley has a first degree in English Language and Literature and has always been interested in language and languages. All her study experience has been in Hong Kong, but she is multilingual, having learned Japanese as well as English, Putonghua and her mother tongue, Cantonese. She was actively involved in English clubs and societies both at school and university, and she has pursued her studies of English to an advanced level, completing an MPhil study of an area of English syntax. Pearl's background is in marked contrast. Pearl is not an English subject specialist. Having attended a Putonghua-medium primary school, and a secondary school where most of the teaching was mixed-code Cantonese and English, she received her tertiary education in the United States, taking a first degree in Accounting followed by a 'Special Major' in Home Economics. Her school public examination results in English were not especially good (a grade C in the HKCEE), and although she is a fluent communicator in English who continues to use the language to some extent in her social life, it is hardly surprising, given her background, to find that she lacks confidence in her ability to deal successfully with grammar, and that the quality of her engagement with content leaves something to be desired. From this analysis, I would suggest that Shirley possesses many of the characteristics of Teacher A above, while the profile of Teacher C appears to be a fairly accurate representation of Pearl, from the evidence available.

5.3 Engagement with the content of learning: the case of Maggie

The complexity of the interaction between engagement and TLA in pedagogical practice may be seen even more clearly if we look at the case of one particular teacher, Maggie, who was mentioned in Chapter 4, particularly in 4.5.8. Maggie's background and interests lead her to describe herself as 'not much of a grammar person'. However, her early years of teaching place her in a situation where she feels obliged to teach grammar. Snapshot 7 below describes one such lesson, which seems to have been fairly typical.

Maggie's own learning of English was mainly through immersion. Although her primary school teachers explicitly 'taught grammar', she had plenty of opportunity to be exposed to English and to use it outside the classroom. Her father (a fluent speaker of English, who used the language all the time in his work) was a role model in this regard, and had

101

a strong influence on Maggie's attitude towards English. She was encouraged to develop the habit of reading English books for pleasure and watching TV in English, and she had opportunities to use the language naturally in communication with her father's Indian business partner.

At her English-medium secondary school, Maggie was in a 'language-rich' environment. In junior forms (Secondary 1–3, i.e. from the age of 11 to 14), grammar was not taught separately, and it was only in Secondary 4 that Maggie encountered a teacher who focused explicitly on grammar. It was not a positive experience: 'It was extremely boring to take grammar lessons. I didn't quite understand her explanation, or maybe I didn't pay attention. The grammar book became a big doodle book. I didn't, and still don't, believe one can really learn how to use grammar this way. I mean one can learn grammar, but not how to use it. There are too many rules and exceptions; I simply couldn't remember them all.' However, this teacher was the exception in employing such an approach: in general, Maggie's own experience of language learning involved acquiring implicit knowledge of grammar through using the language, rather than focusing on the development of explicit grammar knowledge.

After secondary school, Maggie pursued her tertiary studies in the United States as a Business Major. Her undergraduate programme did not involve any attention to grammar. However, Maggie's spoken English continued to develop: as a result of her studies, her close contact with her host family and the whole immersion experience. Then, on her return to Hong Kong, Maggie obtained her first teaching position, in a large, modern co-educational secondary school in one of the 'new towns' in Hong Kong's New Territories. The medium of instruction in the school was officially English, but in reality the teachers of many subjects operated in a Cantonese-English bilingual oral mode and an English written mode. The job was intended to be temporary, but Maggie ended up staying in the school for eight years. At the time of the lesson in Snapshot 7, she was in her third year of teaching, and had just begun her postgraduate in-service initial training (the Postgraduate Certificate in Education, or PCEd).

At this stage of her career, Maggie found that her lack of explicit knowledge about grammar, and particularly terminology, set her apart from her colleagues: 'Teachers around me seemed to have a big vocabulary for grammar, especially my Panel Head. He couldn't read or write [English], but he was very good at throwing those grammatical terms every time we had a meeting. I had to read some grammar text books before I actually knew what they were talking about.' When Maggie began her PCEd course, she also felt that she was different from her peers, because she lacked 'literacy of grammar'. As she recalls the experience: 'Sitting in the PCEd class was a nightmare. The classmates were all grammarians. I had absolutely no idea what they were talking about.'

Although Maggie was, from the beginning, a teacher with an instinctively strong commitment to communicative language teaching, largely as a result of her own experiences as a learner, she nevertheless recognised that the students she was teaching had markedly different expectations and abilities compared with her own and her classmates' when she was at school: 'When I was studying, we don't have grammar lesson at all . . . We just sort of learned it through, I don't know, reading speaking or listening. For some reason it did seem simple to learn when I was young . . . But when I look at my students, they have no idea how to get those things. They have to go formula type. They have to . . . OK, if you have such situation, then you use *-ing* form.'

Maggie therefore made an effort to engage with the content of learning, resenting the pressure from her Panel Head, but recognising that she needed to respond to the expectations of her students. As she did so, however, she was sceptical of the ultimate value of explicit grammar teaching, feeling it had little impact on students' interlanguage: 'When this is like at least their tenth year of learning English, they already have their own whole set of language system, their own version of English. Or their own version of Chinese. So it's like we have to wipe out a little part of what they have and put in my version of it. Well, which I hope it should be the right one, the more appropriate one. So it's difficult sometimes . . . they're refusing to erase that part of their system, or any add-on.'

Snapshot 7 (see p. 104) is a summary of one of Maggie's lessons, given early on in her third year as a secondary school teacher of L2 English.

From the snapshot, we can see Maggie making every effort, in so far as she is able, to engage with the content of learning (with the added 'push', or pressure, of being videotaped as she does so). She is doing something to which, as we have seen, she is committed neither intellectually nor emotionally. Even seven years after the lesson, her inability to engage with the content of learning with any such commitment is unchanged: 'Basically I know how to use it, but when I try to explain it, it's still like really messy, unless I really prepare for it . . . and if they just like ask me, it's really embarrassing as a teacher. But I really am not interested in grammar, and every time I open a book, it's like when I was a kid. I just get really bored.'

Unfortunately, Maggie's attempts to engage with the subject-matter content of this particular lesson might also be described as '*really messy*'. At every stage of the lesson, her TLA seems to impact on the input she provides for her students in a variety of unproductive ways.

Snapshot 7: Maggie

Maggie is teaching a class of 40 Secondary 3 students (13- to 14-year-olds). She is working from a textbook assigned by the Panel Head, entitled *English Usage*. The focus of today's lesson is Unit 3 **Active or Passive?** Each unit of the book follows a similar pattern: exposition of the 'rules' relating to the specific language structure, followed by a series of rather mechanical practice exercises with minimal contextualisation. Maggie decides to supplement the textbook with activities and authentic materials in order to attract the interest of her students.

Maggie begins by introducing the active and passive contrast via a 'role play' situation (acted out by students using cue-cards) involving a robber and a passer-by. A third student (a reporter) writes the following on the blackboard (copying from Maggie's cue-card: 'A passer-by was told by the robber to hold up her hands. All her money was given to the robber'. Maggie uses this to introduce the idea that the robber is doing the action. She therefore writes *active* next to the word *robber* (in the first sentence) and *passive* next to *passer-by*. Maggie's primary focus is on the transformation between active and passive, and she provides a very unclear explanation of use, seeming to suggest that active and passive are almost interchangeable:

> If you want to put it in the active voice, we will have to say *Robber told the passer-by to* . . . But then if we're doing it in the passive way, what is stressing is the person the action that has been done . . . that means the passer-by . . . *Passer-by was told by robber to* . . . So when we're using active and passive voice the sentence means exactly the same . . . they carry exactly the same meaning . . . but what is different is stressing the role, who is doing what . . . or who is being told to do what.

She then gives her students a Calvin and Hobbes strip cartoon to look at and asks them (in groups) to describe the story in the cartoon using active and passive voice. Her students perform the task enthusiastically. However, having been given no reasons for the selection of one form in preference to the other, they produce some very odd sentences, such as *Hobbes is watched by Calvin, The wild sound is made by Hobbes, Hobbes's mouth was put in by Calvin*. Maggie accepts these sentences with no apparent hesitation and concludes the activity by saying 'So it's really simple to use active and passive voice. The question you should be asking yourself is "What is being done?" and "By whom?" "By which person?"'

After that, Maggie turns to the textbook, which provides a partial explanation of when the passive is used. Maggie elaborates briefly on some of the points ('You put your emphasis on the action being done'), before trying to make a connection with two ways of making polite requests, taught the previous day in the context of a letter of application ('It would be appreciated if . . .' and 'I would be grateful if'). She first of all says that both sentences are passive, then concedes of the second 'Well, actually this one is not passive', before switching her attention to making the point that 'It would be appreciated if . . .' is more polite than 'Would you do something for me?'

Finally, she tries to make use of newspaper extracts and their headlines to illustrate the active/passive contrast, giving her students focus questions on her worksheet: 'What is done – and by whom? These are the questions you should ask regarding active/passive voice.'

However, in her preparation, she appears to have underestimated the problems posed by the first and most prominent of her extracts, headlined 'Fired up by Thai cuisine'. Not only is it difficult to relate her focus questions to the headline, but the headline itself is also almost certainly beyond the competence of most of her students, both because of the lexis and also the problem of identifying a subject for the ellipted verb phrase.

- Although Maggie herself is a fluent and extremely effective communicator, who can effortlessly make appropriate choices of active or passive in her own speech and writing, she does not appear to have a clear understanding at an explicit level of the differences in use of the two forms and the reasons for selecting one or the other. As a result, her presentation and practice activities are potentially very confusing when seen from the learners' perspective. They also largely reinforce the view (which students may well have formed on the basis of previous teaching) that active and passive are interchangeable.
- There is little evidence to suggest that Maggie's TLA is actively engaged in monitoring the messages she is sending to students through what she writes on the board, through what she says and through her reactions to the target language samples produced by the students. For

instance, she writes *active* next to the word *robber* in a passive sentence, without appreciating the misunderstanding that could result. She also allows some very odd sentences to be accepted without question as grammatical and as situationally appropriate. For example, in the sentence she cues as part of the presentation, *All her money was given to the robber*, the use of the passive, although grammatically correct, is very hard to justify logically and contextually (since it appears to detach the victim from any involvement in the action of giving the money). As for the student's sentence *Hobbes's mouth was put in by Calvin*, this suggests a number of underlying problems; however, the sentence is accepted without demur by Maggie.

- When Maggie draws on the textbook, her well-intentioned spontaneous attempt to make a connection with the previous day's focus on polite requests is undermined by the limitations of her TLA. This leads her initially to divert students' attention away from the points that should have been made salient at this stage of the lesson – the guidelines on the use of passive voice as outlined in the textbook – and to focus instead on politeness. It also causes her to miss the opportunity, having turned the spotlight on to polite requests, to highlight the role that the passive plays in adding a layer of politeness to the request exponent encountered the previous day *It would be appreciated if. . .* Finally, it results in her sowing the seeds of further potential confusion with her own muddled remarks.

- It also seems that Maggie has not analysed the material she is using from the point of view of her students. This may be partly due to the time pressures that affect any busy teacher, but it is also consistent with the generally superficial level of Maggie's engagement with the content of learning as observed in her preparation and delivery of a number of lessons. The Calvin and Hobbes cartoon was chosen in order to engage the students' interest (which it did) but with seemingly little thought as to the language it might generate and the problems that might arise (both of form and information structure). Maggie's newspaper articles also seem to have been selected without the TLA 'filter' having been brought to bear on the process. Each text contains at least one passive verb form, but during the lesson the articles posed unanticipated challenges and introduced complex language that was clearly inappropriate and distracting for her students.

As we have observed from this particular case, Maggie is a teacher who, at an attitudinal level, finds it hard to engage with grammar. In her own experience of language learning, explicit grammar knowledge seems to have played a very limited role, and when she entered the teaching profession, she found a marked mismatch between her own attitudes towards grammar and the expectations of both senior colleagues in her school and her students. In response to those expectations, she has made the effort to engage with the content of learning. However, as Snapshot 7 reveals, her attempts to engage with language content in her lesson on **Active or Passive?** were fraught with problems. The quality of Maggie's engagement with language content can be seen to have been severely compromised by the limitations of her TLA.

5.4 TLA and engagement with the language content of teaching materials

L2 teachers around the world have varying degrees of autonomy as regards the materials they use in their teaching. Some consider themselves to have total autonomy, while others may feel that they have very little. Maggie is probably typical of many L2 teachers in publicly funded school systems in having some degree of autonomy in her use of materials (and scope for supplementation with her own) while still being expected to cover specified units of the published materials adopted by her school.

Because of such variations in autonomy, and in the ways individual teachers respond to that autonomy at different stages of their careers, the relationship between TLA, teaching materials and engagement with the content of learning is not a simple one, in which, for example, a textbook's treatment of the content of learning determines how the teacher engages with that content. When teachers make regular use of a particular textbook, the way that textbook handles the language content is likely to be a major influence not only on the way teachers conceptualise the possibilities of dealing with language content in their classes but also on the on-going development of their TLA. The textbooks that a teacher makes use of wherever he/she works form part of the context which frames any teacher's professional life and in which the teacher's TLA evolves. If the teacher works with the same textbook for a prolonged period, then the influence of that textbook will be that much greater. Some teachers may regard the influence of published materials as a constraint, particularly teachers who are obliged to work with textbooks that they find uninspiring and/or inappropriate for their students. Others may view textbooks more positively, as a resource containing a wealth of teaching/learning ideas and teacher support, and therefore providing learning opportunities for both student and teacher.

There is little doubt that well-written and appropriately chosen published teaching materials are potentially of great benefit to teachers who are uncertain, for whatever reason, about aspects of their language knowledge (their proficiency and/or their knowledge about the language).

Those materials are likely to offer valuable support for such teachers, via, for example, rules of thumb that achieve a felicitous compromise between simplicity, truth and clarity; well-chosen contextualised examples illustrating the use as well as the formal features of the language to be taught; and samples of spoken and written text providing good models of the target language variety.

However, the relationship between published materials and their users is not one in which teachers can simply 'disengage' their TLA and delegate all content-related responsibility to the textbook, whatever the merits of that textbook. The work of the individual teacher (however inexperienced) inevitably involves some sort of mediation of materials, and therefore some measure of teacher engagement with the content of learning, even when those materials have been carefully designed and well selected, and even if more senior colleagues within an institution have made prior decisions about which parts of a textbook are to be used when, and how. As inexperienced teachers start to overcome their uncertainties and acquire greater self-confidence, they are likely to want to stamp their own personality on their use of the textbook materials, in ways that teachers with less awareness of their own limitations (or fewer inhibitions) may have already been doing from very early on in their careers. As a result, most teachers, by the time they have gained a few years' classroom experience, will have become accustomed to mediating the content of their teaching and learning materials. I would argue that the TLA of the individual teacher will have a significant influence on the quality of any such mediation related to the language content of those materials. It is also TLA which will determine the extent to which the teacher is able to become increasingly discriminating about the way in which the textbook's statements about grammar are made available to the learners, and to intervene constructively in order to reduce the risk of such statements (and their accompanying examples) encouraging the learner to form incorrect hypotheses. It is these influences of TLA that constitute the focus of this and the following section of the chapter.

Unfortunately, the reality in many parts of the world is that there is not an ideal match of materials and learners' needs/abilities. Teachers working in the kind of education system Fotos (2005) describes, for instance, may find themselves constrained by having to use textbooks which are flawed or which, having been prescribed for system-wide use, present an inappropriate level of challenge for many students, given the inevitable range of learners and of teaching/learning contexts within the system. For teachers working in such conditions, there is a particularly pressing need for their TLA to be actively engaged in filtering the textbook's structuring of input for learning. For any teacher, but especially for those with limited autonomy in their selection of materials, it becomes essential to develop the ability to analyse materials critically, to locate potential sources of learner confusion and to take whatever action is feasible within the constraints of the teaching situation to ensure that the language input in the textbooks is made available to the learners in a way that is potentially of maximum usefulness to them. The teacher's language awareness exerts a major influence on the extent to which that teacher is able to engage effectively with the language content of materials in this way.

In spite of such arguments, teachers respond in very different ways to expectations that it is an essential part of their role to form a bridge between what the textbook says and what the students know, to provide the kind of mediation that will facilitate comprehension. Some teachers perform the role with great sensitivity and skill, but others are reluctant to play such a role, especially in relation to grammar. Some appear not to see it as appropriate to do so. Others may lack the confidence to go beyond what the book says, or lack the awareness which would enable them to see the need to do so. Teachers who are less reluctant may see the need to do something, but lack the knowledge, awareness or experience to deal with the problem correctly. Their own interventions may, as a result, serve to increase rather than reduce confusion. All teachers may find their ability to act as a bridge constrained by, for example, lack of preparation time.

5.5 Teachers' engagement with the language content of teaching materials: four contrasting snapshots

Snapshots 8, 9 and 10 (see pp. 110–13) illustrate some of the various ways in which TLA impacts on teachers' engagement with the language content of published materials. Two of the three snapshots involve female teachers we have met before: Rose (Snapshot 3) and Clara (Snapshot 1). The third involves a male teacher, Yan. Snapshot 11 switches the focus to materials produced by the teacher (the teacher in this case being Tony, who we met in 4.5.9), and demonstrates the need for teachers to be as critical in the analysis of their own materials as they are of published materials.

If we look at Snapshots 8, 9 and 10 in the light of the previous discussion, we see three markedly contrasting interactions between TLA, teaching materials and the teacher's engagement with the content of learning as presented in those materials. There are major differences in the extent to which the teachers actively engage in mediating the content of learning, as well as in the quality of their engagement. The three teachers also have varying degrees of success in ensuring that the language

(*cont.* on p. 113)

Snapshot 8: Rose

Late one morning in early December, Rose is giving a lesson on writing to a Secondary 4 class of forty-two girls (aged 14 to 15). The class is working systematically through the assigned textbook (Chamberlain and O'Neill, 1994), which is specifically designed to provide preparation for the integrated skills paper of the HKCEE English examination taken towards the end of Secondary 5.

In this particular 35-minute lesson, the students are examining the characteristics of formal writing. As part of the process, Rose asks them to read the textbook's description of features of formal writing, which begins as follows:

Formal writing
We write in a formal way to *strangers or to people who have power over us.* We also usually write in a formal way when we *write in a public way* (e.g., a letter to a newspaper).
Below are some features of formal writing. Study them carefully.

➢ The subjects of sentences are often abstract:
  • **The idea that noise cannot hurt us** is absurd.
  • **Clearly, the responsibility for solving this problem** lies with the Transport Department.
➢ The passive form is commonly used:
  • Cars **are being driven** far too fast down this road.
  • Women **have never been considered** totally equal to men.
➢ Conditionals are commonly used:
  • We **would appreciate** it if you could arrange . . .
  • It **would be** a good idea to consider . . .

When the students have silently read through the listed characteristics of formal writing, Rose goes through each feature as outlined in the textbook, adding almost nothing to what is stated in the book. The only contribution she makes herself to the structuring of the input is to alert her students to the need to remember these features the next time they are doing a piece of formal writing.

Snapshot 9: Clara

Clara is teaching the same Secondary 5 class (15- to 16-year-olds) as in Snapshot 1. In this particular lesson, on a bright November morning, Clara is devoting the entire 40 minutes to revising modal auxiliaries.

In the first part of the lesson Clara goes through the four rules about modals presented in the textbook. As she deals with each rule in the textbook, she adds her own supplementary comments and examples, which are intended to clarify the precise meaning of the textbook's necessarily brief explanation.

When she deals with the first rule (that modals do not add an *-s* to the third person singular), she reinterprets this to mean that it is not necessary to add an *-s* to the following verb when the modal is in the third person singular. Her illustrative example of the error to avoid is *He can speaks several languages*, and she gives no example of the actual point intended in the textbook.

The second textbook rule is that modals do not have an infinitive or participle form. Clara mediates this rule as follows:

> Rule number 2, so they don't have an infinitive or participle form. That means we don't need to add preposition infinitive *to* in front of the modal verb. And then we don't have to add *-ing* after the modal verb.

Finally she focuses on the third and fourth rules set out in the textbook:

- interrogative and negative uses of modals do not require *do*, and
- modals are followed by the infinitive without *to*, except in the case of *ought*.

In her supplementary comments, Clara joins these two rules together:

> We don't have any negative form, and we don't need to put the *do* into the sentence when we use the modal verb. So except with the exceptional case the modal verb *ought* [writes on blackboard] . . . What can you suggest to put after *ought*? Infinitive *to*. Good.

Snapshot 10: Yan

Yan teaches in a co-educational Chinese-medium secondary school, which has recently moved to new purpose-built premises in a working-class district at the eastern end of Hong Kong Island. Yan has ten years' experience as an English teacher, all in the same school. Yan's own secondary schooling was in a prestigious English-medium school. He is a very proficient and confident communicator in English.

One dank, grey February morning, Yan is teaching a Secondary 3 class (13- to 14-year-olds). His lesson is based upon a unit from the textbook (Sampson, 1994), in which the grammar focus is the use of the present participle to join two sentences with the same subject. According to the textbook:

We can use the present participle, *-ing*, to join together two sentences with the same subject.

Example: *Mr Lee heard a noise. He got up and looked outside.*
Hearing a noise, Mr Lee got up and looked outside.

Yan begins by focusing briefly on the example in the book, and then introduces examples of his own, before asking the students to work through the practice exercise in the textbook. The rubric for the exercise establishes the context of a policeman going to the scene of a robbery and then gives the following instructions:

Rewrite the sentences using the correct *-ing* participle. Follow the example:
(1) *Peter received a call on his radio. He went straight to the scene of the robbery.*
Receiving a call on his radio, Peter went straight to the scene of the robbery.

The first two items in the exercise (numbered (2) and (3)) are straightforward, provided the students follow the example and understand the mechanics of the process. The next item in the exercise is problematic, however, because the two sentences do not have the same subject:

(4) *The ambulance arrived a few minutes later. The man was taken to hospital.*

Fortunately, Yan spotted the problem when he was looking at the textbook before the lesson. As a result, when the students reach number 4, he is able to transform it into an interesting learning challenge, by setting his students the task of resolving the problem. He begins by asking them if there is any problem in combining the two sentences. When one of the students tells him that the subjects of the two sentences are different, Yan asks them how they can overcome the difficulty. After some thought and discussion, another student suggests modifying the two original sentences so that the subjects are the same. Under Yan's guidance, the students are able to do this by making a change to the second sentence: *The ambulance took the man to hospital.* They can then join the sentences in accordance with the desired pattern: *Arriving a few minutes later, the ambulance took the man to hospital.*

input in the textbook is made available to the learners in a way that is potentially of maximum benefit to them. The language awareness of the teacher appears to play a significant role in each of these snapshots of pedagogical practice.

In the case of Rose's lesson (Snapshot 8), the materials that she is working with really need the teacher to act as a bridge, because the listed features of formal writing are open to misinterpretation and leave so much unsaid. To take the remark concerning the passive as an example, this may indeed be true as far as it goes. However, without any accompanying information about when or why the passive is used in formal writing, such a statement is not only unhelpful, but also highly misleading and likely to reinforce the tendency (familiar certainly to Hong Kong teachers) for students to litter their written texts with inappropriate passive verb phrases. The statement regarding 'conditionals' also needs mediation, not least because the second example sentence is not 'conditional' in the sense with which the students are most likely to be familiar (i.e. it does not contain an *if*-clause). Faced with such materials, the L2 teacher finds his/her TLA challenged on at least two levels. The first challenge is one of perceiving that there is indeed a potential weakness or problem in the textbook. The second challenge (which depends on the first challenge having been met) is to think of ways of overcoming the problem so that the learners are presented with more accurate, useful or digestible input. As Snapshot 8 indicates, Rose's handling of the materials suggests that this particular challenge has passed her by. She appears not to perceive any weakness in the textbook extract (and fails to do so even when prompted in post-lesson discussion). Instead, her grammar-related classroom behaviour (on this occasion and in other observed lessons) comes across as unaware, uncritical and accepting of all that the textbook says. To what extent this is due to a lack of declarative knowledge and/or awareness is difficult to judge. It could equally be caused by a lack of confidence in her own TLA (we noted in 4.5.3 Rose's fear of grammar) and an uncritical assumption as a relatively inexperienced teacher that 'the textbook must know best', allowing the TLA 'filter' to be bypassed.

Clara (Snapshot 9), by contrast, is using materials where the limitations are less obvious. Although brief, the explanations of the formal properties of modals contained in the materials are quite clear. However, Clara recognises that the brevity of the explanations may make them difficult for her students to understand. Although Clara is no more experienced a teacher than Rose, she seems to be rather less plagued by self-doubt about her ability to deal with grammar in her teaching. She therefore attempts to engage with the language content of the textbook unit and to play a mediating role by rephrasing and adding to the textbook explanations in order to make each of the rules more accessible to the learners. Unfortunately, however, her TLA appears to be unequal to the task. As a result, each of her interventions adds confusion rather than aiding comprehension, casting doubts not only on her ability to monitor her own output but also on her own understanding of what the textbook says.

Yan's lesson in Snapshot 10 again shows a teacher who is actively engaging with the content of learning as presented by the textbook. However, the quality of the engagement is quite different: with Yan we see an example of textbook mediation in which the teacher's language awareness is engaged to very good effect. In Yan's case, his TLA has both alerted him to the importance of critical evaluation of the textbook treatment of language content and enabled him to screen the materials and identify a major potential problem during his lesson preparation. Then, in harmonious blend with other knowledge-base components of his pedagogical content knowledge, his highly developed TLA (including the ability to view language issues from the learners' perspective) has helped him to work out strategies for modifying his handling of the content, and to devise a highly effective way of providing scaffolding for the students to help them overcome the learning challenge that he sets for them. The strategies he devises also give added salience to the feature of the target language structure that Yan wants to highlight: that the subject of an adverbial participle clause is normally the same as the subject of the main clause.

In Snapshot 11, the focus is different. Rather than looking at a teacher's engagement with the content of learning in published materials, we see a teacher (Tony) designing materials of his own, with the specific intention of shedding light on a grammar point that causes his students continuing problems: the distinction between the Past Simple and Past Perfect.

The reader may recall that earlier in the chapter, in Snapshot 7, we noted examples of language-related problems that can result from supplementing textbook materials with authentic texts, both visual and written. Because Maggie's TLA was insufficiently or inadequately

Snapshot 11: Tony

It is a Friday morning in November. Tony's university supervisor is coming to observe his lesson, and Tony has therefore taken particular care over his lesson preparation.

Tony's aim in his lesson (as outlined in his lesson plan) is to help his students:

> to learn the difference between the Past Perfect tense and Simple Past tense and to understand in what situation these two tenses are used so that they themselves can use the tenses correctly.

As Tony comments in his plan:

> Learners have learnt what Simple Past tense and Past Perfect tense are, but they are confused with the difference between the two. They seldom use the tenses correctly in their writing and can hardly realise the meaning of the Past Perfect tense in their reading.

In order to help his students to understand the difference between the two verb forms, Tony has written a text, which the students are looking at alongside a picture version of the same story.

Tony's written story begins with three simple sentences containing Past Perfect verb groups. However, the tense selection is inappropriate in each case, since there is no past time of orientation justifying the use of Past Perfect rather than Past Simple:

> On the 7th January, a terrible accident had happened. A man and a dog had been killed by a lorry near the road. They had become ghosts! One week later, an old man drove his car near the place where the accident had taken place . . .

engaged with the preparation of her lesson, it seems that she did not spot the language-related pitfalls associated with using either text for her intended purpose. In Snapshot 11, Tony goes one step further than Maggie, by devising his own text with the intention of modelling the target language forms and highlighting the distinctive ways in which they are used. However, in his case too, there seems to be some sort of TLA breakdown: despite his best intentions, Tony's self-produced text will only have reinforced the learner confusion of which Tony is well aware. It seems, in fact, that he is as confused as his students about this particular area of grammar. In both these cases, the teachers' attempts to supplement and/or replace textbook materials were undermined by the apparent inadequacies of their TLA.

Examples like Maggie and Tony should not, of course, deter any teachers from using supplementary published materials or devising model texts of their own. They do, however, underline the need for caution and for the full engagement of one's critical faculties (including TLA) to ensure that such materials offer benefits to the learners rather than simply adding to their problems.

5.5 Conclusion

In this chapter, we have explored various aspects of TLA in pedagogical practice, in particular the complex interrelationship between TLA and teachers' engagement with the content of learning. In doing so, we have noted the following, reflected in a series of classroom snapshots:

- The application of TLA in practice may be significantly affected by the extent to which the teacher seriously engages with content-related issues in his/her teaching;
- In so far as the teacher does engage with content-related issues, the extent and quality of that engagement will potentially be affected by the TLA of that teacher;
- Problems with TLA take various forms; awareness is dependent upon knowledge but is not synonymous with it and there are therefore teachers who have knowledge about language but lack awareness, and vice versa;
- The TLA of the individual teacher can have a significant influence on the extent and quality of that teacher's mediation of the language content of teaching and learning materials, both published and self-produced.

The following chapter focuses on the TLA of expert and novice teachers, with a particular emphasis on the TLA of the expert teacher.

Questions for discussion and reflection

1) In your own teaching, what sorts of issues are the major focus of your planning: issues of methodology, of classroom organisation, or of language content? Why do you prioritise that particular sort of issue?
2) Can you think of a recent occasion when you have faced a challenge to your subject-matter knowledge, (a) in your preparation, or (b) in class? How did you deal with that challenge? With hindsight, do you think you adopted an appropriate strategy?
3) To what extent do you use grammatical terminology in your teaching? What is the rationale for your use/non-use of terminology? Does your practice vary (a) from class to class, or (b) with the same class?
4) Page 99 contains four possible profiles of teachers illustrating different combinations of awareness and engagement. Which profile do you identify with most closely, and why? Can you think of colleagues (past or present) who match any of the other profiles?
5) In your teaching situation, how much autonomy do you have in (a) the selection of the materials you use, and (b) the actual use that you make of selected/assigned materials? To what extent do you rely on the materials (and therefore the textbook-writer) to make decisions about the handling of language content? What is the rationale for your attitude towards published materials?
6) Can you recall a recent lesson in which you modified or supplemented the grammatical 'rule' and/or examples in your textbook? What adaptation did you make, and why? With hindsight, do you think your adaptation was helpful to your students?

6 The TLA of expert and novice teachers

6.1 Introduction

The present chapter examines the TLA of L2 teachers with differing amounts of teaching experience and differing degrees of teaching expertise. It begins with a brief introduction to ideas within the teacher education literature concerning the stages of teacher development and the nature of expertise. This is followed by observations about the TLA of novice and advanced beginner L2 teachers, drawing in the main on quantitative data. The main part of the chapter is then devoted to discussion of research (based mainly on qualitative data) shedding light on the characteristics of the TLA of highly proficient/expert L2 teachers, focusing first on a study of the TLA of three highly proficient L2 teachers, and then on the TLA of one particular teacher, Marina, the 'expert' teacher from Tsui (2003).[1]

6.2 The stages of teacher development

The distinction between 'novice' and 'expert' teachers has been extensively explored in the education literature (Carter et al., 1988; Leinhardt, 1989; Livingston and Borko, 1989; Westerman, 1991; and Berliner, 1994 are just some examples of such studies). Few (if any) of those early studies focused upon the special characteristics of the L2 teacher. More recently, however, as part of the increased attention to L2 teacher cognitions noted in Chapter 4, Tsui's (2003) case studies of four secondary school teachers of L2 English have revealed a great deal about the nature of expertise in language teaching and how such expertise may develop during the teacher's professional life cycle.

In discussions of the development of pedagogical expertise, Dreyfus and Dreyfus's (1986) five-stage model of skill acquisition has been highly influential. In their model, proposed as a characterisation of general human expertise, Dreyfus and Dreyfus assign the following labels to

---

[1] Subsequent to Tsui (2003), I conducted further interviews with Marina and observed her teach. The discussion in 6.5 draws on both Tsui (2003) and my own data.

their five stages: 'novice', 'advanced beginner', 'competent', 'proficient' and 'expert'. Berliner (see, e.g., 1994) has applied the Dreyfus and Dreyfus model to the acquisition of expertise in teaching. Table 5 (see p. 120) sets out the five-stage model of pedagogical expertise development as interpreted by Berliner (1994) and summarises his description of the typical characteristics of teachers at each stage.

Such descriptions provide us with a useful summary of many of the distinctive features of teachers' pedagogical practice at different stages of their careers. For that reason, Berliner's (1994) model is presented here. However, it is important not to over-simplify the nature of teacher development. It should not, for instance, be assumed from such a model that just because the labels for the first two stages suggest some connection with length of experience, all teachers proceed with equal rapidity through all the stages, or that every teacher, given sufficient experience, becomes expert. Berliner (1994), as indicated in Table 5, recognises this, noting that there are some teachers who stay 'fixed' at a level that is less than competent. Berliner (2001) observes that there are only a small percentage of teachers who continue to develop into experts. Tsui (2003) makes a similar point when she emphasises the distinction between expertise and experience, highlighting the crucial difference between the expert teacher and the experienced non-expert. It should also not be assumed from Table 5, despite the note in parentheses in Stage 1, that all new teachers are necessarily less than competent. Hammerness et al. (2005: 381) refer to a number of recent studies suggesting that 'under the right circumstances, with particular kinds of learning experiences, new teachers can develop a more expert practice even as beginning practitioners'. Tsui (2003) notes further limitations of a model of this kind, which focuses on the behaviours characteristic of each stage of teacher development rather than the processes by which expertise is developed and maintained.

Among the teachers we have examined so far, most (with the exception of Yan and, to a lesser extent, Shirley) have illustrated behaviours typically associated with the 'novice' / 'advanced beginner' stages of teacher development. For that reason, the major part of this chapter will concentrate on the TLA and content-related behaviour of 'proficient'/ 'expert' teachers.

6.3 The TLA of the 'novice' teacher

A certain amount of evidence regarding the declarative TLA of novice L2 teachers can be found in Andrews (1999c). The data relate to performance on the test of Language Awareness (LA) referred to in Chapter 4, focusing

Table 5: Berliner's five-stage model of teacher development (based on Berliner, 1994)

Stage 1: Novice level [all student teachers and 1st-year teachers]	• Needs context-free rules/procedures about teaching • Operates rationally, but fairly inflexibly, in following such rules/procedures • Starts to learn the objective facts and features of situations and to gain experience
Stage 2: Advanced beginner level [many 2nd-year and 3rd-year teachers]	• Experience begins to be melded with the verbal knowledge acquired in Stage 1 • Starts to acquire episodic and case knowledge, and to recognise similarities across contexts • Still unsure of self and of what to do when experience / case knowledge is lacking • May still have little sense of what is important in a specific situation
Stage 3: Competent level [many 3rd-year and 4th-year teachers + more experienced teachers]	• Personally in control of events going on around him/her • Makes conscious choices about what to do • Has rational goals and is able to set priorities, decide on goals and choose sensible means for achieving those goals • When teaching, is able to determine what is or is not important • Still not very fast, fluid or flexible in behaviour
Stage 4: Proficient level [a modest number of teachers, from around 5th year of teaching onwards]	• Intuition and know-how become prominent • Is able to view situations holistically and to recognise similarities between events • Can therefore predict events more precisely • Is able to bring case knowledge to bear on a problem • Still analytic and deliberative in deciding what to do
Stage 5: Expert level [a small number of teachers, after at least 5 years]	• Has an intuitive grasp of situations • Seems to sense in non-analytic and non-deliberative ways how to respond appropriately in classroom situations • With routine, repetitive tasks, acts fluidly, effortlessly and without consciously choosing what to do or to attend to • When a problem arises, and with non-routine tasks, is able to bring deliberate, analytic processes to bear • Is willing and able to reflect on and learn from experience

on knowledge of grammar and grammatical terminology (see Appendix for details of the test). In this particular study, 40 prospective teachers took the LA test. Twenty of these novices were a homogeneous group of NNS of English (all Cantonese NS of a similar age starting a Bachelor of Education degree in Hong Kong majoring in L2 English). The other 20 novices were NS of English, all graduates and therefore a little older than the NNS group. The NS novice teachers were all taking a one-year full-time pre-service postgraduate course of initial teacher education in the UK and were about to begin a minor elective in TEFL/TESL. For the purposes of comparison in Andrews (1999c), the NS novices were divided into two groups of ten, depending on whether their first degree was in English Studies or Modern Languages. Table 6 shows the mean percentage scores of the three groups of novice teachers (the mean total scores together with the mean for each of the four parts of the test) compared with the mean percentages for two groups of serving teachers: the group of 20 NNS serving teachers (with an average of two years' full-time teaching experience) who took part in the Andrews (1999c) study, and the 187 serving teachers (at least 90% of whom were NNS of English) referred to in Chapter 4 (Andrews, 1999b).

The performance of the NS groups will be considered in a little more detail in the next chapter. As one might expect, however, given that the error-correction task is essentially a measure of language proficiency, the NS groups scored well on that part of the test, causing the overall mean for the NS Modern Linguist novices, for example, to be substantially closer to that of the serving teachers than would otherwise have been the case. If we focus on the two most demanding components of the LA test (production of metalanguage and explanation of errors), then the performance of the serving teachers is markedly better than that of any of the novice groups. The NNS novice teachers' performance is probably the most appropriate to compare with that of the serving teachers, since the former are recent products of the system in which the latter are teaching. The difference in their scores, which is especially noticeable in the two most challenging components, suggests that L2 teaching experience, particularly in an education system with a long tradition of form-focused teaching, may be associated with a certain degree of continuing development of declarative TLA, at least from the novice to advanced beginner stages. As noted in Chapter 4, however, when three of these serving teachers took the same LA test after an eight-year gap, at a point when they had between 10 and 12 years' full-time teaching experience, their subject-matter knowledge as it relates to grammar seemed to have changed remarkably little (see Andrews, 2006, for further details). The extent to which the declarative TLA of novice teachers evolves and continues to develop is clearly something that needs to be researched systematically in a range of teaching contexts.

Table 6: LA test scores of pre-service and in-service teachers

	NS novice teachers English Studies 1st degree *n = 10* (%)	NNS novice teachers *n = 20* (%)	NS novice teachers Modern Languages 1st degree *n = 10* (%)	NNS serving teachers *n = 20* (%)	Serving teachers (from Andrews, 1999b) *n = 187* (%)
Correction of errors	85.3	76.77	96.0	87.0	80.6
Recognition of metalanguage	50.6	71.9	76.1	82.0	75.1
Production of metalanguage	14.3	48.8	33.4	65.4	63.2
Explanation of errors	11.7	22.3	27.3	42.5	38.9
Total	43.2%	56.1%	60.3%	70.3	65%

As for the procedural TLA of novice L2 teachers, we have seen several examples in previous chapters of teachers with limited teaching experience exhibiting less than 'competent' (i.e. pre-Stage 3) TLA-related behaviours in their pedagogical practice. One characteristic of less-experienced L2 teachers that has been noted in the literature is their relative lack of engagement with the language itself compared with their more experienced counterparts. For instance, in a study of the interactive decision-making (i.e. decisions made in the course of teaching) of nine L2 teachers with experience ranging from 0 to 15 years, Nunan found a marked difference in the extent to which teachers' classroom decisions were driven by language issues (Nunan, 1992). The experienced teachers in his study made nearly twice as many language-related interactive decisions as the inexperienced teachers. The inexperienced teachers focused much more on classroom processes (such as time management, and managing and organising the classroom) rather than content.

Zhu's (2004) study of four advanced beginner L2 teachers in Guangzhou, People's Republic of China, reveals a similar order of priorities among inexperienced teachers. Zhu also makes a number of interesting observations about the limited nature of these teachers' engagement with language-related areas in their teaching. Such engagement occurred in class and occasionally in preparation, but only to the extent of uncritically following the textbook. The four teachers in her study very rarely focused on language in any way in their post-lesson reflections. In other words, there was no real engagement with the content of learning in the 'commitment' sense (as discussed in Chapter 5). According to Zhu (2004:375), 'None of the teachers "problematised" language in the sense of thinking about aspects of language structures which might be difficult for learners, and how best to help learners cope with those potential difficulties.'

In relation to the ability of teachers to predict language likely to prove difficult for learners, McNeill (2005) reports interesting and, at first glance, rather surprising findings concerning the relative merits of novice and more experienced teachers. McNeill's study focused on vocabulary, and the sensitivity of teachers to their students' learning needs as revealed by their awareness of lexical difficulties in a reading text. McNeill compared the performance of four groups of teachers, focusing on the NS/NNS dimension as well as the 'novice' versus 'expert' contrast. The results showed considerable individual variation among teachers, but the 'novice' teachers (i.e. those with no real background in education or applied linguistics) performed the best. McNeill suggests that the fact they performed better than their more experienced counterparts may have been due to their having only recently left school themselves: they were all first-year students on a Bachelor of Education course majoring in L2 English (and therefore total novices with no classroom teaching experience). As McNeill (2005:115–16) observes, 'their closeness in age and experience to the students no doubt allowed them to empathise more with their students' difficulties'.

Andrews (1996) shows something of the shift in priorities that can occur as 'novice' teachers advance beyond the total novice stage and begin to experience the realities of classroom teaching. In this particular study, which replicated research reported by Palfreyman (1993), five pairs of novice teachers (four NNS and one NS) were given the same lesson-planning task: to prepare a lesson presenting the Present Perfect to a class of Secondary 3 (13- to 14-year-old) students. Of the four NNS pairs, two were second-year students on a four-year Bachelor of Education programme majoring in L2 English (i.e. they were total novices, with no experience of classroom teaching from the teacher's side of the fence). The other two NNS pairs were also second-year students studying for a Bachelor of Education, but in their case it was a two-year 'top-up' programme for students who had already completed their initial professional training in a College of Education. Therefore, the four teachers in these two last pairs, although still 'novice', were certificated teachers with at least two significant spells of classroom experience from the practicum on their initial training course. As the analysis in Andrews (1996) reveals, the planning discussions of the two NNS pairs with no classroom experience are focused to a large degree on the specific language structure, with their limited comments on methodology being strongly influenced by their previous experiences as learners. By contrast, the two NNS pairs who are already certificated teachers give much greater priority to methodology, in ways which reveal the impact of both their training and their practical experience. Issues of content still play a part in their discussions, but they are already much more focused on questions of classroom technique, such as whether to use pairwork or group work, and 'information gap' or 'communication gap' activities. The relative lack of importance of language-related issues in the planning of these novice L2 teachers with classroom experience has clear parallels with the findings of Zhu (2004) concerning the advanced beginner teachers in her study.

As the discussion in this section has shown, it is difficult to make too many generalisations about the TLA of novice L2 teachers, partly because of the small sample sizes in the studies discussed. There are likely, for example, to be significant differences among novice teachers depending on whether or not they are total novices and on the nature and expectations of the teaching context in which they are working. Also, as individuals they may well behave in quite different ways because of the prior experiences, especially the L2 learning experiences, which have moulded them, as well as their language background and where they would place themselves on the NS/NNS continuum. All of these factors are likely to have had an impact on their subject-matter cognitions, their confidence about handling the language content of their teaching, and therefore their TLA in pedagogical practice.

However, at the same time as we note the diversity of the 'novice' teacher and the difficulties of generalisation, we should also acknowledge that there do appear to be certain commonalities in their language awareness, as revealed in the studies discussed, which may apply to the majority of novice / advanced beginner L2 teachers in most work situations. It seems, for instance, that they may tend to have lower levels of declarative knowledge of subject matter than their more experienced counterparts, particularly when the latter are employed in educational contexts that oblige the teacher to deal explicitly with language content on a day-to-day basis. There is also evidence to suggest that, once novice teachers move beyond the total novice stage and start to gain experience of the classroom, their engagement with language content tends to be at a relatively superficial level, because their priorities typically lie elsewhere (with classroom management, for example) at this early stage of their professional development. It may also be the case that inexperienced teachers are more liable than more experienced teachers to display the TLA limitations noted in a number of the snapshots in previous chapters.

6.4 The TLA of 'proficient'/'expert' teachers

In this section and the one that follows, we shall look at the TLA of four highly 'proficient'/'expert' L2 teachers. Our focus first of all will be on the three teachers described in detail in Andrews and McNeill (2005). Then, in 6.5, we shall look at the TLA of Marina, the 'expert' teacher in Tsui's (2003) case studies.

As Tsui (2003) notes, when researchers attempt to study the cognitions and practices of 'expert' teachers, they face problems in deciding on the basis for identifying such teachers. Research studies in the past have used various criteria: length of experience, recommendations by school administrators and academic qualifications. Each of these criteria used alone, however, is potentially problematic. Tsui suggests that, with our current level of understanding of expertise in teaching, the best strategy is to employ a combination of criteria, such as experience, reputation and recommendation, supported by classroom observation. In the case of the three teachers in Andrews and McNeill (2005), they were initially singled out as 'Good Language Teachers' and therefore appropriate participants in the study, on the basis of the level of their professional qualifications. Their reputation among colleagues, supported by previous lesson observations by the researchers, provided further confirmation of their suitability. It was also on the basis of such a combination of criteria (experience, reputation and recommendation, supported by classroom observation) that Marina was identified as a suitable participant in Tsui's (2003) study of expertise in L2 teaching.

Among the three teachers (all NNS of English) discussed in Andrews and McNeill (2005), two (Anna and Bonnie) teach L2 English in Hong Kong secondary schools, each being English Panel Chair in her school. The third (Trudi), a German NS, teaches L2 English in a tertiary institution in the UK. In examining the cognitions and practices of these teachers, the study sought to shed light on the following three questions about 'Good Language Teachers' (GLTs):

(1) Do they possess highly developed levels of declarative knowledge of the language systems (i.e. declarative TLA)?
(2) Do they exhibit highly developed levels of TLA in their pedagogical practice (i.e. procedural TLA)?
(3) What are the characteristics of their TLA?

The data gathered were of three types: test data; lesson observation (of two lessons, which were videotaped); and interview (two semi-structured interviews, one a post-lesson interview following the first observation, and one totally unscripted 'stimulated-recall' interview relating to the videotape of the second observation).

In relation to the first question, and the levels of declarative TLA exhibited by the GLTs, the relevant data came from their LA test papers. Each GLT took the LA test (referred to in Chapter 4 and in 6.3 above) testing their explicit knowledge of grammar and grammatical terminology, together with a parallel test focusing on vocabulary knowledge and awareness. On the grammar component, the three teachers performed to a very similar level, with scores ranging from 71.4% to 74.3%. Interestingly, although these scores were several percentage points above the mean (65%) of the 187 teachers tested in Andrews (1999b) and notably higher than the mean (56.1%) achieved by the novice NNS teachers in Andrews (1999c) referred to in 6.3, such performances would not have stood out in comparison with the 17 teachers discussed in Chapter 4. Of that particular group, 8 out of the 17 (including Tony, Snapshot 11) scored better than any of the GLTs, the top score among the 17 being 90%, which was achieved by Shirley (Snapshot 5). Yan (Snapshot 10) scored 80% on the same test. Given that the earlier tests were taken under very different circumstances from the subsequent administrations, it may not be appropriate to draw too many conclusions from such comparisons. Nevertheless, since the teachers discussed in Chapter 4 had no professional qualifications and were in general far less experienced than the GLTs, it is perhaps surprising that the latter did not display markedly higher levels of declarative TLA.

In their pedagogical practice, all three GLTs revealed themselves to be 'language-aware' in broadly similar ways that I shall outline below. At the same time, however, on the evidence from the two observed lessons, the answer to the second question above (concerning the levels of their procedural TLA) can only be a qualified yes. Although the GLTs exhibited many 'language-aware' qualities, none of them could be considered to be the 'finished article' as far as their TLA is concerned. The extent of the limitations of their procedural TLA should not be exaggerated, but with each of them certain minor imperfections became apparent in their mediation of input for learning, those limitations all being vocabulary-related rather than grammar-related. Snapshot 12 describes one of Bonnie's lessons.

Snapshot 12: Bonnie

Bonnie is the English Panel Chair in a co-educational school in an industrial district in the New Territories with an intake of average/below-average academic ability. It is a Monday afternoon in March, and Bonnie is teaching a class of thirty-six Secondary 3 (13- to 14-year-old) students.

One strategy Bonnie frequently employs in her teaching is that of using authentic texts, particularly articles from the *Young Post*, an English language newspaper aimed at readers of secondary-school age. In this particular lesson, the theme is pets, and the advantages and disadvantages of keeping different animals as pets.

Shortly after the lesson begins, Bonnie asks the students to read a letter to the Editor extracted from the *Young Post*. The letter is headed 'Treat your pets with love and respect'. Bonnie has underlined seven words in the text, including *Treat* and *respect* in the headline, and written seven definitions in speech bubbles surrounding the text. The students' task is to match each word to its meaning.

Bonnie tells the students that she herself looked up each word in a dictionary, and used the dictionary definition in the speech bubble. It is this strategy, however, which leads to potential confusion for the students, because Bonnie has taken each word in isolation, without seeming to have paid much attention to its meaning in the text. For example, the definition provided for *respect* in the headline *Treat your pets with love and respect* is 'a feeling of admiration'. Leaving aside the question as to whether students who do not understand *respect* would understand the word *admiration* any more easily, there is clearly something odd about treating a pet with a feeling of admiration. Bonnie's linking of *admiration* to *looking up to* and *wanting to copy* in her subsequent explanation makes the application to pets even stranger.

A similar problem occurs with the word *treat* in the same headline. The definition provided by Bonnie is 'to behave in a nice way', which again fails to fit the headline very well. Its inadequacy as a definition is clearly shown in the second sentence of the letter, which begins 'If you treat your pets badly . . .'

Immediately after the vocabulary-matching task, Bonnie focuses the students' attention on the following pairs of words: *obey/disobey* and *treat/mistreat*. Bonnie asks the students to spot the pattern in the pairs of words, which she then demonstrates on the blackboard by putting ticks next to *obey* and *treat* and crosses next to *disobey* and *mistreat* to indicate positive and negative respectively. Bonnie's focus on the negative meanings associated with the prefixes *dis-* and *mis-* is not in itself confusing. The potential for student confusion arises from Bonnie's treatment of the meaning contrast as if it is the same in each pair, rather than between positive and negative in the case of *obey/disobey* and neutral/negative in the case of *treat/mistreat*.

Given the fact that these limitations became apparent in relation to one area of knowledge about language (i.e. vocabulary), it may be that expertise within TLA has parallels with expertise in teaching more broadly. Just as, in teaching generally, teachers may be 'experts' in some aspects of their professional activity and not others (Tsui, 2003), so in relation to the handling of language content L2 teachers may exhibit greater expertise in some areas than others. In other words, the apparently 'language-aware' teacher may not in fact be equally aware, equally proficient (or indeed equally confident) across all the language systems.

Having said that, however, these GLTs generally exhibited a very high level of TLA in pedagogical practice, with the following major characteristics. The first and perhaps most striking characteristic is their willingness to engage with language, i.e. with the content of learning. In the previous chapter, it was argued that teacher engagement with content-related issues in the classroom is a significant variable influencing the application of TLA in practice. The interviews with all three GLTs show how central the content of learning is both to their thinking about language pedagogy and to their classroom practice. Each GLT engages with content in her own individual way, but for all of them content issues form the core of their thinking, planning and teaching. Trudi's approach to engagement is offered as an illustration.

Trudi characterises herself as a teacher who tries to be both communicative in everything she is doing and 'very well structured at the same time'. She claims that her overall approach to L2 pedagogy is based upon her own school experiences as a learner of Latin and a student of her L1, German, together with her subsequent studies of linguistics, language acquisition and humanistic psychology. She sees her knowledge of linguistics and psychology as going hand in hand, with the latter helping her to understand how best to draw on her linguistic knowledge to assist learners. With the students she currently teaches (post-secondary and adult learners in a tertiary institution), Trudi firmly believes that in order to learn the L2 they need explicit knowledge of grammar as a base on which to build up their implicit knowledge: 'We know this intrinsic structure exists from psycholinguistics . . . so we must give students all possible support to build it up . . . If we teach the implicit way, then it makes the process so much longer . . . If we try to use both the creative and the conscious way, then it helps . . . They're old enough to learn deliberately.' Trudi's teaching in the two observed lessons is noteworthy for its attention to both the cognitive and affective/creative domains, as well as for the way in which she 'scaffolds' learners into using the language forms she is teaching: 'visualising the rules in the first instance . . . giving very carefully selected examples in the beginning . . . make it clear what I'm talking about, and then go over to structured exercises, less structured exercises following, and . . . to come more and more to a transferred situation in which they can speak freely'.

Trudi makes an interesting comparison between herself, as an experienced NNS teacher of English with a study background in modern and classical languages, linguistics and psychology, and some of her NS teacher colleagues with non-relevant degrees and basic TEFL training. She observes in one of the interviews that a number of those colleagues have said to her 'Why are you doing tenses again?' Trudi comments that as a NNS she is constantly aware of her own mistakes and of the complexity of tenses in English. She suggests of her colleagues: 'Maybe they don't understand the difficulties the students face. So some of them said "Why do you teach tenses again?" Sort of tick, tenses done, must understand them . . . They don't know that there is more behind . . . especially behind the English tenses than 's' in the simple present . . . It's how to use it.'

A second characteristic of the TLA of all three of these GLTs is their self-awareness, in particular their awareness of the limitations of their own TLA. As noted above, there seem to be a number of areas of subject-matter knowledge (at least on the evidence provided by the LA test in relation to grammar and vocabulary), which could be improved. Trudi's comments above are indicative of the extent to which these teachers are aware of their limitations. Anna reveals a similar level of self-awareness, when she twice says 'I myself am not very good at vocabulary', and blames herself for any limitations in her students' vocabulary knowledge: 'I may not have given them a good model to stimulate them to know enough. So I still think that they have not enough [vocabulary knowledge] because of me to a certain extent.'

At the same time, among these GLTs such self-awareness does not have the effect (noted among some of the teachers we have met in earlier chapters, such as Rose and Maggie) of inhibiting their engagement with content-related issues or causing any of them to adopt avoidance strategies. These are highly experienced teachers, all with very different classroom personalities but with very similar levels of self-confidence and self-belief. They all therefore confront language issues head on, with (as Trudi's remarks suggest) self-awareness enhancing their sensitivity both to the challenges facing their learners and to those learners' interlingual development. Their self-awareness is also linked to a quest for self-improvement. All three GLTs reveal in their interviews the time and effort spent consulting grammars, dictionaries and other reference materials in order to enhance their subject-matter knowledge to support their teaching. As a further illustration of these GLTs' recognition of the need for continuing professional development, it is worth noting that at the time the study was conducted, one of the two Hong Kong GLTs was about to begin studying for a Master's degree in English Language

Education while the other had been accepted on to a Doctor of Education programme.

Associated with their self-awareness is the willingness of these GLTs to engage in reflection about the content of learning, and the extent to which they engage in such reflection as part of their pedagogical practice. From their interview responses, for example, including their stimulated-recall comments on their teaching, it was evident that for all three GLTs the content of learning, and how best to make input available for learning, was central to their reflections, both their reflection-on-action (before and after teaching) and their reflection-in-action (while teaching).

There are a number of characteristics of the classroom practice of all three GLTs that could be attributed to their TLA and the quality of their reflections about the content of learning. As noted earlier, they all engage fully with the content of learning and share a belief in focusing on language form at appropriate points in their teaching. Anna, for example, describes her own practice as follows: 'I will make the language as a core in the language lesson, and then I think of contexts, situations for them to use the language.' In the same interview she discusses her own pedagogical approach in relation to task-based language teaching (TBLT), the approach upon which the most recent English Language syllabuses for Hong Kong schools are supposedly based.[2] She describes TBLT as 'old wine in new bottles', and says that, for her, 'Language learning is central . . . I mean there is some central element we need to learn: the grammar, the sentence patterns, the vocabulary, the writing, the reading, the listening. Whatever term we give, we still have to teach them [the students], we've to motivate them, to stimulate and engage them into purposeful discussion and purposeful tasks.'

In focusing on form, whether grammar or vocabulary (the areas highlighted in this particular study), all three GLTs appear to have an intuitive understanding of the importance of 'input enhancement' (Sharwood Smith, 1991), making salient within the input the key features of the language area in order to enhance the chances of the learners' 'noticing' as a prerequisite for subsequent 'intake' (Schmidt, 1990). The three GLTs adopt different strategies to this end. Anna, for instance, uses a range of colours on her Powerpoint slides, to highlight particular lexical items, and to indicate contrasts of meaning, such as positive and negative personality traits. Although Anna does not use the term 'noticing', it is clear that this is her goal: 'Only for familiarisation. If they want to use it, they use it. If not then at least they have seen it before, it's not something

---

[2] As noted in Chapter 4, the approach generally adopted in Hong Kong would more accurately be described as 'task-supported' rather than 'task-based' (Ellis, 2004).

totally new . . . Because it's sometimes scary to find there are so many new words. But by association, by thinking "Oh, I've come across this" . . ., then it will make them feel better.'

Meanwhile, Bonnie, relying on rather more basic technology, makes use of the blackboard and different colour chalks to highlight patterns. Trudi, too, relies on the blackboard. Like Bonnie, she frequently builds up patterns on the board at the beginning of the lesson and leaves them there throughout the class in an attempt to promote assimilation by the learners. When interviewed, she talks of her very deliberate use of a combination of drama, colours, gestures and voice to help anchor the patterns she is teaching and to help set up appropriate associations. Bonnie attributes her current practice to observing and reflecting upon the practices of other teachers:

> I've always thought that the organisation on the board is very important for the students . . . When I go for classroom observations, I've seen teachers who, when they explain things, they write on the board and they write everywhere . . . and when they don't have enough space, just clear up one patch and write on it. I thought that what the teacher writes doesn't stay long enough for the students to absorb . . . so I've made a point to be organised when I write on the board.

The motive underlying Bonnie's use of the blackboard is illustrative of another characteristic shown by all three GLTs: their awareness of learners' potential difficulties. This awareness shows itself in the strategies that these GLTs employ to make input available for learning: their strategies for input enhancement, the support they all give individual learners, based on knowledge and understanding of their specific problems and needs, and also the way in which they all skilfully control their own language so that it presents an appropriate level of challenge for the learners. Whether the students are at an advanced level, as in Anna's case, or elementary level (as with Bonnie and Trudi), the teacher-mediated input in each case seems to be pitched at precisely the right level.

6.5 The TLA of an 'expert' teacher: the case of Marina

Berliner's (1994) model of teacher development describes some of the behaviours that are characteristic of the small number of teachers who can justifiably be labelled 'experts'. The following pages will explain why Marina was considered worthy of such a label.

Marina, like Anna and Bonnie, is the English Panel Chair in her school. Marina's school is a co-educational English-medium (EMI) secondary school in Kowloon. The school is situated in a public housing estate, and most of the students are working-class children from the estate. The school's intake has been improving year by year, and students currently entering the school are usually of above-average academic ability compared with the general secondary school population in Hong Kong. In Tsui's (2003) case studies of four teachers of L2 English, all working in the same school, Marina was the 'expert' teacher.

Marina has been teaching for more than 15 years, and has gained all her teaching experience in the same school, becoming the English Panel Chair in her fifth year as a teacher. She has received all her tertiary education at the University of Hong Kong: a Bachelor's degree in Translation, a Postgraduate Certificate in Education (majoring in L2 English) in which she gained a Distinction, and a Master's degree in Education (with a TEFL Major), which was also awarded 'with Distinction'. After obtaining her first degree, Marina worked in administrative positions (as a civil servant, and a hospital administrator) before becoming a teacher, although teaching had always been her ambition (see Tsui, 2003:82–4, for further discussion of Marina's background).

Tsui (2003:200) notes that 'embedded in Marina's teaching of grammar is rich and integrated knowledge'. At the core of that 'rich and integrated knowledge' is Marina's knowledge of subject matter, i.e. her declarative TLA. Like the GLTs above, Marina's performance on the LA test suggests that she is not the 'finished article' as far as her subject-matter knowledge is concerned, as Marina herself acknowledges: 'Even after having taught grammar for years, I still need to consult grammar books . . . I am not a native speaker. I will call myself just a second language learner. So I do need to consult grammar books when I am not sure.' At the same time, she has confidence in her English knowledge and ability, and she is indeed a highly proficient communicator in English both orally and in writing. Although there may still be room for improvement, particularly in the explanation of errors, Marina's total LA test score of 79% compares favourably with the mean scores of the novice NNS teachers (56.1%), the untrained serving teachers (65%), and indeed Anna, Bonnie and Trudi (71.4%, 72.4% and 74.3% respectively), as discussed earlier in the chapter. Marina's scores on the test components were as noted in Table 7.

Interestingly, Marina is (like Maggie, in 5.3), the product of a highly academic EMI girls' school. In Marina's case, she gained admission to her secondary school by virtue of a scholarship as a result of her outstanding performance at primary school. Marina recollects that at secondary school: 'we were immersed in the whole English-rich environment. Yeah, I couldn't recall speaking to teachers other than Chinese teachers [i.e. of Chinese subjects] in Chinese at all. So we were

Table 7: Marina's LA test scores

Correction of errors	Recognition of metalanguage	Production of metalanguage	Explanation of errors	Total
93.3%	88.9%	87.5%	53.3%	79%

forced to speak in English, at least in class and to teachers.' However, whereas for Maggie, as we saw in Chapter 5, using English as a medium of communication at school was a natural extension of her experiences outside the classroom, for Marina the situation was very different. As reported in Tsui (2003:82–4), Marina comes from a working-class background, and her parents speak no English. Therefore, when she left her Chinese-medium primary school, she found adapting to EMI secondary school life extremely challenging. Her response to that challenge was to work as hard as possible on improving her English through, for example, extensive reading. She also, unlike Maggie, actively sought to engage with grammar as part of her learning. In Marina's school, as she recalls it, 'we didn't do a lot of systematic grammar teaching'. As a strategy for self-improvement, Marina therefore made a point of teaching herself grammar: 'My memory of my secondary school years [experience of grammar] was just going out and, you know, buying some grammar exercise books and practising myself those grammar items.'

Marina exhibits a similarly active engagement with the content of learning in her own pedagogical practice in relation to grammar. Just as we saw with Anna, Bonnie and Trudi (in 6.4), the content of learning is at the core of her thinking about language pedagogy and also her classroom practice. Marina describes English Language Teaching in her school as a combination of approaches, including tasks and other features of CLT as well as more 'traditional' elements, but within a syllabus framework that is form- and skill-driven rather than task-driven. Marina sees grammar and vocabulary as central to language learning, even within a context like Hong Kong where a task-based approach to language teaching is being officially promoted: 'I still think grammar and vocabulary are two very important parts. And in order to do a certain task well in terms of both content and language, students need the grammar. So I don't see a task-based approach being simply achieving the task and that's done. It's how the students achieve the task that is important.'

Marina has a clear set of principles that guide her approach to the teaching of grammar (see Tsui, 2003:195–6):

- She firmly believes in an inductive (in the sense of 'discovery learning') approach that requires the active participation of the students: 'Well,

133

when I teach grammar, I avoid just telling students the rules. I know from my experience that if you just tell them "OK, this is like this, that is like that", very often they just forget. So what I always try to do in a grammar lesson is not just telling them the rules, but trying to get them to do something.'

- She tries to ensure that grammar is taught and practised in 'natural', meaningful contexts: 'Of course it's not easy to be authentic, but I try to think of meaningful situations where a certain grammar item is used, and see whether it can be brought into the classroom.'
- She strongly believes in the value of collaborative learning: 'In the selection or design of activities, of course I am trying to get the students to work not only individually, but at least in pairs or in groups, so they help one another.'
- In setting up her activities, she often pushes her students to focus on the quality of their collaborative output by putting it on 'public display': 'Quite often in order to really get them to do something, I tell them that what they do will be discussed, commented on. That would be some sort of public display. That's also important. Because they know "OK, we have to work together and then in ten minutes' time the teacher will ask us to show the class our product."'

Planning is an extremely important aspect of Marina's engagement with the content of learning in her enactment of the curriculum. As Tsui (2003: 188) notes, 'Marina never goes to class without preparation and a lesson plan, no matter how busy she is.' The e-mail below (Snapshot 13), which Marina sent to me two days before I was due to watch her teach, illustrates both the intensity of Marina's engagement with the content of learning, and also the non-routine nature of her planning and teaching: even though she is teaching language items she has taught many times before, and even though she is extremely busy, she is challenging herself to think of fresh ways to handle the content rather than taking the 'safe' option.

Snapshot 13: Marina's pre-lesson e-mail

Date: Mon, 10 Jan 2005 09:03:02
From: Marina Tam
Subject: Your visit
To: Stephen Andrews

Dear Steve

My plan for this Wed's lesson is still fuzzy as I didn't have time to plan it in detail. I might make modifications as well.

Tomorrow's lesson and Wednesday's are related. My class is clipping some news articles on the tsunami and tomorrow we're going to look at one story in the *South China Morning Post* dated 7.1.2005. The headline is "I watched as my wife was sucked into the mud". It's mainly on comprehension – understanding the content.

On Wednesday, we'll use the same article. I'll do a quick revision. Then I'll draw students' attention to some verbs in the article followed by either gerunds/to-infinitives. Then we'll look at some other verbs from their Longman Express 3B textbook (there's a grammar page on this grammar point). There's very little I can tell you now regarding how I am going to use the grammar page. I'm still thinking. At this stage I'm inclined to draw students' attention to 3 categories: verbs + gerunds, verbs + to-infinitives & verbs + gerunds/to-infinitives. There are 3 verbs I plan to spend more time on: remember, forget and stop, as these mean differently when followed by gerunds and by to-infinitives. I might use a very simple corpus to get students to work out the difference in meaning. But I still need to work on it, and if I think of a better alternative I'll change my idea.

I'm still thinking of an activity for students to use the verbs + gerunds/to-infinitives productively.

I should've let you have more details but these days are really hectic. I'm doing English Panel book inspection and was in the school browsing students' writing and exercises on Saturday and Sunday. Well, this is the real picture of English teaching in secondary schools. Sometimes we don't have time to plan lessons until the day before.

Will keep you informed of my plan.

Best wishes
Marina

Like the GLTs in 6.4, Marina's procedural TLA is distinguished from that of less expert teachers by her ability to view the content of learning and the challenges it poses from the learners' perspective: 'I found it really helpful if I put myself into their shoes again. Because I learned English maybe in a similar way . . . a slightly different way, but then still like a second language learner.' This affects Marina's planning: 'whenever I plan something I try to put myself in the shoes of my students. I try to sort of think what they need, and how far they go, and whether they can manage something or not.' This ability also guides her as she builds scaffolding into her lesson.

Scaffolding the students' learning is something that Marina takes great pains over. Scaffolding plays a key role in maximising the effectiveness of her inductive ('discovery learning') approach to the teaching of grammar. It is a technique she picked up herself from her own foreign-language learning experience: 'I got this sort of scaffolding when I was doing my German lessons at the Goethe Institut. That was many years ago. I was still in the university. I went there, and there was a very good teacher. He introduced me to the idea of pairwork. And he was able to scaffold his lessons very well' (see also Tsui, 2003:86–7). Snapshot 14 shows how Marina scaffolds students' learning in the observed lesson referred to in Snapshot 13.

Snapshot 14: Marina's lesson

It is 8.15 on a cold Wednesday morning in January. Marina has a double (2 × 40 minutes) period with the forty students in her Secondary 3 class (13- to 14-year-olds).

The lesson proceeds as follows:

- Marina begins by getting the students to retell to a partner the story of the newspaper article studied the previous day. Each student uses as a cue the pictures he/she has drawn to illustrate the sequence of events in the story.

- Marina then writes on the board five verbs from the first two columns of the story (*love, wanted, kept, began* and *started*) and gives the students one minute to find and circle those verbs.

- She uses the board to focus briefly on the verb-chain patterns with the first two verbs as used in the article, eliciting the terms *to-infinitive* and *gerund* from the students. She draws two columns on the board (headed 'verb + gerund, verb + *to*-infinitive'), writing *love* in the first and *want* in the second. She asks the students to assign the other three verbs to one or other of the columns, based on the way they are used in the article. Then she alerts the students to cases where the verb can be followed by either a *gerund* or a *to-infinitive*, using *love* as an example. She draws a third column on the board (headed 'verb + gerund or *to*-infinitive') and the students agree to move *love* to that column.

- Marina directs the students' attention to the textbook (Longman Express 3B) and the list of 21 verbs in the 'HELP' box on page 92. The students discuss (in pairs) which of the three categories each verb belongs to. Different students then volunteer their guesses.

Marina records their hypotheses on the board, without comment or correction, using her three columns.

- Marina introduces the idea of using concordances to check patterns of grammar usage. Using a visualiser, she illustrates the process with two verbs from the list of 21 (*want* and *start*).

- She divides the class into groups of four. Each group has a set of concordances (ten per verb) for the 19 remaining verbs from the list, plus *stop*. Each member of the group has concordances for five of the verbs. Individual group members, having arrived at conclusions about the verb-chain patterns commonly found with their own five verbs, report to the others in the group. Marina then gets the groups to focus on their previous hypotheses, as listed on the board, and to come forward to volunteer any necessary corrections.

- Marina then focuses specifically on verbs where there is a meaning difference associated with the selection of + *gerund* or + *to-infinitive*. She highlights three such verbs: *remember*, *forget* and *stop*. Marina gives the students three short texts, relating true incidents from her own life. Each text contains two examples (illustrating the two patterns) of one of the three verbs, and some guiding questions. The students work individually and then in groups to work out a general rule that holds for all three verbs. They report to the class.

- Marina concludes by assigning two tasks. First, the students are to write something true about their own life experiences, using one or more of the verbs used by Marina in her own texts. Then, they are asked, while they are fulfilling the school's requirement to read the *South China Morning Post* (Hong Kong's major English-language newspaper) every day, to note in the articles they read examples of the different patterns of verb-chaining and to copy sample sentences into their grammar notebooks.

Two important features of Marina's planning, both of which are indicative of the nature of her TLA, are her alertness in spotting opportunities for focusing on language content and her ability to recognise how and in what ways the textbook treatment of content needs to be supplemented. These features are clearly illustrated in Snapshot 14 in her teaching of gerunds and infinitives. First, when Marina was using the newspaper article (referred to in Snapshot 13) for reading comprehension during her Tuesday class, she had already realised, as the e-mail suggests, that she could make use of it the following day: 'I noticed those patterns when I was reading and I thought "Oh yeah, it would be a good idea to have that as a start, just to draw their attention to those patterns first."' She had also concluded that there were limitations with the textbook's treatment of the grammar point, which would not actively engage the students: 'We need a bit of work. Instead of me telling them, I prefer their looking for some sort of answers. That is why I thought "OK, in this case why don't I ask them to look at the newspaper article first and single out some words and introduce the three different categories . . .?" '

In her planning, Marina constantly reviews what she is thinking of doing in light of her students' needs and abilities. In the lesson in Snapshot 14, for instance, the starting point was students' needs and Marina's familiarity with their problems: 'I particularly picked words like *remember* and *stop* because I've noticed that some students do have difficulty understanding how to use them and I think they are pretty common words and it would be good if they were able to master them.' The students are at the forefront of Marina's thinking throughout the planning process. Immediately after the lesson, she reports how she decided against her original idea of using concordances to focus on *remember*, *forget* and *stop* (an idea she was borrowing from Thornbury, 1999): 'When I looked at the lines, looked at the corpus, I was a little bit worried that the students may not find it easy to understand. So I finally came up with – it was yesterday – I came up with my own experience, trying to share with them something about me, using the different patterns.'

Marina is constantly thinking about her teaching and contemplating modifications to her lesson plan, even as the lesson is proceeding (reflection-in-action). The idea for the second post-lesson task in Snapshot 14, for example, arises spontaneously mid-class, stimulated by Marina's desire to encourage students to make meaningful use of their newspaper reading: 'the idea suddenly came . . . "Why don't I ask them to start reading the newspaper and looking for examples?" That came in the lesson, yeah.'

As we saw with Anna, Bonnie and Trudi earlier, reflection is a central characteristic of Marina's approach to teaching – not in a formal sense but, as she says, 'This is something I do.' Her immediate post-lesson reflections cover various aspects of her teaching, but content-related issues are a central part of the process:

> The first thing that I would think about would be whether students really learned from it. Yeah, and from that, I look at what makes it possible for them to learn it, acquire it and what hinders their acquisition. And then reflect on the activities I used, and how I presented the grammar point . . . Because sometimes it did happen, you know, I thought 'OK in this certain activity they might need a certain grammar point', but it turned out to be not exactly the case. It was those things I reflected on.

Then as she prepares to teach something that she has taught before, she uses her previous lesson plans as a stimulus for reflection on past experience: 'I try to just keep the very rough plans I have. So when I have to use the same idea again, it helps me to recall what I did. But it doesn't mean I just do step 1 to step 10 again. I would look at it again and see how I can change it.'

Like Anna, Bonnie and Trudi, Marina's TLA in pedagogical practice is also characterised by self-awareness. As we noted earlier, she is aware of her own limitations, but at the same time she has sufficient self-confidence that she does not feel the need to appear omniscient in front of her students: 'I don't want them to think that what I say is always true. Because it may not be the case at all . . . Sometimes I may say something wrong, and I have to go back in the next lesson and say "Sorry! I made a mistake."'

Linked to Marina's self-awareness is her sensitivity to the fact that she is at a very different stage of professional development from the 'novice' teachers in her English Panel, who would (she believes) find it quite difficult to admit to the class 'I am not sure about this.' Marina's experience of such teachers and their engagement with the content of learning is that they lack the sort of understanding of grammar items, particularly the understanding of the 'natural use' of those items, that would enable them to develop teaching strategies and activities. She understands the extent to which concerns about classroom management dominate the thinking of the inexperienced teacher (as noted, for instance, by Nunan, 1992, and discussed in 6.3 above). Marina recalls having experienced such uncertainties herself: 'I did undergo all these, you know, the whole process of like how I experiment with the activities.' However, Marina recalls these experiences positively as challenges, rather than negatively as problems: 'Of course if you look at it in a positive way, it's so challenging at the same time.'

Tsui (2003:227–8) describes expertise as 'constant engagement in exploration and experimentation, in problematising the unproblematic, and responding to challenges'. As our detailed examination of Marina's TLA has shown, she possesses all these qualities. At the same time, it is clear that in her pedagogical practice relating to grammar, as exemplified in Snapshots 13 and 14, her expertise is not based solely upon a highly developed TLA. Her pedagogical content knowledge in her enactment of the curriculum is functioning as an 'integrated and coherent whole' (ibid.:250), with her TLA (including knowledge of students) and other knowledge bases (such as knowledge of general pedagogy, knowledge of language pedagogy, knowledge of language learning strategies and knowledge of context) working seamlessly together to underpin her exemplary performance.

Tsui (2003) points out that her own characterisation of expertise is different from that of Dreyfus and Dreyfus (1986), who emphasise the intuitive, non-reflective nature of expertise. Tsui (2003) suggests that this difference in conceptualisation may be in part due to Dreyfus and Dreyfus's confusion of expert performance on the one hand, and the ways in which experts develop and maintain the ability to perform at 'expert' level on the other. It is also worth noting the discussion in the education literature (see, e.g., Hatano and Inagaki, 1986; Hatano and Oura, 2003) of the contrast between 'routine experts' and 'adaptive experts'. Bransford et al. (2005b:48–9) note that both types of expert continue to learn throughout their lifetimes: 'Routine experts develop a core set of competencies that they apply throughout their lives with greater and greater efficiency. In contrast, adaptive experts are much more likely to change their core competencies and continually expand the breadth and depth of their expertise.' Routine expertise is seen as being associated with efficiency, while adaptive expertise emphasises innovation. The adaptive expert is seen as possessing not only efficiency, but also the ability to adapt and innovate, even when this means 'unlearning' previous routines, 'letting go' of previously held beliefs and tolerating the ambiguity of having to rethink one's perspective. Marina undoubtedly fits into the category of the 'adaptive expert': she is highly efficient in every aspect of her pedagogical practice, but at the same time she is constantly questioning herself, re-assessing her teaching and her beliefs about what she does, and challenging herself to broaden and deepen her knowledge and her expertise as a teacher.

6.6 Conclusion

In this chapter, we have looked at the TLA of teachers with a range of experience and expertise, from total novices to highly experienced teachers. We have also examined in detail the TLA of highly proficient and expert teachers. In our discussion, we have noted the following:

- The process of teacher development is complex. Teachers do not develop at the same pace. In particular, only a small percentage ever become expert, and experience does not necessarily equate with expertise.
- There are problems with the terms 'novice teacher' and 'expert teacher'. With 'novice', the issue is one of coverage: the term does not differentiate between total novices and beginner teachers with some experience of classroom teaching. With 'expert', the problem relates to the criteria used to identify such teachers.

- There is an apparent tendency for novice teachers to have lower levels of declarative TLA than their more experienced counterparts working in a similar context.
- Less experienced teachers' engagement with the language content of their lessons appears to be relatively superficial, because their attention is focused more on issues, for example, of classroom management.
- The highly proficient NNS teachers of L2 English in the study discussed (Andrews and McNeill, 2005), while appearing to have markedly higher levels of declarative TLA than the sample of novice NNS teachers referred to in 6.3, still had room for improvement in their knowledge of subject matter.
- The procedural TLA of those highly proficient L2 teachers also revealed minor imperfections, but they generally exhibited a very high level of TLA, characterised by willingness to engage with the language content of learning, self-awareness (in particular, awareness of the limitations of their own TLA) and a readiness to engage in reflection about the content of learning as part of their everyday pedagogical practice.
- Expertise in L2 teaching requires the teacher to be language-aware, but that language awareness is a fully integrated part of the pedagogical content knowledge (PCK) of the expert teacher: the various knowledge bases making up the PCK of the L2 teacher (including TLA) work seamlessly together to underpin expert performance.
- Adaptive experts differ from routine experts in that, in addition to the efficiency of the latter, the former possess the ability to adapt and innovate.

In the following chapter, our attention turns to the language awareness of native-speaker and non-native-speaker L2 teachers.

Questions for discussion and reflection

1) Based on Berliner's (1994) five-stage model of teacher development, where would you place yourself, and why? Are there some aspects of (a) your overall teaching, and/or (b) your TLA that are at a different stage of development from others? If so, which aspects are more developed, which are less developed, and why?
2) When you first started L2 teaching, to what extent did you prioritise issues of language content? Did your attitude change at any stage? If so, when, and for what reasons?
3) In the teaching context with which you are most familiar, what levels of subject-matter knowledge (declarative TLA) would you

estimate that novice L2 teachers typically have? What are the reasons for this situation? Is it a situation that is generally considered problematic?

4) The minor imperfections observed in the procedural TLA of the three 'Good Language Teachers' (Andrews and McNeill, 2005) all concern vocabulary rather than grammar. How would you explain that? Would you expect to find a similar situation among L2 teachers in the context with which you are most familiar?

5) The 'expert' teacher in this chapter and two of the three 'Good Language Teachers' are non-native-speaker teachers of English working within a particular teaching context: the Hong Kong secondary school. In the teaching context(s) with which you are familiar, would you expect the TLA of 'expert' L2 teachers to take a similar or a different form?

6) Is an 'expert' teacher necessarily a 'perfect' teacher? Is it appropriate, for example, to label as an expert teacher of L2 English anyone who does not achieve a score approaching 100% in the Language Awareness test (Appendix)?

7 TLA and the native-speaker and non-native-speaker debate

7.1 Introduction

The issue of native-speaker (NS) and non-native-speaker (NNS) teachers of language, especially of L2 English, has been extensively discussed in recent years. It is an issue that inspires passionate debate, both within and outside the profession. The present chapter attempts a dispassionate analysis of the issue, with particular reference to the TLA of teachers of L2 English. The chapter begins by outlining some of the background to the debate. It then goes on to examine the arguments and research findings concerning the relative merits of NS and NNS teachers in relation to the three types of language-related knowledge encompassed by the label TLA: knowledge *of* language (i.e. language proficiency), knowledge *about* language (i.e. declarative knowledge of subject matter) and knowledge of students (especially the cognitive knowledge of learners as it relates to subject matter). It concludes with a brief discussion of English as a Lingua Franca (ELF) and the potential impact of ELF on any consideration of the relative merits of NS and NNS teachers.

7.2 The background to the issue: letters to the editor

At the time that I was writing this book, the two letters below appeared in the *South China Morning Post*. As the opening sentence of the first letter indicates, they formed part of a correspondence relating to professional standards among Hong Kong's teachers of L2 English, and to the role of NS teachers of English, including those, known as NETs (Native English Teachers) in the Hong Kong context, who have been recruited as part of the Hong Kong Government's drive to improve standards of English Language teaching in Hong Kong schools.

Although Letter 1 is unsigned, the writer is evidently a senior secondary school student (i.e. in Secondary 6 or 7) in a local (as opposed to 'international') school, and almost certainly a Cantonese NS. Readers will no doubt react in different ways to the sentiments that are expressed or implied in the letters, and perhaps also to the examples chosen by the writer of Letter 1 as indicators of the alleged inadequacies of 'local', i.e.

Letter 1

Reason for teacher bias

Correspondent Beda Chan is right in saying that racial discrimination exists in Hong Kong ('HK teacher bias, too', December 1). However, this is, in fact, necessary and unavoidable.

The vast majority of local English-language teachers today do not possess adequate language skills. They have a poor understanding of formal vocabulary – words such as 'divulge' and 'propound'. Their oral skills, especially, are rather poor; many are unable to speak fluently, while some even mispronounce certain words (examples of this are the teachers who served as my examiners in the Hong Kong Certificate of Education Examination, English syllabus B. They gave me a D in oral fluency).

[*Note: a 'D' grade represents a fairly low pass level*]

As students, many of our English-language teachers got a C or D in HKCEE English. They managed to enter the English or linguistics stream simply because no one else wanted to. My point is not to voice my grief over the HKCEE scores, but I have to say that such teachers are not worthy of their positions. They simply mislead their students. I am not saying that all non-native English teachers are bad; there are indeed some able ones.

Yet what's wrong with recruiting more native speakers? This is the only means by which we can create a proper English-speaking environment for our school children. Remember that native English speaker does not refer to a white skin, but to anyone whose mother tongue is English. For example, the school in which I am studying has seven native-English teachers, three of them ethnic Chinese, and one an African.

NAME AND ADDRESS SUPPLIED

(*South China Morning Post*, Letters page, 8 December 2005)

non-native-speaker (NNS) teachers. My purpose in quoting the two letters in full is simply to illustrate the strength of feeling which the NS/NNS teacher issue can inspire, not just among teachers themselves but among all stakeholders in the education process, and to highlight the concerns which provoke such correspondence.

At the heart of the issue is the question of language competence. Each of the writers of the two letters has his/her personal 'take' on the relative merits of NS and NNS teachers of L2 English. However, as their

Letter 2

Unqualified teachers

Is recruiting more native speakers the solution to Hong Kong's deteriorating English standards and a better option than the inadequate language skills of many local English teachers ('Reason for teacher bias', December 8)?

I doubt it. Many foreign institutes offer English-teaching courses in Hong Kong. They are not strict about participants' academic qualifications. It is not surprising that many enrol because they cannot find a job in their own profession, or they are visiting and need pocket money.

A British man I know paid $5,000 [*roughly £350 or US$640*] and attended a one-month course. He has been teaching English to 3- to 10-year-old children at a famous kindergarten in Kowloon Tong for over two years. A hairdresser, he has a secondary school education level. Although he speaks fluent English, he cannot spell and does not understand grammar. But no one will question his language skills because he is white.

None of his mates on the course were teachers by training, but yoga instructors, real estate agents and salesmen. Most were unemployed. Shouldn't they have the same qualifications as local teachers of English?

NAME AND ADDRESS SUPPLIED

(*South China Morning Post*, Letters page, 12 December 2005)

letters make clear, there are common perceptions among the general public that NS and NNS teachers of L2 English possess different strengths and weaknesses: while NS teachers may, for obvious reasons, have greater oral fluency and wider knowledge of vocabulary than the majority of their NNS counterparts, the subject-matter knowledge of the latter (in particular, their explicit knowledge of grammar) may be markedly better.

The NS/NNS comparison would no doubt inspire heated debate even if discussion were confined solely to the sensitive question of language competence. What makes the issue especially highly charged emotionally is the ideological and racial (racist) dimension. The privileging of the NS teacher of English has been seen by a number of critics (see, e.g., Phillipson, 1992) as being ideologically, politically and economically motivated, part of the 'linguistic imperialism' that is said to lie behind the worldwide spread of English. According to Kramsch (1999:34, cited in Llurda, 2004), 'it is the teaching of ESL within an assimilationist ideology that has canonised (or beatified) the native speaker around the world'. Kachru (1997:9) has described the idealisation of the NS as one of a number of myths hanging 'like a linguistic albatross around the necks of the users of the language', while Rajagopalan (1999:203) describes the NS/NNS distinction as 'at best a convenient myth the linguists have got used to working with, and at worst the visible tip of an insidious ideological iceberg'.

As the letters above point out, the debate about NS/NNS teachers of English has also become linked to questions of race. Rajagopalan (2005:287), for example, notes that the native speaker, instead of being an 'innocent theoretical reference point in language teaching, . . . is increasingly being seen today as a concept shot through with ideological, indeed often *racist*, connotations'. The impact of such racism, as experienced by the NNS teacher, is perhaps most evident in employment practices, where an employer's stated preference for a NS teacher of English may often translate into a preference for a white Anglo-Saxon. A recent editorial in the Education section of the *South China Morning Post* confirms that racist employment practices (though apparently not in operation at the school attended by the writer of Letter 1 above) are fairly commonplace in the Hong Kong primary and secondary schools for which NETs are recruited. The editorial suggests that Hong Kong, in its recruitment of teachers of English, might tap the expertise of nearby countries such as the Philippines, Singapore and India. However, as the writer then notes, 'there are huge barriers to such a move, not least prejudice and racism. Already, there is a tendency among many schools to prefer white, western NETs ahead of others' (Forestier, 2005).

The issue of the NS/NNS teacher is far from simple, and a detailed examination of all its complexities is beyond the scope of the current volume. However, my view is that L2 teacher competence does not depend on where one happens to be placed (or where one chooses to place oneself) on the NS/NNS continuum, and most certainly not on one's ethnicity. As we have seen from previous chapters, such competence requires any teacher, from whatever background, to develop a number of knowledge bases, both generic and subject-specific, and to maintain them at a level at which they can work harmoniously, mutually informing and supporting each other to underpin the teacher's enactment of the curriculum. Central among these knowledge bases is TLA, a label that encompasses three types of knowledge integral to the debate on NS/NNS teachers: knowledge *of* language (i.e. language proficiency), knowledge *about* language (i.e. declarative knowledge of subject matter) and knowledge of students (especially the cognitive knowledge of learners as it relates to subject matter). In the following sections, we shall look at arguments and research findings relating to each of these in turn. First, though, we shall look briefly at some of the history of the NS/NNS teacher debate.

7.3 The NS/NNS teacher issue: why it is not a simple dichotomy

In recent years, there has been a significant growth in the literature focusing on the NNS teacher (see, e.g., Braine, 1999; Kamhi-Stein, 2004; and Llurda, 2005a). The contributors to those volumes generally elect to use the terms NS and NNS teachers, although they sometimes prefer to refer to the latter as 'non-native English-speaking professionals' or 'non-native educators in ELT'. As the use of these alternative phrases suggests, the terms NS and NNS are felt to be potentially problematic in a number of ways.

First, their use suggests that there is a simple dichotomy. On the one hand, there are those who satisfy what Davies (1996a:156) calls the 'bio-developmental definition' of native speaker, a definition which is based on Bloomfield's use of the term: 'The first language a human being learns to speak is his [sic] native language; he is a native speaker of that language' (Bloomfield, 1933:43). On the other hand, there are all the rest, who do not fulfil that criterion and who are therefore by definition NNS of that language. Such a dichotomy is, however, an over-simplification, as Table 8 illustrates.

Table 8 profiles six student teachers, chosen randomly from an intake of 120, all about to embark on a one-year full-time postgraduate pre-service teacher education course at the University of Hong Kong, majoring in L2 English. The majority who register for that course are Cantonese NS (i.e. NNS of English), like Clarice and Grace in Table 8, and would unhesitatingly label themselves in that way. Each year, there is also a minority of participants (roughly 10%) who are prototypical NS of English, like Veronica below. But then there are also several, like Jennifer, Sejal and Wilma, who are much more difficult to classify. They may not be NS of English by the 'bio-developmental' definition referred to above, but they nevertheless regard English as their major language. In other words, there is a contrast between their 'language inheritance' and their 'language affiliation' (Rampton, 1990). The situation in Hong Kong may be unusual in certain respects, but Table 8 shows some of the variations that may be masked when labelling teachers as 'native speakers', or indeed 'novices' (see Chapter 6), and highlights the individuality of each teacher's formative experiences.

147

Table 8: The profiles of six student teachers on a pre-service L2 teacher education course

Name	Age	Own description of language background	First degree	Teaching/work experience
Clarice	22	Cantonese NS	BA English and Translation, Hong Kong	Small amount of one-to-one L2 English teaching
Grace	23	Cantonese NS	BA TESL, Hong Kong	Some teaching experience including practicum on 1st degree
Jennifer	30	Cantonese mother tongue ('now poor'); regards English as 1st language	BSc in Accounting, UK	Worked in business in the UK; no teaching experience
Sejal	36	Gujarati mother tongue; regards English as 1st language	BSc in Zoology, India	Two years' experience of Science teaching in India, and some years of work in banking in the US
Wilma	32	Tagalog mother tongue; regards English as 1st language	BSc in Business Administration, the Philippines	Several years' business experience in Hong Kong; has RSA/ UCLES CELTA and some limited L2 English teaching experience
Veronica	34	English NS; born and educated in the UK	BA in Modern Languages (French and Spanish), UK	Small amount of one-to-one L2 English teaching since coming to Hong Kong as dependent spouse; previous experience in publishing

It is with such variations in mind that I referred in 7.2 to the NS/NNS continuum. In this way one can acknowledge that, while there are large numbers who could/would not be ascribed (by themselves or by others) as anything but NS or NNS, there are many who fall somewhere in between. Towards the NS end of the continuum, for instance, as shown in Figure 4, we find teachers like Jennifer, Sejal and Wilma in Table 8, who distinguish, in their terms, a 'first' (i.e. most important) language from their native language in the bio-developmental sense. Then, towards the NNS end, there are teachers like Maggie (as seen in Chapter 5), who would describe herself as a Cantonese NS and a NNS of English, but many of whose 'difficulties' in dealing with the content of learning may be linked at least in part to her experience of having acquired her English largely through immersion, i.e. like a NS.

	Jennifer				*Grace*
Veronica	*Sejal*	*Wilma*		*Maggie*	*Clarice*
NS ◄───► NNS

Figure 4:   The NS/NNS 'continuum' – an illustration[1]

A second potential problem with the terms NS and NNS teacher arises from the privileging of the former and the resulting negative perceptions associated with the latter. In spite of the fact that, as Canagarajah (1999) has noted, NNS teachers make up more than 80% of the EFL/ESL teaching force worldwide, they have not been generally accepted in English-speaking countries until recently, however well qualified they may be (Braine, 2005:275), and even in their own countries, as Letter 1 above reveals, they are not always well regarded. Rajagopalan (2005:284) writes of the low self-esteem of NNS teachers, whom he describes as being marginalised, discriminated against and, until recently, largely 'resigned to their pariah status'. Braine (1999) recalls the difficulty he and colleagues had in trying to find a name for the proposed caucus for non-native educators within the TESOL organisation, citing the suggestion made by one prospective member of the caucus that using the term NNS was akin to using the slave-owner's language. Braine (1999:xvii) ascribes this difficulty to the struggle for self-definition and the identity crisis prevailing among non-native professionals.

The argument of those who contest the use of the term NNS (e.g., Garvey and Murray, 2004) is that it continues to privilege the NS model, defining NNS teachers in terms of what they lack, rather than what they possess: their bi- or multilingualism. This is the point made by Seidlhofer (2004:229) when she speaks of a 'counterproductive and divisive terminology which hinges on a negative particle, and which has

---

[1] In speaking of a NS/NNS continuum, I recognise that I am simplifying the interaction of a complex set of factors (see, e.g., Rampton, 1990; Leung, Harris and Rampton, 1997). The way I have placed individuals on the continuum in Figure 4 is based on a combination of factors: the bio-developmental criterion; individuals' experiences of acquiring English; and the extent to which they identify with English because of the role it plays in their lives. It is not intended to reflect language proficiency ('language expertise' in the terms used by Rampton, 1990), the issue discussed in 7.4.

had correspondingly negative effects on English language pedagogy'. Garvey and Murray (2004) prefer to use the term 'multilingual teacher' rather than NNS teacher, because they perceive the former to be both more inclusive and more accurate. While acknowledging the complexity of the issue of NS identity and the fact that the term 'multilingual teacher' succeeds in avoiding the negative connotations of 'NNS teacher', the creation of a new dichotomy between NS teachers and multilingual teachers is also problematic, because such a distinction implies that the former are, by definition, monolingual. A sizeable proportion of NS teachers may indeed be effectively monolingual, having achieved little or no success as L2 learners. However, there are a significant number of other NS teachers, such as Veronica in Table 8, who could justifiably claim to be multilingual. Given the usefulness of the NS/NNS continuum (borrowed from Medgyes, 1994, who uses the phrase 'interlanguage continuum') as a way of dealing with the infinite variety of individuals' language backgrounds, the remainder of this chapter and the book will continue to refer to that continuum and to employ the terms NS and NNS teacher, because (whatever their limitations) these terms are widely used in the literature, including that which is written by NNS educators themselves.

Many aspects of the NS/NNS teacher issue (as it relates to English) can be linked to the on-going debate about the status of non-native World Englishes (see, e.g., Kachru, 1985; 1990) and the implications of using them as pedagogical models in the classroom (as discussed by, for instance, Quirk, 1990; Bhatt, 1995; and Nelson, 1995; Kirkpatrick, 2007). Quirk (1985:6) has articulated the view that the pedagogical model for EFL/ESL should be exonormative, i.e. derived from standard British or American English: 'The relatively narrow range of purposes for which the non-native needs to use English (even in ESL countries) is arguably well catered for by a single monochrome standard form that looks as good on paper as it sounds in speech.' Kachru (1991), meanwhile, has adopted the opposing position, arguing that learners of English outside the so-called Inner Circle (where English functions primarily as L1) should aim at an endonormative model of English, based on an educated indigenous variety. For writers such as Phillipson (1992), the dominance of British and American varieties of English associated with the exonormative view represents linguistic hegemony (the 'linguistic imperialism', referred to in 7.1). The perceived danger of such hegemony is that it may damage the vitality of local multilingualism (Canagarajah, 1999:208) and lead to the undermining of the cultural identity of both the NNS learner and the NNS teacher.

Linked to this association of American and British English with the worst aspects of economic globalisation and the legacy of colonialism is what Phillipson (1992:193–9) describes as the 'native-speaker fallacy', that 'the ideal teacher of English is a native speaker'. This was the conventional wisdom in the early days of the TEFL/TESL profession, as evidenced, according to Phillipson, by the 1961 Makerere Conference (discussed in Phillipson, 1992:183–5,193–9).[2] As a number of commentators have observed (for instance, Braine, 2005; Rajagopalan, 2005), this 'apotheosis of the native speaker' (Rajagopalan, 1997) can also be associated (though not as an intended outcome) with developments in theoretical linguistics at the time. Chomsky's Generative Grammar (the dominant theory in the 1960s) saw the goal of linguistic theory as being to describe the knowledge of the language that provides the basis for the actual use of knowledge by a speaker-hearer. Such descriptions, in Chomskyan linguistics, were based upon the 'ideal speaker-listener, in a completely homogeneous speech community, who knows its language perfectly' (Chomsky, 1965:3). For Chomsky, a grammar was only descriptively adequate 'to the extent that it correctly describes the intrinsic competence of the idealised native speaker' (1965:24).

At the same time, however, there were those in the 'real world' of TEFL/TESL who were already aware of the potential limitations of the NS teacher. With the growth of the EFL industry during this period, it was very easy for untrained NS graduates to find employment teaching English, and many such graduates entered the EFL profession with the attitude, according to John Haycraft, the founder of International House (IH), " ' I'm English, aren't I? So I can teach my own language, can't I?" ' (Haycraft, 1988). In response to the inadequacy of such minimal qualifications for language teaching, Haycraft and his wife set up short, highly practical TEFL courses. NS graduates of that generation had typically learned about the grammar of English while at school, but they had no experience of analysing language from the perspectives of learning and the learner. Because of this, the IH courses included from the beginning a certain amount of 'language analysis' (i.e. TLA). These short intensive TEFL courses developed into the 'IH four-week courses', which in turn gave rise to similar EFL teacher-training programmes throughout the world (via the RSA/Cambridge CTEFLA scheme, now known as the CELTA).

The need for increased attention to TLA on such programmes became more and more apparent in the 1980s and 1990s, particularly as providers of training realised that most native speakers of English below a certain age had no experience of studying English grammar, even at

---

[2] Phillipson asserts that this was the view of the Makerere Conference. However, this interpretation has been strongly challenged by Davies (1996b:493), who quotes as counter-evidence recommendation (b) from page 6 of the conference report: 'Our aim is to provide at all levels qualified teachers who are indigenous to the country in which the teaching takes place.'

school (see Andrews, 1994). The experience of one NS teacher of English working in Hungary is perhaps typical: 'Most native teachers I know never really came across grammar until they started teaching it. So you have to learn it as you go along' (Arva and Medgyes, 2000:361). Recognition of a growing concern with TLA issues among teacher education providers is implicit in the greater emphasis given to the teaching and assessment of language awareness within such TEFL programmes as the revamped and unified RSA/Cambridge Diploma for English Language teachers (now known as DELTA).

By contrast, there have usually been fewer doubts about the TLA of non-native-speaker teachers of English. While it may be generally perceived, as Arva and Medgyes (2000:357) suggest, that such teachers 'speak poorer English, use "bookish" language, and use English less confidently' than NS teachers, it has also been assumed that NNS teachers have 'more insight into and better meta-cognitive knowledge of grammar' than their NS counterparts (ibid.:364), because of their educational background and training. In recent years, however, this assumption has been called into question in many parts of the world because the demand for appropriately qualified teachers of English has far outgrown the supply. The inevitable result of this shortage is that there are large numbers of inadequately prepared EFL/ESL teachers working in both the public and private sectors.

This particular problem does not only affect developing countries: in Hong Kong, for example, a survey carried out in 1991 suggested that only 27% of graduate secondary school English teachers were subject-trained, while a mere 21% had both subject training and professional training (Tsui et al., 1994). The situation in Hong Kong prompted the following comment in a government report: 'One of the major problems besetting the teaching of languages in schools in Hong Kong is the large number of language teachers who are not "subject-trained"' (Education Commission, 1995:18). According to the Commission, many teachers of English in Hong Kong 'lack depth of knowledge in the subject, or skills in teaching it as a subject, or both' (ibid.:49). Government concerns about the negative impact of these alleged deficiencies on student learning have led directly to a range of requirements, designed 'to ensure that language teachers are adequately prepared for their work, i.e. proficient in the language they teach, well grounded in subject knowledge and acquainted with the latest theories and practices in language teaching and learning' (SCOLAR, 2003:3). The Government's measures include the establishment of a Language Proficiency Requirement (LPR), with one route to the attainment of this 'benchmark' being the achievement of a Pass in the specially created Language Proficiency Assessment for Teachers (or LPAT) (see, e.g., Coniam and Falvey, 2002, for further discussion). The LPR applies both to NNS and to NS teachers of English.

As noted earlier, the arguments about the relative merits of NS and NNS L2 teachers centre on their language-related competences, particularly their knowledge *of* language (i.e. language proficiency) and their knowledge *about* language (i.e. their declarative knowledge of subject matter), together with their knowledge of their students. Each of these competences will now be discussed in turn.

7.4 The language proficiency of NS and NNS teachers

Conventional wisdom regarding the language proficiency of NS and NNS teachers suggests, not surprisingly, that this is the area in which the NS teacher has the edge. This commonsense view is supported by various studies of stakeholder perceptions. Benke and Medgyes (2005:207), for instance, reporting the results of a survey of 422 Hungarian learners of English in various types of institution, note a number of favourable comments associated with NS teachers' oral proficiency: 'With respect to NS teachers, learners spoke highly of their ability to teach conversation classes and to serve as perfect models for imitation. They were also found to be more capable of getting their learners to speak.' Meanwhile, Llurda (2005b), in a survey investigating practicum supervisors' views of NNS TESOL students in North America, reports that, although the vast majority of such students are perceived to be highly competent English speakers, they are generally seen to have some limitations in their command of English in comparison with their NS counterparts. Llurda also records that 'a relatively important proportion' (from 14% to 28%) of international students in North American TESOL programmes are considered to be 'weak' or 'problematic' in fluency, grammar, listening comprehension, accent and also, interestingly, in language awareness.

Medgyes, in his groundbreaking 1994 book *The non-native teacher*, refers to language proficiency limitations as the 'dark side of being a non-native'. Medgyes speaks of the 'language deficit' of the NNS teacher, describing the NNS teacher as 'more or less handicapped in terms of a command of English' (p. 76). According to Medgyes, who uses the terms NESTs (native-speaking teachers of English) and non-NESTs:

> On the whole, non-NESTs are well aware of their linguistic handicap and of its all-pervasive nature: in no area of English-language proficiency can we emulate NESTs: we are poorer listeners, speakers, readers and writers. True enough, long stays in English-speaking countries, hard work and dedication can help us to narrow the gap between 'us' and 'them', but very few of us will

153

> ever be able to catch up. To achieve native-like proficiency is
> wishful thinking.
>
> (Medgyes, 1994:33)

As Rajagopalan (2005:293) notes, such self-awareness can be very demoralising for the NNS teacher: 'the very idea that they can never be equal to their NS colleagues often makes them enter into a spirit of conformity or even defeatism, paving the way for frustration and lack of enthusiasm to go on investing in themselves'.

It could, however, be argued that Medgyes is being excessively modest in his observations and is underrating the abilities of the NNS teacher as well as overestimating, by comparison, the merits of the NS teacher. NSs are not, by right of birth, automatically endowed with the ability to be articulate orally or coherent in the writing of their L1. Davies (2001:273), for instance, refers to the problems even educated NSs experience because of their lack of 'fluency in the written elaborate code', saying that they often have 'an inability to control the resources of the standard language in such a way that they can communicate their meanings in written English to their readers' (ibid.). Anecdotal evidence suggests that such abilities are not always present even among those who teach their L1 as a foreign or second language. It is also worth noting that NS teachers of English in Hong Kong, obliged like their NNS counterparts to fulfil the Language Proficiency Requirement referred to above, have not necessarily performed especially well on the 'benchmark' tests.

Rajagopalan (2005) explores this issue further, arguing very persuasively that it is wrong to assume that being a NS means that one is perfect in all the four language skills. As he points out, 'the so-called native is native only in speaking, that too at a none-too-exciting level of practical utility (by any standard, far from the kind of competence an L2 learner is typically looking for)' (Rajagopalan, 2005:296). Rajagopalan observes that the communicative abilities that L2 students typically seek to acquire involve being able to do things with language, and are therefore concerned with discursive or rhetorical skills rather then purely linguistic skills. He observes that the development of such skills requires hard work and years of practice, with the NS on almost the same footing as the NNS, because these skills draw on competences other than the purely linguistic, 'which are nobody's monopoly, howsoever well endowed by birth' (ibid.:297).

Any discussion of the relative merits of NS and NNS teachers in terms of their language proficiency also needs to be contextualised. If the target language model is exonormative, and the learners are being trained principally in order to communicate with native speakers, then the NS teacher (assuming he/she is educated and articulate) may possess certain advantages as a model. However, if the learning goals relate primarily to English as a Lingua Franca (ELF), i.e. with preparing the learners to function internationally using English as a means of communication with other NNSs of English, then any assets the NS teacher of English possesses in terms of native proficiency in, for example, British, American or Australian English become largely irrelevant, because effective communication in lingua franca uses of English is not dependent on conforming to NS norms. This issue is discussed further in 7.7.

7.5 The declarative TLA of NS and NNS teachers

If language proficiency is the domain in which NS teachers are generally assumed to have the advantage, the reverse is true in any comparison of NS and NNS teachers in terms of their knowledge of subject matter, i.e their declarative TLA. Medgyes (1994), for instance, notes that NNS teachers are more insightful than NS teachers, which he attributes to differences in the processes by which they have developed mastery of the language:

> Acquisition being largely unconscious, NESTs [i.e. NS teachers] are not aware of the internal mechanisms operating language use and are therefore unable to give their students relevant information about language learning. On the other hand, during their own learning process, non-NESTs have amassed a wealth of knowledge about the English language. Their antennae can intercept even the minutest item as a possible source of problems, of which NESTs are likely to take no notice.
>
> (Medgyes, 1994:60)

Seidlhofer (1999:242) also emphasises the advantages of the NNS teacher in comparison with the NS teacher, that 'because of their own language learning experience, they have usually developed a high degree of conscious, or declarative, knowledge of the internal organisation of the code itself – unlike native-speaker teachers, whose access to the code is usually firmly anchored in context and who may therefore find it more difficult to abstract from specific instances'.

Two of the studies referred to in the previous chapter shed some light on the differences between NS and NNS teachers of English in terms of their declarative knowledge of grammar and grammatical terminology. Andrews (1996), for instance, illustrates some of the difficulties novice NS teachers encounter when attempting to deal with issues of language

155

content. In that study (described briefly in 6.3 above), five pairs of novice teachers were videotaped as they planned a lesson on the Present Perfect. The four NNS pairs, although exhibiting the differences in priority noted in 6.3, could all talk quite knowledgeably and confidently about the Present Perfect. The performance of the two NSs, Kylie and Mary (Snapshot 15 below), was, by contrast, noticeably different.

Snapshot 15: Kylie and Mary planning a lesson on the Present Perfect

Kylie and Mary are very aware of their own lack of explicit knowledge. Kylie confesses her ignorance at the outset, and even half an hour into the task, following extensive consultation of the grammar book with her partner, she is no more confident:

Kylie: [looking at book] *I don't think I'd actually be able to teach this . . . Being serious cos I don't really understand it enough myself.*

Much of their discussion consists of an attempt to overcome their lack of previous explicit knowledge, and of efforts to wrestle with the uses of the Present Perfect as listed in the grammar book by working out examples themselves.

During the planning discussion, Mary recognises a number of parallels with her own experiences as a learner of French. This is linked to a dawning realisation (after almost 40 minutes of discussion) of the connection between English grammar and French grammar: the similarities and the differences:

Mary: *Well I probably learned this when I was doing French . . .* [looking at grammar book with puzzled expression]

Kylie: *A-level . . . there's no way we learned the Present Perfect in GCSE*

Mary: *I think we might have done*

Kylie: *I don't think we did . . . I don't think I've ever heard of it in my life* [laughs]

Mary: *I think we might have done . . .* [looking at book] *. . . hang on . . . of course you have . . .*

Kylie: *Or have we done the wrong one?* [laughs]

Mary: *Oh I'm going to say something that's going to sound so stupid*

Kylie: *Go on . . . say it*

Mary: [looking at book] *This is the same as the Perfect Tense in French . . . This is the Perfect Tense*

Kylie: *Is it?* [laughs]

> Mary: *Past Tense . . . yeah . . . je suis allée, I have been . . . or I went . . . no it's not actually . . . the Present no . . . in French it's something different . . .*
>
> Such exchanges as they had about how to teach the Present Perfect focused mainly on the extent to which the explicit teaching of grammar and grammatical terminology was a good thing:
>
> Mary: *I'd do the Present Perfect forms . . .*
> Kylie: *Yeah I'd do that but I don't know whether I'd tell them 'This is the negative form', 'This is the negative question' . . . cos that's just . . . well just all confusing . . .*
> Mary: *Yeah but how else . . . would you say it?*
> Kylie: *. . . I'd say . . . well I don't know . . . I'd say 'You can use the Present Perfect if you're wanting to ask a question.'*
> Mary: *Yeah . . . which is the question*
> Kylie: *Yeah but it's not giving them a name for it . . . cos that's just gonna confuse them . . . what I'm saying is that I wouldn't give them all these like little name things . . . cos it'll just get too confusing.*

Kylie and Mary are, of course, only one pair of NSs, who in this case had not had the benefit of either tertiary education or professional training. They were 'gap year' students, between school and university, who were working in Hong Kong as English Language Teaching Assistants (ELTAs) giving conversation classes in local secondary schools. Nevertheless, such difficulties are not uncommon among NS teachers. In Arva and Medgyes' (2000) study of NS and NNS teachers of English in Hungarian classrooms, the NS teachers are well aware of their weaknesses. One, for instance, acknowledges that 'The non-native teacher has learnt grammar and is able to convey that to people very clearly with no wastage, whereas I would have to more often look up to find out what I was being asked about' (Arva and Medgyes, 2000:362), while another ruefully observes 'This is wrong and this is the correct way you should say it, I know, but I can't explain why it's wrong or right' (ibid.:361).

Andrews (1999c), also discussed in 6.3, examines data comparing the declarative knowledge of grammar and grammatical terminology of NS and NNS teachers of English as measured by a 60-item Language Awareness (LA) test. As the earlier discussion indicated, the NNS teachers in the study generally performed better than the NS teachers. The overall mean score for the serving NNS teachers was 70.3%, compared with 56.1% for the novice NNS teachers and 51.75% for the combined novice NS teacher groups. Performance on the three most demanding parts of the test revealed a similar pattern. As noted previously, however, significant differences became apparent among the results achieved by the NS novice teachers when the scores of those with first degrees in Modern Languages were compared with the scores of those with an English Studies background, with the former outperforming the latter (see Table 6, p. 122).

It would, of course, be a mistake to read too much into these results, given the nature of the test, the small sample size (n = 10 in each NS novice teacher sub-group) and the lack of detailed information about participants' tertiary studies or the nature/extent of their bi- or multilingualism. It may be tempting to attribute the better performance of the NS Modern Languages group to the impact of their multilingualism on their language awareness. That would, however, entail an assumption that most if not all of the NS English Studies group were monolingual. A more likely explanation is that the NS Modern Languages group overall had more in-depth experience of the formal study of language(s) and a more recent need to show familiarity with grammatical terminology (albeit in relation to languages other than English) as part of their PGCE Major studies. Whatever the explanation, the markedly better performance of the NS novices from a Modern Languages background was an interesting finding, which could usefully be explored in greater depth and in other contexts.

In addition to comparing the LA test performance of NS and NNS teachers, Andrews (1999c) also reveals the kind of problem that novice NS teachers often experience with 'all these like little name things', i.e. grammatical terminology. One of the four tasks in the LA test (see Appendix) requires the test-taker to supply an appropriate grammatical term for the item underlined in each of twelve sentences. Some of the labels suggested by the NS novice teachers are shown in the samples below.

- Alice fell asleep <u>during</u> the lecture.
  'passive verb'; 'conjunction'; 'adjective'; 'present continuous'; 'present participle'

- Mrs Wong <u>has been living</u> in that flat for years.
  'past participle'; 'verb imperfect tense'; 'past tense verb'; 'present passive'; 'pluperfect'; 'past perfect'; 'past continuous'; 'continuous imperfect'

- There are still a lot of things <u>to be done</u>.
  'conjunction'; 'future verb'; 'auxiliary verb'; 'verb to be past tense'; 'future perfect'; 'past perfect'

However, just as in relation to language proficiency we noted the danger of oversimplification and over-generalising the assumed advantages of the NS teacher, so in considering declarative knowledge of subject matter we should be equally cautious in assuming that NNS teachers are necessarily adequately equipped or better equipped than their NS counterparts. Well-educated, professionally trained and experienced NNS teachers should certainly be expected to have higher levels of subject-matter knowledge than NS teachers with irrelevant first degrees (if any) and limited professional training, alongside whom they may find themselves working. But, as we have seen in earlier chapters, not all NNS teachers have relevant study backgrounds, and many of them have weaknesses in their TLA that are attributable at least in part to gaps in their declarative knowledge of subject matter. At the same time, not all NS teachers lack appropriate qualifications and professional training, and not all of them have the impoverished levels of subject-matter knowledge described above.

7.6 NS and NNS teachers' knowledge of students

Our third TLA-related area of comparison is another in which the NNS teacher is generally acknowledged to have the edge over the NS, as seen, for example, in Llurda's study of TESOL practicum supervisors' perceptions of their NNS and NS students. The supervisors' perception of their NNS students' 'Language Awareness', defined by Llurda (2005b:152) as 'the capacity to understand and to help L2 students understand the complexities and the generalisable aspects of language', was that it was better or equal to that of NSs (in 34% of cases better and in 50% equal).

As Medgyes (1994:61) points out, this advantage may be especially apparent in situations where teacher and students have the same L1: 'Non-NESTs [i.e. NNS teachers] sharing the learners' mother tongue are in a particularly favourable position. Since we have jumped off the same springboard as our students, both in a linguistic and cultural sense, we are intrinsically more sensitive to their difficulties than NESTs.' Seidlhofer (1999:242) refers to the advantage that NNS teachers have in being 'distanced' from the language they teach because they have had to learn it themselves: 'This distancing from the context can be an important advantage since all learning involves abstracting from context, via a conceptual rather than a contextual apprehension of meaning. Non-native teachers of a foreign language are already at a remove from the language, quite naturally distanced.' According to Seidlhofer, this enables the NNS teacher to 'get into the skin of the foreign learner' in ways that would be much more difficult for the NS teacher (ibid.:243).

Meanwhile, Cook (2005) makes the separate but related point that the NNS teacher presents learners with the encouraging example of someone who has become a successful L2 user:

> The non-native teacher has been through the same route as the students and has acquired another language, a living demonstration that this is possible for non-native learners. They [i.e. NNS teachers] have shared the student's own experience at some time in their lives and have learnt the language by the same route that the students are taking. The native speaker teacher cannot appreciate their experiences and problems except at second hand.
>
> (Cook, 2005:57)

The NS teacher, on the other hand, may actually be a source of discouragement for some students, because of the unattainable level of language proficiency such a teacher exemplifies.

Although arguments of the sort quoted in the preceding paragraphs are increasingly common in the literature, there has been relatively little research comparing NS and NNS teachers' sensitivity to language difficulty from the learner/learning perspective, in spite of the fact that (as noted in Chapter 2) such sensitivity forms an important part of TLA. McNeill (2005) is, however, one such study: in this case a comparison of NS and NNS teachers' ability to identify sources of difficulty in a pedagogical text. As McNeill observes, the assumption motivating such research is that

> teachers who are aware of the language which their students find difficult are more likely to be effective in teaching because they can focus their attention on learners' actual needs. Conversely, it is assumed that teachers who are less aware of their students' language problems will be less effective because they devote teaching time to language which may not be required by students and neglect areas where a teacher's help would be beneficial.
>
> (McNeill, 2005:108)

In McNeill's study (also discussed in Chapter 6), four groups of teachers were asked to make predictions about lexical difficulty in a reading text. Students at an appropriate level were tested on their understanding of the lexical content of the text, and the predictions made by the teachers were compared with the actual difficulties experienced by the students. Two of McNeill's teacher groups were NNS and two were NS. One group in each pair comprised experienced, trained teachers, while the other consisted of teachers receiving their initial training. What McNeill (2005) found was that the teachers in both the NS groups generally failed to identify the words that students found difficult, whereas 'the NNS teachers were much more in tune with the learners' problems' (p. 115).

At the same time, however, as McNeill makes clear, there were among the teachers within each group large individual differences in their ability to predict lexical difficulty. Also, as noted in Chapter 6, the novice NNS teachers (rather surprisingly) performed more successfully than their more experienced counterparts. From such findings it seems that this particular aspect of TLA is not found in all NNS teachers to the same extent, with any teacher's sensitivity to learner difficulty being affected by a range of other factors. As McNeill (2005) suggests, it would be interesting to carry out follow-up research with NNS teachers whose students have a different L1 or who teach multilingual groups, in order to see how far the NNS teacher's apparent edge in this aspect of TLA carries across to a wider range of teaching and learning contexts.

Although NNS teachers who share their learners' L1 are in principle at an advantage in terms of their ability to predict learner difficulty, it appears that not all NNS teachers are able to exploit that advantage. This suggests parallels with the situation noted in relation to declarative TLA, that the possession of a high level of subject-matter knowledge is in itself no guarantee that the teacher will make effective use of such knowledge in the classroom. In Chapter 5, it was suggested that the procedural dimension of TLA requires qualities of perception, reflectiveness and sensitivity which each individual L2 teacher (whether NS or NNS) possesses to a different degree. These same qualities affect the extent to which any teacher can empathise with and respond appropriately to the difficulties experienced by his/her students.

7.7 English as a Lingua Franca: implications for NS and NNS teachers

As suggested in 7.4, much of the discussion of the relative merits of NS and NNS teachers has been premised on the assumption that the teaching of L2 English should be based on NS norms and models. In recent years, however, the work of a number of scholars has called this assumption into question, because of the increasing use worldwide of English as a Lingua Franca. The term English as a Lingua Franca (ELF) is used to refer to the fact that, in so much international communication, English is used as the means of communication, even when it is not the L1 of any of the interlocutors.

House (1999:74) defines ELF interactions as 'interactions between members of two or more different linguacultures in English, for none of whom English is the mother tongue', although most ELF researchers accept that NSs also participate in intercultural communication (Jenkins, 2006). House (1999) suggests that this type of interaction, which is extremely frequent now, will increase exponentially in the future. The widespread availability of the Internet and of mobile phones has helped to promote the growing use of ELF, with the resulting interactions often taking place between people with different levels of English proficiency, whose pronunciation and command of English grammar and lexis are non-standard. As Seidlhofer (2004) observes, ELF has taken on a life of its own, largely independent of the norms established by native users of English.

In spite of the growing importance of such forms of interaction, there has been little interest until recently in attempting to describe ELF, and the exonormative model of English (derived from standard British or American English) has continued to be the one on which most L2 teaching is based around the world. Increasingly, however, researchers have begun to examine the nature of ELF and to explore the implications for the teaching of L2 English (see, e.g., Seidlhofer, 2004, for a summary of research in this area). Jenkins (2000) was the first major study of ELF interaction, focusing on ELF phonology. Since then, ELF research has extended into other areas of the language. Seidlhofer (see, e.g., 2002) has begun to compile a corpus of spoken ELF, which is already revealing characteristics of the lexico-grammar of ELF that appear to be common irrespective of the speaker's L1. Such features include dropping the third person present tense -*s*; confusing the relative pronouns *who* and *which*; and omitting definite and indefinite articles where they are obligatory in NS language use, and inserting them where they do not occur in NS language use (Seidlhofer, 2002; 2004). Although much ELF research aims to identify patterns of common use among speakers from a wide range of backgrounds, some researchers limit their focus to ELF in a specific region. Seidlhofer (2004), for example, refers to the efforts of linguists to establish whether there are distinct regional varieties of ELF in Asia and Europe.

When considering the pedagogical implications of their work on ELF, researchers are not proposing that all learners should aim to learn a monolithic variety of English as an International Language. Instead, they argue that insisting on students' conforming to NS norms is both unrealistic and inappropriate in the context of international uses of English, where what is important is mutual intelligibility. This rejection of NS norms is not based solely on practical pedagogical considerations. According to Widdowson (2004:361), there is an ideological dimension, too, with conformity to NS norms being seen as 'the authoritarian imposition of socio-cultural values which makes learners subservient and prevents them from appropriating the language as an expression of their own identity'.

The potential pedagogical implications of ELF are still being debated. As Jenkins (2006:161) puts it, ELF researchers 'believe that anyone participating in international communication needs to be familiar with, and have in their linguistic repertoire for use, as and when appropriate, certain forms (phonological, lexicogrammatical, etc.) that are widely used and widely intelligible across groups of English speakers from different first language backgrounds'. The most obvious applicability of an ELF approach is in any multilingual classes where the students' primary motivation is instrumental: to develop the ability to communicate in international contexts. For such students, mutual intelligibility would seem an appropriate target. In monolingual classes, however, even if the goals of learning and teaching are similar, an emphasis on mutual intelligibility might well be counterproductive, leading to a reinforcement of learners' L1 identities and their L1 accents (Jenkins, 2000). Even in the multilingual class, it cannot be assumed that all students would necessarily accept a target of international intelligibility. Timmis (2002) and Kuo (2006), for instance, both note a tendency for students to continue to look to a NS model to meet their future needs, even when their future English use is likely to be primarily with NNSs. Jenkins (1998:125) gives a salutary warning when she notes that 'we should all guard against political correctness in the sense of telling our students what their goals should be: in particular that they should not want to sound like native speakers if they clearly wish to do so'.

The impact of ELF on language pedagogy worldwide has yet to become fully apparent. The challenge to the conventional preference for teaching to be based on NS norms will undoubtedly be resisted by many employers, parents and other stakeholders in many parts of the world, even in contexts where the primary purpose of learning English is to be able to communicate effectively with other NNSs (see Andrews, 2002, for discussion of related issues in the Hong Kong context). However, the implications of ELF for our evaluation of the relative merits of NS and NNS teachers in terms of their Teacher Language Awareness are potentially far-reaching, because the target variety of English (the 'E') in ELF classrooms is no longer the English of NSs. As a result, the language-related competences (i.e. the TLA) required of the teacher no longer relate to a model of language based upon NS norms.

For NS teachers, Widdowson (2004:362) suggests that an ELF approach completely undermines the basis of their authority: 'It is not only a matter of calling into question how reliable native speakers can be as informants about a language no longer their own, but of how far their linguistic experience qualifies them in their pedagogic role as

instructors.' For NNS teachers ('the world's majority of English teachers'), on the other hand, Seidlhofer (2004:229) suggests that an ELF
perspective can have a very positive impact, transforming the way in
which such teachers perceive and define themselves: 'instead of being
nonnative speakers and perennial, error-prone learners of English as a
Native Language, they can be competent and authoritative users of
ELF'.

7.8 Conclusion

In this chapter, we have explored some of the background to the NS/NNS
teacher 'debate', and discussed the relative merits of NS and NNS teachers in relation to their TLA, examining in turn their knowledge *of* language, their knowledge *about* language and their knowledge of students.
We have also considered the potential impact of the increasing interest
in English as a Lingua Franca on any evaluation of the strengths and
weaknesses of NS and NNS teachers (both their self-perceptions and the
perceptions of others).

During the discussion, the following specific observations were made:

- The NS/NNS issue is highly emotive, with emotions being heightened
  by the ideological and racial/racist dimension;
- The NS/NNS dichotomy is unsatisfactory, because it oversimplifies
  the complex realities of individuals' language backgrounds, and
  because it defines NNS teachers in terms of what they lack, rather
  than what they possess (their bi- or multilingualism);
- The so-called 'native-speaker fallacy' (that 'the ideal teacher of
  English is a native speaker') was the conventional wisdom in the early
  days of the TEFL/TESL profession, and has had a demoralising effect
  upon many NNS teachers;
- At the heart of the debate about the relative merits of NS and NNS
  teachers is their TLA, and specifically their knowledge *of* language
  (language proficiency), their knowledge *about* language (subject-
  matter knowledge) and their knowledge of students;
- In terms of knowledge *of* language, NS teachers may generally have
  the edge over NNSs as regards oral fluency; however, being a NS is
  no guarantee that one is perfect in all the four language skills:
  writing, for example, is a skill that has to be learned by NS and NNS
  alike;
- In their knowledge *about* language, NNS teachers are generally
  assumed to be superior to NSs; however, this is not necessarily the
  case;

- As far as their knowledge of students is concerned, NNS teachers who share their students' L1 generally appear to be better at predicting learners' difficulties; however, not all NNS teachers have this ability to the same extent;
- The adoption of an ELF approach in any teaching and learning context would undermine any claims to superiority of the NS teacher, because the target language variety would no longer conform to NS norms.

On the basis of the evidence and arguments discussed in this chapter, it seems that even where the prevailing pedagogical model is exonormative (i.e. derived from standard British or American English, however defined) NNS teachers may well have an advantage over their NS counterparts in two of the three areas of knowledge that make up TLA. Certainly, from the available evidence it would appear that the idealisation of the NS teacher is indeed a fallacy. At the same time, however, as we have seen from previous chapters, in which all the teachers featured have been NNSs, it would be equally fallacious to idealise the NNS teacher. What is important is to recognise that, as I have argued in 7.2, all L2 teachers require a certain level of TLA, much of which is dependent on hard work, practice, reflection and sensitivity rather than an accident of birth.

The following chapter focuses on TLA and student learning, examining research evidence relevant to the central assumption underlying this book: that there is a relationship between the language awareness of any individual teacher and the language learning achievements of his/her students.

Questions for discussion and reflection

1) To what extent do Letters 1 and 2 (in 7.2) reflect attitudes that are commonplace in your own society? In the teaching context(s) with which you are familiar, are NS teachers of English generally regarded more highly then NNS teachers? If so, why? If not, why not? Are the perceptions of different stakeholders within the community (students, parents, employers, the Ministry of Education) the same or different?
2) In the institution in which you currently work, are there both NS and NNS teachers? How are they deployed? Do they perform similar or different roles (a) in their teaching, (b) in their wider duties? Do you think that they are deployed appropriately?
3) Where would you place yourself on the NS/NNS 'continuum', and why?
4) From your experience, and your perspective (given where you have placed yourself on the NS/NNS continuum), what do you

---

consider to be the relative strengths and weaknesses of NS and NNS teachers of English?

5) In the teaching context(s) with which you are familiar, would it be appropriate to make English for international communication the target of L2 English teaching? If it were suggested that English teaching should be based on ELF norms rather than NS norms, what would be the likely reaction of (a) students, (b) teachers, (c) parents, (d) employers, (e) the press, (f) the Ministry of Education?

6) What is your own view of teaching based on ELF norms? If mutual intelligibility were the agreed goal in your classroom, would you be equally tolerant of non-standard grammar, non-standard lexis and non-standard pronunciation? If not, why not?

8 TLA and student learning

8.1 Introduction

In this chapter, the focus of discussion is the relationship between Teacher Language Awareness and student learning: to what extent is any L2 teacher's effectiveness (as indicated by the learning outcomes of his/her students) attributable to his/her TLA? The chapter begins by setting out some of the difficulties associated with trying to make causative links between TLA and student learning. The remainder of the chapter discusses research that is relevant to any examination of the relationship between TLA and student learning. That research is discussed in relation to three themes: teachers' subject-matter knowledge; teacher engagement with the content of learning; and teachers' awareness of learner difficulties.

The basic argument throughout this book has been that Teacher Language Awareness is an essential attribute of any competent L2 teacher. The assumption underlying that argument is that there is a relationship between the language awareness of the L2 teacher and the effectiveness of that teacher as indicated by the language learning achieved by his/her students. Put simply, the book assumes that TLA has a positive impact on student learning: TLA is seen as a potentially crucial variable in the language teaching / language learning enterprise, in the sense that the language-aware L2 teacher is more likely to be effective in promoting student learning than the teacher who is less language-aware.

At the same time, however, all such statements about the impact of TLA on student learning have been cautiously worded and carefully hedged. Even in the previous paragraph, for example, TLA is described as '**potentially** crucial' and is identified as '**a** potentially crucial variable' rather than '**the** potentially crucial variable'. Such hedging is necessary for two main reasons. First, there are a number of variables that have the potential to exert an influence, positive or negative, upon student achievement in L2 learning. These variables may be factors about the learner, including his/her background, and about the context of teaching and learning: they are certainly not confined to attributes of the teacher, least of all to one specific attribute such as TLA. Second, we currently know very little about the precise nature of the relationship between TLA and student learning: we may make certain logical deductions

Table 9: TLA and variables potentially influencing its impact on student learning

---

Teacher variables
TLA is just one attribute of the L2 teacher. Its interaction with other attributes of the individual teacher makes it difficult to predict its specific impact on student learning. For instance:
- A teacher with relatively high levels of TLA may find his/her effectiveness (i.e. as measured by learner achievement) undermined by weaknesses in other aspects of pedagogical content knowledge, or general teaching skills (such as the ability to manage a class).
- A teacher with limited TLA may nonetheless produce successful learners if other aspects of that teacher's competence and/or personality engage students' interest and motivate them to make an effort to achieve.

Teacher/learner variables
Whatever the attributes of the individual teacher, learning is a task undertaken by students and is therefore potentially affected by learner variables at least as much as by teacher variables. For example:
- A teacher may have a highly developed TLA and be very proficient in other areas of pedagogy, but individual students taught by that teacher may, for a variety of reasons (such as background, and/or motivation), fail to make significant progress in their L2 learning.
- A teacher who exhibits major TLA weaknesses may have individual students who nevertheless make substantial advances in their language proficiency as a result of factors unrelated to the teacher, such as the students' own intrinsic motivation and/or desire for success.

Contextual variables
In addition to variables relating to the teacher and learners, a wide variety of contextual variables (such as class size, teaching and learning resources, the regularity and intensity of teaching, and the role of high-stakes tests) have the potential to affect the extent of student achievement.

---

about the impact of TLA, but there is relatively little research evidence to support such deductions.

The examples in Table 9 illustrate some of the possible interrelationships between variables that would make it so difficult to identify consistent causative associations between TLA, or any other individual variable, and learning outcomes. Those examples represent only a small sample of the combinations of variables that potentially affect students' learning. Faced with such complexity, and the lack of evidence to suggest that any single variable in L2 teaching and learning is more significant than any other, there is clearly no justification for making strong claims about the specific impact of TLA. Nevertheless, there is a certain amount of research that is relevant to any discussion of the relationship between

TLA and student learning. In the sections that follow, the implications of that research will be examined.

8.2 TLA, subject-matter knowledge and student learning

It has been argued in the preceding chapters that knowledge *about* language constitutes the declarative dimension of TLA, and that this knowledge of the subject matter of L2 teaching is at the core of TLA in pedagogical practice. But what evidence is there to support the belief that any teacher's possession or lack of such subject-matter knowledge is likely to affect student achievement? In order to address this question, we shall first of all examine evidence from general education research. We shall then consider some initial findings from a study of L2 teaching and learning.

As a starting point, it is worth noting what the education literature tells us about the link between students' achievement and teacher variables generally. Bransford, Darling-Hammond and LePage (2005a) cite a number of studies suggesting that teacher quality can have at least as large an effect on student achievement as factors relating to students' background (such as parental income, parents' education and other family factors). For example, Ferguson (1991), in an analysis of nearly 700 Texas school districts, found that teacher expertise (as measured by scores on a certification examination, possession of a Master's degree and amount of experience) accounted for more of the inter-district variation in students' achievement in reading and mathematics from grades 1 to 11 than students' socioeconomic status. Bransford, Darling-Hammond and LePage (2005a:15) report that in Ferguson's study: 'The effects were so strong and the variations in teacher expertise so great that, after controlling for socioeconomic status, the large disparities in achievement between black and white students were almost entirely accounted for by differences in the qualifications of their teachers.' Meanwhile, a study conducted by Strauss and Sawyer (1986) in North Carolina, also discussed by Bransford, Darling-Hammond and LePage (2005a:15), found that, after school and student background factors had been accounted for, teacher quality had a 'strikingly large' effect on student achievement: a 1% increase in teacher quality (as measured by National Teacher Examination scores) was associated with a 3% to 5% decline in students failing state competency tests. From both these studies, then, there is clear evidence that the quality of the teacher has a major impact on student learning.

The evidence regarding subject-matter knowledge specifically is rather more equivocal. As Darling-Hammond (2000) notes in her review of previous research on teacher quality and student achievement, there is some support in the literature for relating subject-matter knowledge to teacher effectiveness, but the findings are neither as strong nor as consistent as one might expect, with some studies showing a positive relationship while others show none. According to Darling-Hammond (2000:3), 'It may be that these results are mixed because subject matter knowledge is a positive influence up to some level of basic competence in the subject but is less important thereafter.' This observation is consistent with the findings (discussed in Chapter 6) relating to the TLA of 'expert' L2 teachers. It was suggested in that chapter that, while 'expert' L2 teachers appear to possess a certain level of subject-matter knowledge (as measured by a test of their declarative TLA), this level being generally above that of the less expert teacher but not dramatically so, what sets such teachers apart is their ability to draw upon that subject-matter knowledge and integrate it with other aspects of their TLA and pedagogical content knowledge (PCK) in their enactment of the curriculum.

Darling-Hammond (2000) suggests that differences in the findings of the studies she reviews may be caused by the different measures of subject-matter knowledge, noting that measures of the number of courses taken in a subject area have more frequently been found to be related to teacher performance than have scores on tests of subject-matter knowledge. This comment highlights a problem that is equally relevant to TLA and to indicators of L2 subject-matter knowledge. The limitations of measures such as the LA test I have used on a number of occasions have been remarked upon in previous chapters. As Darling-Hammond (2000:3) observes, 'tests necessarily capture a narrower slice of any domain'. At the same time, however, indicators such as the possession of a relevant first degree also have their limitations, particularly, one might suggest, in relation to L2 education, where the teaching may be wholly concerned with language and communicative skills while the potentially relevant degree may have been primarily focused on literature. The results of Andrews (1999c), as discussed in Chapters 6 and 7, illustrate some of the difficulties associated with assuming a degree in English Studies to be a reliable measure of the subject-matter knowledge required to teach L2 English. Nevertheless, for the time being, we may still have to rely, in any relatively large-scale studies, on measures such as tests and/or 'relevant' qualifications, whatever their limitations: the relative complexity of the TLA construct and the importance of the procedural dimension mean that we are still a long way from the successful development of specific measures of L2 teachers' TLA. As Wilson, Floden and Ferrini-Mundy (2001) conclude in their review of research on teacher education, 'although subject matter knowledge of some form is important, the field needs to learn more about the specific kinds of subject matter knowledge that matter in teaching' (Grossman and Schoenfeld, 2005:206). This point applies to the subject-matter knowledge of the L2 teacher (and his/her TLA) just as much as it does to teaching in general.

Interestingly, Darling-Hammond's findings from her own research (2000) are much less equivocal about the link between teacher quality characteristics and student achievement when those characteristics include both possession of a relevant degree and full certification as a teacher. In her study, Darling-Hammond examines the ways in which teacher qualifications and other school inputs are related to student achievement in reading and mathematics in states across the United States. She reports that the most consistent highly significant predictor of student achievement in reading and mathematics in each year tested was the proportion of well-qualified teachers in a state (i.e. those with a relevant degree and full certification), while the strongest consistently negative predictors were the proportion of new teachers who were uncertified, and the proportion of teachers with less than a minor degree qualification in their teaching subject. She notes the similarity between these findings and those of Ferguson (1991) and Strauss and Sawyer (1986), referred to earlier, and observes that the strength of the 'well-qualified teacher' variable may be due to the fact that it incorporates both strong disciplinary knowledge and substantial knowledge of education: 'If the two kinds of knowledge are interdependent as suggested in much of the literature, it makes sense that this variable would be more powerful than either subject-matter knowledge or teaching knowledge alone' (Darling-Hammond, 2000:26). On this basis, given that TLA embraces domains of PCK that go beyond mere subject-matter knowledge, one might expect TLA to be an equally significant predictor of student achievement in L2 learning. However, the relevant research remains to be conducted.

In the specific area of L2 education, there is a certain amount of evidence concerning the relationship between the subject-matter knowledge of L2 teachers of English and student learning in the data gathered as part of the 'Good Practices' project (Tsui et al., 2005), a large-scale investigation recently conducted in Hong Kong. The aim of this study was to identify good practices in the teaching of English in local secondary schools, i.e. practices that bring about positive English language learning outcomes, and to investigate the conditions that maximise English language learning. From the start, therefore, good practices were associated with student learning outcomes, with positive learning outcomes being seen in terms of both overall improvement in language proficiency and the development of a positive attitude towards learning English.

Given the highly context-specific nature of 'good practices', and their dependence on the complex interplay of contextual factors, a case-study approach was adopted. Various potential case-study schools were identified, based on whether there was evidence of consistent improvement or decline in English language proficiency from Secondary 1 to Secondary 3 (i.e. between the ages of 11 and 14). Students' performance on the Hong Kong English Attainment Test (HKEAT) over a three-year period was used as an indicator of their language proficiency. Thirty-seven schools eventually took part in the first part of the study, which involved the administration of a questionnaire to those English teachers currently teaching Secondary 1 to 3 or with experience of teaching those forms.

In order to ensure that the study focused on the practices of teachers working with lower-ability students as well as those working with higher-ability students, the concept of value-addedness was used to identify schools (and effective teachers within those schools). This involved comparing the observed performance of students in each school with their expected performance. A school was therefore classified as 'improving' on the basis of a positive value-added score, i.e. the observed English performance of students exceeded the expected performance by a sufficiently large amount. A similar approach was used to classify teachers as effective, ineffective or non-effective (where they fell into neither of the two preceding categories). In classifying the teachers, value-addedness was assessed at the class level rather than the school level. The value-added score of each teacher was referred to as the Teacher Effectiveness Index (TEI).

So what do the data from the 'Good Practices' study reveal about the relationship between L2 teachers' knowledge of subject matter (i.e. their declarative TLA) and student learning? In order to address this question, the possession of a relevant first degree was taken as an indicator of subject-matter knowledge (with the limitations acknowledged earlier) while the TEI was used as an indicator of student learning. A total of 388 teachers of English from the 37 secondary schools completed the teacher questionnaire. In the case of 248 of them, their TEI was also available. For these 248, it was therefore possible to explore the association between their degree qualification and their TEI. In examining this association, two definitions of 'relevant degree' were used: (a) a narrow definition, where the degree was specifically identified as English, Linguistics or TEFL/TESL/TESOL, and (b) a broader definition (similar to that used by the Hong Kong Government), which also includes degrees in subjects such as Translation and Communication, provided that some form of English study has been a substantial component.

With both definitions of 'relevant degree', the results turned out to be inconclusive. A comparison of the mean TEI scores of those teachers with relevant degrees and those with non-relevant degrees revealed that, with both definitions of relevant degree, the TEI of relevant degree holders was higher than the TEI of non-relevant degree holders. The mean TEI of relevant degree holders was also slightly higher when the narrower definition of relevant degree was applied. However, the differences were not statistically significant. This is consistent with what Darling-Hammond found in her survey of research in general education on subject-matter knowledge and teacher effectiveness. Unfortunately, with the 'Good Practices' data, no attempt could be made to examine the relationship between the TEI and the possession of a relevant degree plus a relevant teacher education qualification, because precise information about participants' teacher education major subjects was not available. A similar problem made it impossible to compare the TEIs of those with English degrees mainly focusing on language/linguistics and those whose English degree focused primarily on literature. Clearly, therefore, there is a need for further research in this area.

8.3 TLA, teacher engagement with language content and student learning

It was argued in Chapter 5 that a teacher's engagement (in the 'commitment' sense) with the language content of learning has a major impact on TLA: that the application of TLA in pedagogical practice may be significantly influenced by the extent to which the teacher seriously engages with content-related issues at all, and by the priority which that teacher accords to the language focus of the lesson. In Chapter 5 and in various other parts of the book we have seen evidence to support this argument in terms of the impact of such engagement on teacher decision-making and teacher behaviour. But are there data about learning outcomes, data that might shed light on the relationship, if any, between teacher engagement with the language content of learning and student achievement?

Some possible evidence concerning this question can be found from the 'Good Practices' project (Tsui et al., 2005), discussed in the previous section. As noted above, there were 248 Hong Kong secondary school teachers of L2 English for whom a Teacher Effectiveness Index was computed and who also completed a questionnaire. The 106-item teacher questionnaire used in the study was made up of six sections:

- Teachers' academic and professional background
- Management of learning (pedagogical knowledge)
- Enactment of the ESL curriculum (pedagogical content knowledge)
- Engagement with the content of learning (teachers' language awareness: subject-matter knowledge)
- Teaching efficacy
- Teachers' professional learning.

Each section of the questionnaire except the first consisted of two or more sub-scales. 'Engagement with the content of learning' (EWLC), for example, comprised three sub-scales: 'Pre-lesson thinking about language content' (PTLC), 'Post-lesson thinking about language content' (POLC) and 'Dealing with "input for learning" in the classroom' (DILC). In responding to each item in this section of the questionnaire, teachers were required to rate the frequency with which they employed the stated strategy, using a six-point scale ranging from 1 (never) to 6 (regularly/always). The ten items in this section are set out in Table 10. Factor analysis was used to assess the construct validity of the teacher questionnaire: if the factor structure of the questionnaire agreed with the logical structure of the questionnaire, then there would be empirical support for the construct validity of the teacher questionnaire. In this case, the factor analysis suggested that the teacher questionnaire measured 12 major dimensions broadly following the logical structure of the teacher questionnaire, and that therefore the teacher questionnaire could be said to have construct validity. One of the 12 dimensions was 'Pre- and post-lesson thinking about language content' (i.e. the PTLC and POLC sub-scales combined), and another was 'Dealing with "input for learning" in the classroom' (DILC).

*Table 10: Section 4 of the 'Good Practices' teacher questionnaire –
'Engagement with the content of learning'*

---

56) When I plan my teaching, I set clear linguistic/language skills objectives (PTLC)

57) When planning language skills lessons, I look for opportunities to draw students' attention to important grammar points (PTLC)

58) Before teaching a grammar item, I evaluate the adequacy and clarity of the grammatical information provided by the textbook (PTLC)

59) When I design or select activities, I consider whether they help to achieve the linguistic objectives of the lesson (PTLC)

60) When reflecting on a lesson, I think more about how well students coped with the language content than their participation (POLC)

61) In planning future lessons, I take account of students' difficulties with the language content of earlier lessons (POLC)

62) I design follow-up materials that will raise my students' awareness of their recurrent language errors (POLC)

63) I make extensive use of grammar terms when I teach grammar (DILC)

64) When explaining a grammar item, I aim to be as complete and comprehensive as possible (DILC)

65) When I have difficulty explaining a grammar point to the students, I just use examples (DILC)

In order to examine the relationship between teacher engagement with language content and student learning, the correlations between the Teacher Effectiveness Index and various combinations of the 'Engagement with the content of learning' (EWLC) sub-scales were calculated. The analysis revealed that there was a statistically significant relationship between the Teacher Effectiveness Index and 'Pre- and post-lesson thinking about language content' (the combination of the PTLC and POLC sub-scales which was one of the major dimensions of the teacher questionnaire indicated by the factor analysis). The relationship between the Teacher Effectiveness Index and 'Pre-lesson thinking about language content' alone was also statistically significant. The effect size in each case was small (0.130 for PTLC plus POLC, 0.138 for PTLC alone), but there was a consistent association, hence the statistical significance. This would appear to provide some confirmation that teacher engagement with the content of learning, particularly in the form of pre- and post-lesson thinking about the content of lessons, does indeed affect student learning. The effect may not be dramatic, but it appears to be consistent. Again, however, there is a clear need for further research examining this relationship, research that focuses on teachers from different backgrounds working in different teaching and learning contexts.

8.4 TLA, teachers' awareness of the learner and student learning

In the model of TLA outlined in Chapter 2, awareness of language from the learners' perspective was viewed as being of central importance. This awareness was seen as optimally taking a variety of forms:

- Awareness of the state of learners' interlanguage and of its likely developmental path;
- Awareness of the processes of interlingual development; and
- Awareness (given the learners' current state of knowledge) of the challenges posed for the learners by the language content of pedagogic materials and tasks.

This is the aspect of TLA that is most obviously linked to student learning, since it is explicitly learner-related. It will therefore be discussed in the present chapter in order to evaluate the research evidence linking such awareness to student learning.

In fact, what research there is in this area has generally tended to stop short of examining learner outcomes. One example of such research is McNeill (2005), discussed in Chapters 6 and 7. As noted previously, McNeill's study focuses on the ability of teachers to predict learners' vocabulary difficulties in reading texts. It is therefore specifically concerned with teachers' awareness of their students' prior L2 knowledge and of the difficulty level of L2 language items for students at a particular stage of their learning. The study does involve the learner perspective to the extent of requiring the collection of data from students. However, those data were gathered at the beginning of the study, so that teachers' predictions of learner difficulty with different lexical items could be compared with the actual difficulties experienced by learners. There was no attempt in the study to investigate the student learning outcomes associated with teachers' subsequent vocabulary-related decisions.

Another study concerned with L2 teachers' awareness of the learner is Berry (1997), with the specific focus of the research in this case being grammatical terminology rather than vocabulary. Like McNeill (2005), Berry's study involved student data, provided in this case by a questionnaire administered to 372 undergraduates. The questionnaire contained 50 items of grammatical terminology, and the students were asked (a) to say if they were familiar with each item, and (b) if so, to provide an example. At the same time, the ten teachers of those students were given a questionnaire with the same 50 items and asked (a) if they thought their students would know the items, and (b) whether they would wish to make explicit use of those items in their teaching of that class. From his analysis of the data, Berry found wide discrepancies between the learners' knowledge of grammatical terminology and the teachers' estimation of it, with the teachers generally lacking awareness of their students' knowledge of metalanguage despite the fact that they had all taught the course and similar students before. Those discrepancies were seen as having serious potential consequences for student learning when the teachers' desire to use those terms in class was included in the analysis. Berry (1997:143) suggests that 'the weakest will encounter problems with any teacher and there are some teachers with whom even the most knowledgeable students will have difficulty'. As with McNeill's (2005) study described above, Berry's research did not focus on actual learning outcomes. However, the implied consequences for student learning are very clear and consistent with those in McNeill (2005): L2 teachers' awareness of their students' language knowledge and likely difficulties varies greatly, and where such awareness is lacking, teachers may make inappropriate pedagogical decisions, with potentially negative classroom consequences.

A certain number of studies relevant to this aspect of TLA have also been conducted from the perspective of a Vygotskyan sociocultural theory of learning. Sociocultural theory (referred to briefly in 2.5) is based on the view that knowledge is essentially social in nature, and that it is constructed through processes of collaboration, interaction and communication among individuals in social settings (see, e.g., Vygotsky, 1978). One of the central notions within the Vygotskyan framework is the zone of proximal development (ZPD), defined by Vygotsky (1978:86) as 'the distance between the actual developmental level as determined by independent problem solving and the level of potential development as determined through problem solving under adult guidance or in collaboration with more capable peers'. According to Aljaafreh and Lantolf (1994:468), 'the ZPD is the framework, par excellence, which brings all of the pieces of the learning setting together – the teacher, the learner, their social and cultural history, their goals and motives, as well as the resources available to them, including those that are dialogically constructed together'. The second central notion in Vygotskyan sociocultural theory is that of scaffolding, whereby support is extended to the less knowledgeable partner (e.g., the student) as he/she collaborates with a more knowledgeable partner (e.g., the teacher). In order for the teacher (expert) to provide appropriate scaffolding within the student's (novice's) ZPD, it is clear that 'the expert . . . must try to be sensitive to the learners' actual level of competence' (Aljaafreh and Lantolf, 1994:469). In other words, the teacher needs awareness of the learner of the type outlined at the beginning of this section.

Two studies from this perspective, both concerned with error correction, offer some evidence of the relationship between this aspect of TLA and student learning. Aljaafreh and Lantolf (1994), for example, report on three learners of English, each of whom received corrective feedback collaboratively and within their ZPD. Their analysis indicates that various approaches to error treatment (both explicit and implicit) are potentially relevant for learning: the crucial condition for such treatment to be effective is that it should be the result of a collaborative endeavour involving other individuals, with the corrective feedback being provided at the right point or within the learner's ZPD. In other words, it requires the teacher to have an awareness of the state of the learner's interlanguage and of the scaffolding required to overcome a particular language difficulty and provide mediation to support learning.

Nassaji and Swain (2000) provide further insights in this regard, in a study of two learners of English, which sought to examine whether negotiated help provided within a learner's ZPD is more effective than help provided randomly and irrespective of the learner's ZPD. Nassaji and Swain's study focused on the use of the article and involved four tutorial sessions of individual feedback on compositions written by the learners. After the four tutorials, the two students were also tested for improvement in their knowledge of articles, using cloze tests focusing on the article errors in their original compositions. Both qualitative and quantitative analysis demonstrated the effectiveness of the ZPD

177

corrective feedback. The student receiving ZPD feedback, despite showing less accuracy in her article use than her non-ZPD counterpart in her first composition, performed the better of the two in her final composition. The ZPD student also showed consistent progress in her article use across the four compositions, unlike her counterpart, whose performance reached a high point in the second composition and then worsened steadily. Although this study does not explicitly focus on TLA, and the random feedback that disregarded the ZPD was a deliberate strategy rather than a consequence of the tutor's lack of learner awareness, there are nevertheless implications that the teacher's awareness of the state of the individual learner's interlanguage and the provision of appropriate scaffolding can indeed have a positive impact on student learning.

These are, however, very small-scale studies focusing on a limited range of areas of grammar. Clearly, there is a need for further research concerning the impact of teachers' awareness of the learner on student learning. It is also important to emphasise that these studies took place under conditions far removed from those obtaining in most L2 classrooms. While it may be feasible to have such awareness of the learner's interlingual development when teaching one-to-one, the situation is rather different for the teacher who is faced with a class of 40 students. Ellis (2005), for instance, suggests that it is impossible for any teacher to have a precise understanding of each learner's on-going interlanguage development. Nevertheless, I would argue that the more the teacher gains evidence from learners' performance in speaking and writing, and reflects on the learning and the learning gaps which that evidence reveals, the more likely that teacher is to make sensible content-related pedagogical decisions. Precise understanding of learners' interlingual development may be an unrealistic expectation, but heightened awareness would seem both a realistic and a worthwhile aspiration. Also, as Ellis (2005) suggests, it may not be the *precision* of, for example, the timing of focusing on a particular language feature that is crucial: as long as the 'focus on form' is not too far ahead of the learners' current state of interlanguage development, it may still 'push them along' in the development of their 'built-in' syllabus.

8.5 Conclusion

In this chapter, we have looked at some of the research evidence that is potentially relevant to any examination of the relationship between TLA and student learning. That research was discussed in relation to three themes: teachers' subject-matter knowledge; teacher engagement with the content of learning; and teachers' awareness of learner difficulties. In the discussion, the following major points emerged:

- It is very difficult to identify consistent causative associations between TLA and learning outcomes, because of the number of variables that potentially affect student learning;
- Research in general education on the relationship between the teacher's subject-matter knowledge and student learning appears to suggest that there is some link between teacher quality characteristics (including subject-matter knowledge) and student learning; research from L2 education indicates a possible link between subject-matter knowledge and teacher effectiveness (as measured by student learning outcomes), but the evidence from research in both areas is inconclusive;
- Research from L2 education appears to indicate that teacher engagement with the content of learning, especially in the form of pre- and post-lesson thinking about language content, has a positive impact on student learning;
- Research evidence relating to the impact of teacher awareness of the learner on student learning is also inconclusive. Two Hong Kong-based studies indicate a significant potential impact, but neither gathered evidence of students' learning outcomes. Two studies conducted within a sociocultural framework suggest a link, but they are very small-scale studies.

As the arguments in the previous sections illustrate, we are once again largely obliged to fall back on inference and logical deduction to support the link between TLA and student learning. Although there is a certain amount of evidence to support the assumption of such a link, the most obvious conclusion to be drawn from the discussion in the present chapter is that we need more research that might shed light on this relationship. Potentially valuable data might be drawn not only from relatively large-scale research like the 'Good Practices' project referred to in 8.2 and 8.3 above, but also from TLA-focused case studies of both individual teachers and of learners. Only as a result of such research can we begin to understand more generally what makes an L2 teacher effective in a particular teaching/learning context, and the specific role that TLA plays in helping a teacher to be effective in promoting student learning. At the same time, however, we would have to recognise the need to treat the findings from such research with caution, given the number of variables with the potential to influence student learning (as noted in 8.1).

The following chapter looks at TLA and teacher learning, focusing on issues relating to the development of the L2 teacher's language awareness.

Questions for discussion and reflection

1) Do you believe that there is any connection between a teacher's language awareness and the L2 learning achievements of that teacher's students? What evidence, anecdotal or otherwise, do you have to support your viewpoint?

2) Table 9 illustrates some of the possible interrelationships between variables that make it so difficult to identify consistent causative associations between TLA, or any other individual variable, and learning outcomes. Do you conclude from this statement that research focusing on the possible relationship between TLA and student learning is a waste of time? If so, why? If not, why not?

3) The discussion in 8.2 talks of the difficulties for researchers of finding suitable indicators of teachers' subject-matter knowledge. Some studies take the possession of a relevant (however defined) first degree as an indicator. Do you think that a 'relevant' first degree is a reliable indicator of subject-matter knowledge? Do you have a 'relevant' first degree yourself? Is your possession or lack of a 'relevant' first degree a good indicator of your own subject-matter knowledge of L2 English?

4) The questionnaire in 8.3 focuses on teachers' engagement with the content of learning. How would you respond to each of the ten items, using a six-point scale from 1 (never) to 6 (regularly/always)? If possible, compare your responses with those of a classmate or colleague. What do you think those responses reveal about your engagement with the content of learning?

5) Both of the small-scale studies from a sociocultural perspective described in 8.4 focus on error correction. How can awareness of the learner's 'zone of proximal development' (ZPD) help the teacher to provide the sort of feedback that might improve student learning? When you give feedback to a learner in your own teaching (either orally or in writing), to what extent do you take account of that learner's ZPD? How does this affect the form/content/style of your feedback?

6) In your own teaching context, to what extent is it realistic for the teacher to be aware of individual students' interlanguage development? What strategies can you employ to enhance your awareness of learners' on-going interlanguage development?

9 TLA and teacher learning

9.1 Introduction

In the earlier chapters of this book, we explored the nature of the content knowledge required by L2 teachers and the potential impact of that knowledge on pedagogical practice. In the previous chapter, we considered the relationship between subject-matter knowledge (together with other aspects of TLA) and students' learning outcomes. In all of these chapters, the arguments put forward have generally lent support to the assertion of Wright and Bolitho (1993:292), cited in Chapter 1, that: 'the more aware a teacher is of language and how it works, the better', although, as we saw in Chapter 8, further research is needed before we can claim with any degree of certainty that TLA has a demonstrable impact on students' learning.

In a number of the previous chapters, we have looked at snapshots of the TLA of various teachers. These snapshots appeared in the context of discussions of TLA in pedagogical practice; TLA and teachers' subject-matter cognitions; the TLA of expert and novice teachers; and the TLA of NS and NNS teachers. However, we have devoted little or no attention so far to the development of TLA, i.e. to the specific matter of teachers' own learning. In this case, the key question is how we can help teachers – whether they are novices on pre-service courses or experienced practitioners taking part in in-service programmes – to develop the knowledge, skills and sensitivity required to be 'language-aware'. In this final chapter of the book, we will examine some of the issues relating to the development of the L2 teacher's language awareness and some of the principles that might be applied to the planning of TLA-related courses and activities. We shall then look in detail at the design of one particular course focusing on the development of L2 teachers' language awareness as it relates to grammar.

9.2 The development of LA courses for L2 teachers: background and issues

The vast majority of courses for teachers of L2 English probably involve some kind of language work. This focus on language often takes the form of a component labelled 'Language Analysis', 'Language Awareness' or simply (and ambiguously) 'LA'. The inclusion of such a component is especially common on initial (pre-service) courses, but 'Language Awareness' is increasingly the focus of in-service professional development, too. As seen from a UK perspective, the emergence of courses (or components of courses) intended to enhance the language awareness of teachers of L2 English has occurred principally, although by no means exclusively, in response to two trends within the profession: the demand for NS teachers who would be capable of teaching beginner- and elementary-level students possessing little or no English; and the demand from NNS teachers and their employers for professional upgrading focusing on the knowledge and competences that might help those teachers to cope successfully with the implementation of ELT curriculum innovations in their schools and education systems.

The first of these demands became apparent when the EFL industry began to take off in the early 1960s, and English language schools opened up in Britain and around the world. As noted in Chapter 7, it was very easy at that time for untrained NS graduates to find employment teaching English, in spite of their lack of training. In 1962, recognising the need for such teachers to engage in some form of pre-service preparation for their work in the classroom, John Haycraft and his wife, Brita, started to offer two-week intensive courses of TEFL training, based loosely on the training models used in business and industry. From the beginning, these courses included a certain amount of language analysis. The Haycrafts' courses were initially created in order to prepare teachers to work for their own school, International House (IH), which opened in London in 1959 (Haycraft, 1988). However, there was clearly a wider demand for such training. Before long, as that demand grew, the courses became four weeks (100 hours) in length, and the IH 'four-week' model eventually provided a blueprint for similar programmes of initial TEFL training all over the world, via the Royal Society of Arts (RSA) Preparatory Certificate in TEFL, popularly known as the 'Prep. Cert.' or simply the 'RSA'. The 'Prep. Cert.' training scheme was established in 1978, and subsequently updated (as CTEFLA and CELTA) under the administration of the University of Cambridge Local Examinations Syndicate (UCLES) (see 1.6 and the footnote on page 19). LA continues to play a central role in these widely taken courses wherever they are taught.

The second type of demand revealed itself a little later, when the growing influence of communicative language teaching (CLT) on EFL/ESL curriculum developments worldwide acted as a catalyst for the creation of in-service refresher courses for NNS teachers of L2 English. Many of these focused on (or included a component of) Language

Awareness / Language Analysis. Such courses provided an opportunity for teachers to explore the connections between language form, meaning, context and use in ways that they generally had not done during their previous studies at university and/or teachers' college. The activities on such courses, particularly if they bore the 'Language Awareness' label, were typically inductive data-based 'consciousness-raising' tasks designed to stimulate participants' reflections on and insights into the workings of different parts of the language systems, and to encourage them to question pre-digested facts and their own pre-conceptions about language. The first published LA materials aimed primarily at teachers (Bolitho and Tomlinson, 1980) contain an imaginative range of such activities. More recent published materials, such as Wright (1994) and Thornbury (1997), expand the task repertoire, but they basically follow the established pattern of discovery-focused analysis of language data in order to extend users' awareness of how the language works.

One of the main issues arising in relation to both published LA materials and to the training courses that include a 'Language Awareness' / 'Language Analysis' component is the extent to which either fully succeeds in helping teachers to make the bridge between the declarative and procedural dimensions of TLA. It may well be, for example, that the tasks in published LA materials enhance teachers' language awareness in the sense of increasing their knowledge about aspects of English grammar, lexis, discourse and phonology. But according to Wright (2002), those materials may not always manage to make the links needed to create the 'shift from new knowledge to classroom reality' that Wright considers to be the greatest challenge for those working in the area of LA development for teachers.

Bartels (2005b) explores this issue of knowledge transfer, by examining the implication underlying Fillmore and Snow's (2002) recommendations that teachers should know, among other things, the principles of word-formation. According to Bartels (2005b:405), the hypothesis upon which such advice is based is that 'armed with this knowledge about language, teachers will . . . be able to understand and diagnose student problems better, provide better explanations and representations for aspects of language, and have a clearer idea of what they are teaching'. While it may be reasonable to assume (as I have argued throughout this book) that such knowledge has the potential to be of value to the teacher, Bartels (2005b) concludes from the findings in the various papers in his edited volume (Bartels, 2005a) that helping teachers to acquire knowledge and conceptions about language and language learning is not in itself enough to promote significant changes in their pedagogical practice. He suggests that this view is supported by evidence from the teacher education literature, citing Wideen, Mayer-Smith and Moon's (1998:160) meta-analysis of research on teacher education: 'In this review of recent empirical research, we found very little evidence to support an approach to learning to teach which focuses primarily on the provision of propositional knowledge.' Bartels speculates that in the specific domain of language teacher education, problems with knowledge transfer may perhaps arise because the activities in which teachers engage on applied linguistics courses are not analogous to the activities they would normally engage in as teachers.

The focus in Bartels (2005a) is primarily on university-level courses for language teachers. However, a similar knowledge-transfer problem has been noted in relation to the short intensive pre-service courses of the four-week type mentioned above. Kerr (1993), for instance, claims that much of the LA work on courses following the IH or CTEFLA model has emphasised the analytical process of studying language at the expense of the application of any insights that might be gained from such analysis. According to Kerr (1993:41), LA activity has typically focused on the transmission of knowledge about language rather than on fostering an awareness of implications for the learner or the teaching/learning process. Kerr cites as examples of the resulting difficulties experienced by participants on CTEFLA courses 'the trainee who elicits the stress on a monosyllabic word or the one who asks a class of beginners if they wouldn't "mind just jotting down a few notes and then working out the answers in pairs"' (ibid.), and he suggests that problems of this nature are rather more frequent than gaps in knowledge. In 1996, the CTEFLA scheme gave way to CELTA, which had a more enlightened Language Awareness syllabus than its predecessor, one that was intended to address such problems. However, in a follow-up to his 1993 paper, Kerr (1998) found that the LA component of training courses in 30 CELTA centres was largely unchanged, with recent developments both in the syllabus and the study of language generally having had 'very little impact in the way that CELTA trainers have conceived of and packaged language awareness for their trainees' (p. 5).

The problem noted by Kerr in his two papers is, at least in part, linked to a second issue in TLA course design, which is a particular dilemma for those involved with pre-service programmes. On the one hand, participants in such programmes clearly need and want the security of pre-digested 'facts' about language that will enable them to survive their initial classroom experience without their confidence being too severely dented. On the other hand, however, if they are to develop professionally, they must be ready to question and reflect on the adequacy of such facts. Wright and Bolitho (1993) make the point that LA work is potentially destabilising for all teachers, whether pre-service or in-service, because it is a challenging way of approaching language, which obliges teachers to confront their linguistic preconceptions. For pre-service trainees, who tend to lack confidence in relation to many aspects of managing a language lesson, there may be severe limits on their readiness to look at language in 'different' ways and on their willingness and ability to 'tolerate open-endedness and ambiguity' (Wright and Bolitho, 1993:299). Nevertheless, as Wright and Bolitho suggest, it is important on such courses, even when there are severe time constraints, to avoid focusing excessively on the transmission of 'factual' knowledge. On any course, there is an appropriate balance between establishing the necessary foundation of a basic knowledge about language, and arousing the kind of sensitivity to the diversity and complexity of language that is essential to any thinking L2 teacher. The challenge for the teacher educator is to find the right balance each time, and to address the specific TLA needs and concerns of the individual participants on each course. Achieving such a balance may be rather easier on some courses than others: on an intensive four-week CELTA course, for instance, it may be virtually impossible.

9.3 The development of LA courses for L2 teachers: models and principles

The design of TLA courses and course components has been influenced by ideas from general education as well as language education. But one of the major influences on TLA work in the past two decades has been the model outlined in Edge's 1988 paper, referred to in Chapter 1. In that paper, Edge sets out what he sees as the three major roles that the trainee teacher of L2 English needs to take on: those of language *user*, language *analyst* and language *teacher*. These roles refer to three interrelated competences. The language *user* role concerns the teacher's language proficiency and determines that teacher's adequacy as a model for students. The language *analyst* role relates to the teacher's language systems knowledge base, and his/her ability to understand the workings of the target language. The third role, that of language *teacher*, is dependent on the teacher's familiarity with a range of TEFL procedures and the possession of underlying theoretical knowledge about language pedagogy, and involves making appropriate and principled decisions about the use of those procedures. The sort of explicit study of language and language learning required for the second of these roles, that of language *analyst*, is referred to by Edge (1988:12–13) as 'applying linguistics' and is seen as playing an integrative role on any L2 teacher education course, facilitating language learning for the trainee as 'user' and pedagogical decisions for the trainee as 'teacher'. In other words, knowledge about language is seen as 'enabling knowledge' (Wright, 1991:63).

Edge's paper illustrates how these three components may be integrated, taking as his example the design of a four-year pre-service L2 teacher education programme, in which the overt emphasis shifts from Language Improvement through Applied Linguistics to Methodology, as the student develops from user to analyst to teacher of language. Edge implies that this is just one way in which these three components may be integrated. Wright (1991) develops that point, suggesting that while a programme with such progression might reflect the needs of the pre-service trainee, for in-service programmes the situation is different, because serving teachers have already gone through the user/analyst/teacher developmental process once.

Wright and Bolitho acknowledge Edge's influence on their own approach to the development of L2 teachers' language awareness, which they have described in a series of papers since the early 1990s. In their 1993 paper, for instance, they propose a methodological framework for LA activities (Figure 5), which is explicitly based on Edge's three competences. The model in Figure 5 illustrates their conceptualisation of the interrelationship between the user, analyst and teacher competences, in which LA is viewed as playing a mediating role. In LA work they expect teachers to draw on and continuously develop these three competences, while different types of LA activity are seen to offer different points of entry to the framework. In a 1997 paper, Wright and Bolitho describe LA as an integral part of continuing professional development for L2 teachers, and they outline an experiential approach (see, e.g., Kolb, 1984) to LA work on in-service programmes, which

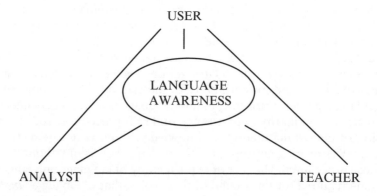

Figure 5: Relationships between user, analyst and teacher of language (Wright and Bolitho, 1993:298)

186

specifically aims to address the knowledge-transfer issue referred to in 9.2 above. The starting point for the sequence of LA activities is a problem derived from the teachers' own classroom experiences with language. The teachers analyse and review those experiences in order to explore the linguistic and pedagogic dimensions of the problem and gain deeper insights into the particular area of language, before planning future classroom action. The trainer's role in such a cycle is seen as essentially facilitative: 'providing a secure environment for learning, helping participants to keep focused, listening carefully and responding appropriately, probing with questions at the right moment, ensuring that the necessary learning resources are available, setting relevant tasks, negotiating deadlines and outcomes' (Wright and Bolitho, 1997:175).

Wright (2002) develops these ideas, setting out a five-stage cycle for LA activities, designed to interconnect the user, analyst and teacher domains. The stages are as follows:

Stage 1: *Working on language data*. Participants are invited to engage with language via, for example, a language-related teaching issue. They work with linguistic data, draw on their previous experiences and their present understandings, and share their thoughts with their fellow course participants.

Stage 2: *Looking back – reviewing*. Participants reflect on the processes they have just experienced and confront the potentially disturbing impact of new linguistic insights. Stages 1 and 2 together are seen as the 'awareness-raising process' (Wright, 2002:126).

Stage 3: *Making sense*. The aim at this stage is to make sense of the insights emerging from Stages 1 and 2, by formulating rules about the language that may be of direct use in the classroom. Participants work collectively to develop and refine their ideas.

Stage 4: *Linking*. At this Stage the aim is to promote the transfer of this new linguistic knowledge to the classroom. Wright (2002: 127) describes this as a shift from 'thinking about language to thinking about the practical side of working with language for teaching purposes'. One way in which it is suggested this shift can be promoted is by getting participants to look at how published teaching materials deal with the language points focused on in Stages 1 to 3.

Stage 5: *To the classroom*. The last stage in the cycle (before any direct transfer to a classroom situation) involves participants engaging in planning language activities, taking account of the insights about language acquired at the earlier stages.

Wright also proposes a series of principles for LA work, drawing on ideas first outlined in Wright and Bolitho (1993). Those eight principles are: (i) LA work needs data; (ii) LA work needs talk; (iii) Integrate participants' responses (intellectual, emotional) to LA issues; (iv) Provide time; (v) Build on participants' initial responses; (vi) Give help with rules and metalanguage; (vii) Be ready with 'expert' input; and (viii) Look for a payoff in terms of classroom practice (Wright, 2002:127–8).

The cycle of TLA activities that Wright describes and the principles that inform its design place an emphasis on engaging with preconceptions about language, developing and organising knowledge about language, and on critical reflection. They therefore have much in common with the three learning principles for facilitating the development of prospective teachers of all subjects discussed by Hammerness et al. (2005):

1. Prospective teachers come to the classroom with preconceptions about teaching, based on their previous classroom experience over many years as learners (the 'apprenticeship of observation' noted by Lortie, 1975). Those initial understandings need to be engaged in any teacher development programme: if not, then new concepts and information may be misunderstood, or taken on board only to the extent required to perform satisfactorily in an exam or an assessed lesson.

2. Prospective teachers need to be helped to 'enact' what they know, i.e. to develop the kinds of organised understanding and skills that support effective action. This means that they must '(i) have a deep foundation of factual and theoretical knowledge, (ii) understand facts and ideas in the context of a conceptual framework, and (iii) organise knowledge in ways that facilitate retrieval and action' (Hammerness et al., 2005:366).

3. Teaching is an extremely complex and demanding task. If prospective teachers are going to be given the tools to help them ultimately become 'adaptive experts' (see the discussion in Chapter 6, and Bransford et al., 2005b) who can manage complexity, they need to develop the ability to think about their own thinking, i.e. their metacognition. Hammerness et al. (2005:376–7) characterise people with high levels of metacognitive awareness as having the mental habits of continually assessing their own performance and modifying their assumptions and actions as necessary: 'Effective teachers particularly need to be metacognitive about their work. The more they learn about teaching and learning the more accurately they can reflect on what they are doing well and on what needs to be improved.'

The approach to TLA development advocated by Wright (2002) and the teacher development principles outlined by Hammerness et al. (2005) also reflect the view of teacher learning embodied in the professional development activities for language teachers described in Richards and Farrell (2005). The strategies that Richards and Farrell discuss, such as the use of journals and teaching portfolios, analysing critical incidents, case analysis and action research, could all be applied to TLA-focused professional development activity. The view of teacher learning under-pinning such strategies essentially represents an integration of three different theories:

- Teacher learning as *a cognitive process*: teacher development requires teachers to explore their own beliefs and thinking processes in order to examine how these influence their classroom practices;
- Teacher learning as *personal construction*: teachers should be helped to develop self-awareness, understanding of their classrooms and personal interpretations of knowledge; and
- Teacher learning as *reflective practice*: teacher learning is enhanced by engaging in critical reflection on the nature, meaning and impact of classroom experiences.

Wright's (2002) emphasis on LA work needing talk (echoing Wright and Bolitho, 1993) also highlights the importance of collective activity and the co-construction of knowledge. Self-monitoring of classroom experiences and other individual continuing professional development activities undoubtedly have their value. But the benefits of sharing reflections and working collectively to analyse past actions and their consequences cannot be overemphasised. Busy L2 teachers might not always have the formal opportunities for the co-construction of understanding about language that may be afforded by participation in an in-service course with a focus on TLA developments. They should nevertheless endeavour to make use of or to set up informal discussion groups and networks, or 'communities of practice' (defined by Wenger, 2004, as 'groups of people who share a concern or a passion for something they do and learn how to do it better as they interact regularly'). Shulman and Shulman (2004:267) make the point that 'learning proceeds most effectively if it is accompanied by metacognitive awareness and analysis of one's own learning processes, and is supported by membership in a learning community'.

From the preceding discussion, I would argue that a combination of language-related self-reflection and focused collaborative activity of the sort described represents the most effective way of helping L2 teachers to achieve enhanced levels of language awareness and the development of pedagogical strategies for dealing with language that are of direct relevance to their specific teaching context. The principles and five-stage cycle proposed by Wright (2002) provide an excellent basis for such collaborative activity.

9.4 The development of LA courses for L2 teachers: a case study

Contextual factors generally play a large part in determining the design of any course: LA courses for teachers are no exception. The course described in this part of the chapter is very much a product of the Hong Kong context, which has provided a backdrop for all the examples in this book. It is slightly different from some LA courses in that it focuses less on language per se and more on the transfer of knowledge about language to pedagogical practice. However, it embodies many of the principles of TLA course design and teacher learning discussed earlier.

9.4.1 The context of the course

The course, entitled 'Pedagogic Grammar' (PG), takes place as part of a four-year pre-service Bachelor of Education programme of the type referred to in Edge (1988). This particular programme (the Bachelor of Education in Language Education offered by the University of Hong Kong) was introduced in the early 1990s, as an alternative to the conventional approach to the preparation of future teachers of L2 English in Hong Kong secondary schools. Instead of three years of subject-matter study followed by one year of teacher education (the typical pattern of separating the first degree from professional training), the BEd was planned as a fully integrated programme, in which all four years would include the four strands of main subject study, educational studies, professional studies (i.e. methodology) and school experience.

During the time that the BEd programme has been offered, the vast majority of those studying for the degree have been local Cantonese-speaking students, who are themselves recent products of the schools for which they are being prepared. In the past two or three years, however, the intake has changed slightly, with an increase in the number of mature students and of students with an international background whose L1 is a language other than Cantonese.

The PG course takes place in the second semester of Year 3. By the time they reach that stage of their BEd studies, the students have already taken a course of 'Language Awareness' (in the first semester of Year 1). The BEd Year 1 LA course pays particular attention to some of the preconceptions about language that Hong Kong students tend to have after twelve or more years of often very 'traditional' form-focused English lessons, encouraging them to open their minds to alternative interpretations and analyses of language phenomena. By the second semester of Year 3, the BEd students have also taken a number of courses focusing on specific aspects of the English language systems, including phonology, written discourse and the grammar of written and spoken English.

9.4.2 The timing of the course

The PG course is timed to take place immediately after the students have spent nine weeks on teaching practice in a local secondary school. The school experience strand of the BEd is spread over the four years of the programme: in Year 1 students undertake a series of visits to different types of school (including international schools and special schools); in Year 2 students spend three weeks in a school, observing lessons and gaining their first experience of classroom teaching; in Years 3 and 4 students spend a total of 18 weeks on teaching practice (a nine-week block each year in different secondary schools), supported in each placement by a mentoring teacher, a classmate and a visiting university tutor. The nine-week block in Year 3 represents the students' first prolonged experience of secondary school English teaching in the role of teacher.

The timing of the PG course is especially significant in relation to the aim of providing a 'push' to the transfer of knowledge, and sparking the process by which declarative knowledge becomes proceduralised. By scheduling the course to take place immediately after the Year 3 practicum, the intention is to provide an opportunity for the students to reflect in depth on their very recent experiences of dealing with grammar in the secondary school classroom and to re-evaluate some of their grammar-related pedagogical decisions in light of knowledge gained on the course. Such reflections are intended to lay the foundations for further knowledge-building and personal exploration, as well as for their next practical classroom experience during the fourth and final year of the programme. It is also hoped that the students may be encouraged to develop habits of self-monitoring and of sharing with colleagues their reflections about language and language pedagogy, habits that may become an integral part of their professional practice as L2 teachers.

There is strong support in the education literature for purposefully scheduling a course in order to integrate theory and practice, with evidence from a number of studies suggesting that the way teacher education is conducted can affect the extent to which teachers are able to enact what they are learning. According to Hammerness et al. (2005:375), 'These studies have found that, when a well-supervised student teaching experience precedes or is conducted jointly with coursework, students appear more able to connect theoretical learning to practice, become more comfortable with the process of learning to teach, and are more able to enact what they are learning in practice.'

9.4.3 The course description and course aims

The PG course has evolved in various ways since it was first offered. The current outline (Table 11) describes the course and its aims.

Table 11: The BEd Pedagogic Grammar course – description and aims

---

Description of the course
This is a 6-credit course during which we will explore the relationship between grammar and pedagogy. There are eight timetabled three-hour sessions. These will take the form of workshops, during which you will explore different areas of grammar, and/or approaches to the teaching of grammar. There will be assigned readings for each session. Assessment will be based upon a portfolio.

Aims of the course
(A) By the end of the course, you should have an enhanced understanding of:
- the arguments for and against the teaching of grammar;
- the importance of 'Teacher Language Awareness' and its relationship with content-related pedagogical decisions;
- the rationale for and characteristics of different approaches to the teaching of grammar.

(B) By the end of the course, you should be able to:
- make efficient, informed and critical use of reference grammar sources to locate relevant grammatical information;
- analyse and evaluate the treatment of grammar in textbooks / teaching materials;
- make principled decisions in relation to your own grammar teaching, based on sound knowledge of the grammar area, understanding of the language/learning needs of your students and familiarity with different approaches to grammar pedagogy.

9.4.4 The structure of the course

Although the first session of the course takes place after teaching practice, the course effectively begins beforehand, with a pre-practicum meeting. At that meeting, the students are given a memo containing instructions and a set of questions. This pre-course memo (Table 12) is intended to achieve two objectives:

- to encourage reflection and discussion during the practicum (both with the BEd classmate at their assigned school and the mentoring teacher) about their lessons and also about broader issues relating to grammar pedagogy; and

- to ensure that they note those reflections and that they gather the materials they will need both for the course and for the portfolio on which they will be assessed.

The questions in the memo, with one minor addition, are from Borg (1999c).

Table 12: The BEd Pedagogic Grammar course – the pre-course memo

Memo to	: All BEd (English – Year 3) students
From	: Steve Andrews

Pedagogic Grammar

As you know, after your Teaching Practice, we shall be meeting for a course on 'Pedagogic Grammar'. I want to ensure that this course is as relevant as possible to your experiences and needs in relation to grammar and grammar teaching. I am therefore going to ask you to collect some materials on a regular basis during your TP, and to carry out one or two **small** (!!) related tasks, so that we can build on your experience during the course.

Please note that this preparatory work will be the beginning of a portfolio, which will form the basis of the assessment of the Pedagogic Grammar course. It is therefore **very important** that you take it seriously, and arrive at the first session of the course with the requested materials.

Materials to be collected
1) Photocopies of all grammar-related materials used in your teaching.
2) Plans of any of your lessons that involved the teaching of grammar.
3) Photocopies of written feedback from TP supervisors on any lessons involving the teaching of grammar.
4) Reflections on a **sample** of the lessons in (2). Please make sure that you reflect on a **minimum** of four such lessons – preferably those that have caused you the most difficulty. These reflections should be **brief**, and should focus specifically on issues relating to the grammar items you have had to teach. Note down, for example:
    - Uncertainties you may have had about your own knowledge of the grammar item to be taught;
    - Questions you may have had about the textbook treatment of the grammar item: either the explanation of the rule(s), or the methodology employed;
    - Doubts you may have had about any materials/advice given to you by the school in relation to the lesson;
    - Queries you may have had about the best way to teach the grammar item;
    - Impressions you may have formed about the approach to grammar preferred by the students in your school.

Table 12: (cont.)

Task

On the following page you will find a set of questions. They concern decisions that every teacher has to make in relation to the teaching of grammar.

Please look at the set of questions at the beginning of your Teaching Practice, and think about them as you teach any lessons involving grammar.

Then, at the end of your Teaching Practice, note your response to each of the questions, based on your experiences.

BEd (Lang. Ed. – English) Year 3 2005–2006 Pedagogic Grammar

How do you teach grammar?

The questions below are intended to make you think about your experience of dealing with grammar during Teaching Practice.

N.B. *There are NO right or wrong answers to any of the questions!!!!*

Materials

1) What are the sources of the grammar materials I use?

Lesson structure

2) Do I devote whole lessons to grammar teaching? Or does grammar teaching take place as just **part** of a lesson?
3) Do I sequence my grammar teaching activities in any particular way(s)?
4) Within the context of a lesson involving other things as well as grammar, at what stage(s) does the grammar work occur?

Strategies

5) Do I tell students that we are doing grammar work? Or do I keep it implicit?
6) To what extent do I explain grammar? How? When?
7) Do I ever refer to Cantonese when teaching grammar? If so, when? If not, why not?
8) To what extent do I encourage students to discover things for themselves? How?
9) Do I encourage students to become aware of grammar rules? How? When?
10) How much grammatical terminology do I use when I teach grammar? How much terminology do my materials use?
11) Do I provide students with opportunities to use grammar? How? When?

Outcomes

12) Do the students have an opportunity to keep a record of the grammar I cover?
13) Do I check students' understanding of grammar? How? When?

Questions about grammar

14) What kinds of questions about grammar do I ask the students?
15) How do I respond to students' answers to those questions?

Table 12: (cont.)

16) Do I encourage students to ask questions about grammar?
17) Do students ask questions about grammar?
18) How do I respond to such questions?

Grammar errors

19) How do I deal with students' spoken and written grammatical errors during accuracy and fluency work?

(Questions adapted from Borg. 1999c)

In the first session of the course, participants are given details of the portfolio assessment which forms an integral part of the course structure (Table 13).

Table 13: The BEd Pedagogic Grammar course – the portfolio assessment

Aims of the portfolio assessment

In designing the assessment for this course, I wanted you to demonstrate understanding of the issues we will be exploring together. More importantly, however, I wanted to give you the opportunity to reflect on the relevance and applicability of those issues to the practical realities of teaching, and also to your developing personal theories of language pedagogy.

In the portfolio, you will therefore be expected to demonstrate the abilities outlined in the **Aims of the course**. In my grading of your portfolio, I will be looking for evidence of those abilities. In addition, I shall be looking for evidence of the ability to engage seriously with issues relating to the teaching and learning of grammar, and for reflections that demonstrate an attempt to form a principled personal view of grammar/language pedagogy.

Requirements of the portfolio

Your portfolio should contain the following:
1. The materials you gathered during School Experience (outlined in my earlier memo to you), including your reflections on four lessons involving the teaching of grammar;
2. The post-session reflection tasks you are assigned during the course;
3. **Three** more extended pieces of reflective writing (suggested length: about 1,000 words each). In order to produce these reflections, you are advised to select three of the four lessons referred to in 1. above. The instructions for the three tasks are as follows:
   (a) **Task 1**
   In the first lesson you select, focus on the **grammar area** itself. Outline which features of the grammar area you taught. Critically evaluate your selection of what was to be taught in the light of your understanding

195

Table 13: (cont.)

of the grammar area from reference grammars. Discuss how you would handle these content-related issues if you were teaching the same area of grammar in a similar teaching situation in future.

(b) **Task 2**

In the second lesson you select, focus on the **treatment** of the grammar area in the **materials** you were given by the school (either the textbook or in-house materials). Critically evaluate how the grammar area is treated in those materials. Pay particular attention to content-related issues (e.g. the accuracy of the information provided, the clarity of the explanations, the quality of the examples) rather than to issues of methodology.

(c) **Task 3**

In the third lesson you select, focus on the **approach** you adopted. Briefly describe which approach you adopted, and why. Reflect on possible alternatives, and discuss how you might approach the teaching of the same grammar area in future.

The reflections that students include in their portfolios are of two main types. First, at various points during the course, they are invited to note down their immediate reactions to issues discussed, particularly their thoughts about any practical implications for grammar teaching in the classroom context that they have just experienced. Then, at the end of the course, they are required to revisit three of their practicum lessons and reflect critically on them. Each of these three extended reflections has a different focus: one on the grammar area itself, one on the textbook's treatment of that grammar area and one on the pedagogical approach adopted by the student in the selected lesson.

As noted in the course outline, the eight sessions of the course all take the form of workshops. The students are expected to have done assigned readings before each class, and they then participate in a series of workshop tasks in groups, with the tutor acting as a facilitator. The eight workshop sessions are sequenced as follows. In **Session 1**, the students are grouped with classmates who did their teaching practice in different schools. Each group then uses the questions in Table 12 as a framework for comparing grammar-related aspects of their practicum experience: both the practices they adopted, and the reasoning (including the response to specific contextual factors) that guided them. Then, towards the end of the session, they are invited to negotiate the content of four of the remaining seven workshop sessions. They nominate grammar topics that they found challenging or problematic during their teaching practice, and then vote to make a final selection of four areas of grammar, each of which becomes the focus of one workshop. Typical areas nominated for inclusion are: Conditional sentences, Indirect and direct speech, Relative clauses, Articles, Perfect verb forms, and Gerunds and infinitives. **Session 2** focuses on two fundamental questions: 'Why do we teach grammar?' and 'Why do teachers need to know about grammar?' **Session 3** is a Pedagogic Grammar case study. The specific grammatical focus of this session has changed from year to year (depending on the students' selection of items for the four PG workshops), but typically the case study has three phases: (a) awareness-raising about the grammar area and analysis of what reference grammars say about it (drawing on a variety of reference grammar sources, including both books and the Telenex database);[1] (b) critical analysis of a textbook treatment of the grammar area (with particular attention to the textbook's presentation of grammar rules and choice of examples); and (c) analysis of transcribed extracts of teacher talk in a lesson (recorded in a local secondary school) in which that teacher is dealing with aspects of the grammar area, and making use of the textbook materials discussed in (b). The snapshots in earlier chapters are examples of the type of 'critical incident' that the students are invited to consider in (c). In **Sessions 4–8**, four of the classes are given over to PG workshops, in which the students work collectively to explore issues relating to their chosen grammar topics. The specific aims in these sessions are to broaden students' understanding of each grammar area, to heighten their awareness of their students' potential difficulties, to help them make informed and appropriate choices about how the grammar area should be handled with students of different ages and proficiency levels, and to enable them to reflect critically on the choices made by the writers of textbooks used in Hong Kong secondary schools. The remaining session focuses on approaches to the teaching of grammar, looking at the rationale behind different ways of introducing new grammar in form-focused P-P-P lessons, and of integrating a 'focus on form' within activities where the primary focus seems to be on meaning and/or on the practice of skills.

9.5 Conclusion

In this chapter we have looked at TLA and teacher development, exploring the crucial question of how we can help teachers to develop the knowledge, skills and sensitivity that will enable them to be

[1] Telenex is an English-teacher support network set up at the University of Hong Kong by a team led by Amy Tsui. Telenex incorporates two grammar databases: TeleGram (for secondary teachers) and PrimeGram (for primary teachers).

'language-aware' in their pedagogical practice. In our discussion, we have noted the following:

- 'Language Awareness' / 'Language Analysis' (LA) work forms an increasingly important part of teacher development courses worldwide;
- One of the major concerns for those planning or teaching such courses is the issue of knowledge transfer, and the extent to which the course helps participants to make the bridge between the declarative and procedural dimensions of TLA, i.e. between the possession of knowledge and the application of that knowledge;
- Another concern in planning such courses is the difficulty of reconciling participants' conflicting needs: their immediate need (especially on pre-service courses) for simplified, pre-digested 'facts' about language, to help them survive their initial experience of classroom teaching; and their longer-term need to develop a questioning attitude towards such 'facts' and an awareness of the diversity and complexity of language;
- Successful LA courses help participants to draw on and continuously develop the three competences: language user, language analyst and language teacher; on in-service programmes, LA activities are particularly effective when they are based on an experiential approach;
- L2 teachers' continuing development of enhanced levels of language awareness and of pedagogical strategies for dealing with language that are appropriate to their teaching context is best achieved through a combination of language-related self-reflection and focused collaborative activity.

As noted in the earlier part of the chapter and again in the summary above, promoting the transfer of teachers' enhanced knowledge about language (the declarative dimension of TLA) to their pedagogical practice (the procedural dimension of their TLA) remains one of the principal challenges for those involved with TLA development. The ideas outlined in 9.4 are not a guaranteed solution to the problem of knowledge transfer. They do, however, represent a systematic and principled attempt to confront that challenge. As such, they may be of some help to others facing similar issues in different teacher development contexts.

Questions for discussion and reflection

1) Have you taken an LA course, or course component, at any stage in your own professional development? If so, how was that LA course organised? What sort of activities did you

---

participate in? Did those activities attempt to promote 'knowledge transfer'? If so, to what extent do you think they were successful, and why?

2) If you were planning the 12-hour LA component of a course for pre-service trainees in a teaching context with which you are familiar, what would your main objectives be, and why? Which areas of language and specific features of language would you focus on? What sort of activities would you include?

3) If you were planning a 24-hour in-service LA course for teachers with three to five years' full-time teaching experience, again in a teaching context with which you are familiar, how would your objectives, your language focus and your chosen activities differ from those you proposed for the pre-service course? Why would they differ in these ways?

4) With a colleague or classmate, try to plan a cycle of LA activities based on Wright's (2002) five-stage model and his principles for LA work. Provide a rationale for the unit of LA work that you plan.

5) Arrange to make a video recording of one of your lessons in which some form-focused teaching is likely to take place. View the videotaped lesson and try to identify at least two content-related 'incidents', planned or unplanned, where you are dealing with either a grammar-related issue or a lexis-related issue (e.g. explaining, dealing with student output). Transcribe each incident, and then critically evaluate your handling of the language content in each lesson extract. Write a brief contextual description to accompany your transcriptions and then show them to a colleague or classmate as snapshots of your TLA in pedagogical practice. Discuss the snapshots together.

Epilogue: TLA and teacher professionalism

The preceding chapters of this book have argued that TLA is of crucial importance in the language teaching / language learning enterprise, because of its potential impact on student learning: the language-aware L2 teacher is more likely to be effective in promoting student learning than the teacher who is not language-aware. The language awareness of the L2 teacher has been explored from a variety of perspectives, and illustrated with snapshots from L2 English classrooms in the specific context of the Hong Kong secondary school. Now, in these final few pages, I feel it is important to return once more to the motivation for writing such a book, and to set its central argument within the context of more general educational debate.

The arguments in this book – that Teacher Language Awareness (TLA) is a core component of the L2 teacher's knowledge base and that it is a growing concern for those involved in setting professional standards for L2 teachers – accord with wider trends, both in language education and general education, associated with the establishment and maintenance of professional standards. These include, for instance, the various moves in recent years towards the professionalisation of TESOL (among them the ill-fated BIELT, the British Institute of English Language Teaching, set up with the goals of establishing a framework of professional qualifications and a professional code of practice), the initiatives in various parts of the world to set professional standards for teachers of all subjects (such as the frameworks developed by the National Board of Professional Standards in the United States) and the growth of interest in the generic notion of the teacher as professional that is evident in the education literature (see, e.g., the various papers in Darling-Hammond and Sykes, 1999).

If teaching in general (and L2 teaching in particular) is to be considered a profession, then there is an underlying assumption that the practitioner needs to be in possession of a knowledge base or set of knowledge bases that are distinctive to the profession. The nature of teacher knowledge and teacher learning has been extensively researched (Freeman, 2002, provides a review of the North American literature in this area). The view of TLA outlined in Chapter 2 draws mainly on Shulman (for instance, 1986a; 1986b; 1987), but also on Turner-Bisset (2001) and Tsui (2003), to put forward an argument for regarding TLA as one closely interrelated set of knowledge bases that are drawn upon in L2 teaching, a set of knowledge bases that is on the one hand integrated with the other knowledge bases in the enactment of expert teaching, but that is nevertheless worthy of investigation and treatment as a separate component of teacher cognition, because it is a cluster of knowledge bases that are all specifically related to language.

Shulman (1999) makes a particularly powerful argument to support the notion that teaching should be regarded as a profession. He begins by affirming that the nature of teaching, with its constant demand for principled responses to unpredictable situations, places it on a par with other professions: 'We have come to understand that teachers are professionals precisely because they operate under conditions of inherent novelty, uncertainty, and chance. Although there may be curricula that strive to prescribe teachers' behaviour with great precision, for most teachers a typical day is fraught with surprises' (Shulman, 1999:xii–xiii). Because of this, according to Shulman, teachers' work 'cannot be controlled by rules, even though it must be governed by standards' (1999:xiii).

Shulman then develops his argument regarding standards, saying that 'Professionalism demands thoughtful, grounded actions under complex and uncertain conditions that are nevertheless guided by, rooted in, and framed by clear professional standards. A professional both acts wisely and can explain his or her actions' (ibid.). He then expresses his view that knowledge of subject matter is at the core of teacher professionalism. As he puts it, 'deep, flexible and confident understanding of subject matter makes possible the kinds of professional autonomy and responsiveness that the teaching of all youngsters requires' (ibid.). Shulman makes clear that such knowledge is necessary but by no means sufficient: the professional teacher needs a range of other knowledge bases. Nevertheless, subject-matter knowledge is the core. Therefore, he argues, 'professional teachers must be well educated, especially in the subject matter they teach, and . . . their career-long professional education experiences must continue to be grounded in the centrality of that content' (ibid.).

Such arguments from general education provide support for the assumption underlying the whole of this book: that L2 teaching, like the teaching of any other subject, is a profession, and that those who wish to be recognised as L2 teachers should fulfil the requirements of any professional (i.e. 'reaching a standard or having the quality expected of a professional person or his work; competent in the manner of a professional', Oxford English Dictionary Online, 2004). In other words, they should possess competences and qualities (and perhaps also qualifications certifying possession of those qualities) equivalent to those expected of a professional in any other field.

If this seems to be a case of stating the obvious, in the way referred to in the Prologue of this book, then it is perhaps worth pointing out that the topic of professionalism in L2 teaching and the relevance of subject-matter knowledge have provoked considerable debate, especially in the United Kingdom in relation to the teaching of English as a Foreign Language. For example, Thornbury, in a paper provocatively entitled 'The unbearable lightness of EFL' (2001b), remarks that '[m]uch has been made of the need to raise and/or maintain standards in order to ensure the professionalism of EFL. But the question remains: is TEFL really a profession? And, if so, what standards should it be judged by?' (p. 392).

According to Thornbury (2001b), Widdowson (1998) proposes that professionalism in TEFL is at least in part dependent upon a knowledge of linguistics:

> Like other professional people (doctors, lawyers, accountants), teachers claim authority because of specialised knowledge and expertise . . . The subject for language teachers is a language, and so it is obviously this that they need to know about . . . A knowledge of the subject, English as a foreign language, presupposes some knowledge at least about language as a whole . . . In other words, knowing the language subject depends in some degree on the study of linguistics.
>
> (Widdowson, 1998, cited by Thornbury, 2001b:392)

Thornbury (2001b) cites Widdowson in order to argue against this 'academic model' of TEFL, suggesting that such an aspiration to what he describes as 'sham' respectability is misguided in a number of ways. First, placing language as subject on a par with, for example, medicine and law as subjects ignores the uniqueness of language, which can be both content and medium of instruction. Second, according to Thornbury, this 'academic model' over-inflates the importance of declarative knowledge of subject matter: the 'what' of teaching. In so doing, it downplays the importance of the 'how' of teaching.[1]

The points that Thornbury makes here are important. The first relates to one of the central arguments in this book: that much of the complexity of TLA (as we have seen it reflected in the practices of the teachers cited in previous chapters, for instance) is associated with the intertwining of L2 as content and medium of instruction, which is a feature of L2 classes in many parts of the world. The second point – that L2 teachers

---

[1] In fairness to Thornbury, he does make clear in a footnote to his paper that his comments relate primarily to native-speaker teachers of EFL, rather than to non-native-speaker teachers, most of whom have, in his words, 'trained long and hard to achieve a measure of local respect, and can claim to have earned the professionalism that still eludes the so-called native speaker EFL teacher' (Thornbury 2001b:396).

need more than just declarative knowledge – is equally valid. Earlier chapters have provided more than one example where declarative knowledge is shown to be a mixed blessing in the hands of the teacher who is an over-zealous transmitter of such knowledge.

Nevertheless, the validity of these two specific points does not, to me at least, justify Thornbury's dismissal of the importance of subject-matter knowledge and of what he caricatures as an 'academic model' of TEFL. Rather than discounting the significance of such knowledge, I have tried to propose in this book that we need to rethink and reconceptualise our understanding of subject-matter knowledge in the context of L2 pedagogical practice in a way that takes account of the central importance to our endeavours as L2 teachers of both the declarative and procedural dimensions of that knowledge (TLA). It is absolutely correct to suggest, as Thornbury implies, that L2 teachers demonstrate their professionalism in the way they handle language-related issues in their teaching, and not solely by their possession of qualifications that attest to their knowledge of linguistics. However, I would argue (in the belief that the argument is supported by evidence in the preceding chapters) that any L2 teacher, except possibly those employed solely as native-speaker conversation partners, requires an adequate level of subject-matter knowledge to inform the handling of all content-related decisions. At the same time, this is only one component (the declarative dimension) of the TLA required of the professional L2 teacher: the procedural dimension is at least as important in the context of pedagogical practice.

An assertion of this kind inevitably provokes a series of related questions, among them:

- What constitutes an adequate level of subject-matter knowledge (declarative TLA) for the L2 teacher?
- What constitutes an adequate level of procedural TLA for the L2 teacher?
- Can valid and reliable instruments for measuring declarative and procedural TLA be identified as a step towards the certification of L2 teachers' professional competence? If so, how?

These questions in turn raise a number of awkward issues. However, I would suggest that in any attempt to specify the professional standards expected of the L2 teacher that may be happening as part of the process of the professionalisation of L2 teachers and teaching taking place in various parts of the world, such questions cannot be ignored. In the responses to those questions that are formulated in different educational contexts, I would also argue that the specifications of what is required of a professional L2 teacher should include a thorough, context-specific analysis of TLA-related competences, focusing on both knowledge and behaviour, i.e. the declarative and procedural dimensions of TLA.

The process of resolving such issues and conducting such analyses is likely to be both time-consuming and challenging. But it is essential if the standards set for the TEFL profession are to be robust, comprehensive and contextually appropriate.

Appendix: Language Awareness test – rubrics and sample test items

(The LA grammar test is largely based on Alderson, Clapham and Steel's test (1996), which in turn drew on Bloor (1986).)

Grammar component

Section 1: Grammatical terms

A. Metalanguage recognition

Exercise 1
From the sentence below select one example of the grammatical item requested and write it in the space provided. NOTE: You may select the same word(s) more than once if appropriate.
[*14 grammatical items are requested, such as countable noun, relative pronoun*]

Exercise 2
In the following sentences, underline the item requested in brackets.
[*Four items are requested, focusing on sentence functions*]

B. Metalanguage production

Exercise 3
Look at the twelve sentences below. What grammatical terms would you use to describe the item underlined in each of the sentences? NOTE: For each item provide a full description.

> Examples:
> 1. It was the <u>most exciting</u> film she had ever seen.
>   *superlative adjective*
> 2. I <u>saw</u> Jenny last Saturday.
>   *verb in past simple tense*

Section 2: English error correction and explanation

This section consists of 15 English sentences, each of which contains a grammar mistake.

Appendix

For each sentence:

1. Rewrite the faulty part of the sentence correctly. (There is only one part that is wrong.) Do NOT rewrite the whole sentence.
2. Underneath each sentence explain the error.

[*This task contributes marks to two components of the test. The first part of each item contributes to 'Correction of errors', the second to 'Explanation of errors'*]

> Example:
> I often goes to the cinema.
> *Correct version*: **go**
> *Explanation*: **The verb must agree with the subject**
> [**Do NOT write** : *Change 'goes' to 'go'*]

References

Alderson, J. C., Clapham, C. and Steel, D. (1996). *Metalinguistic knowledge, language aptitude and language proficiency*, Working Papers, 26. University of Lancaster.

Aljaafreh, A. and Lantolf, J. P. (1994). Negative feedback as regulation and second language learning in the zone of proximal development. *Modern Language Journal*, 17(4), 465–83.

Anderson, J. (1983). *The architecture of cognition*. Cambridge, MA: Harvard University Press.

(1995). *Cognitive psychology and its implications*. New York: W. H. Freeman.

Andrews, S. J. (1994). The grammatical knowledge/awareness of native-speaker EFL teachers: What the trainers say. In M. Bygate, A. Tonkyn and E. Williams (eds.), *Grammar and the language teacher* (pp. 69–89). Hemel Hempstead: Prentice Hall.

(1996). Metalinguistic awareness and lesson planning. In P. Storey, V. Berry, D. Bunton and P. Hoare (eds.), *Issues in language in education* (pp. 191–210). Hong Kong: Hong Kong Institute of Education.

(1997). Metalinguistic awareness and teacher explanation. *Language Awareness*, 6(2/3), 147–61.

(1999a). Why do L2 teachers need to 'Know About Language'? Teacher metalinguistic awareness and input for learning. *Language and Education*, 13(3), 161–77.

(1999b). The metalinguistic awareness of Hong Kong secondary school teachers of English. Unpublished PhD thesis, University of Southampton.

(1999c). 'All these like little name things': A comparative study of language teachers' explicit knowledge of grammar and grammatical terminology. *Language Awareness*, 8(3/4),143–59.

(2001). The language awareness of the L2 teacher: Its impact upon pedagogical practice. *Language Awareness*, 13(3), 75–90.

(2002). Teacher language awareness and language standards. *Journal of Asian Pacific Communication*, 12(1), 39–62.

(2003). Teacher language awareness and the professional knowledge base of the L2 teacher. *Language Awareness*, 12(2), 81–95.

(2006). The evolution of teachers' language awareness. *Language Awareness*, 15(1), 1–19.

Andrews, S. J. and McNeill, A. (2005). Knowledge about language and 'good' language teachers. In N. Bartels (ed.), *Applied linguistics and language teacher education* (pp. 159–78). New York: Springer.

References

Arva, V. and Medgyes, P. (2000). Native and non-native teachers in the classroom. *System*, 28, 355–72.

Ausubel, D., Novak, J. and Hanesian, H. (1978). *Educational psychology: A cognitive view* (2nd edn). New York: Holt, Rinehart and Winston.

Bachman, L. (1990). *Fundamental considerations in language testing*. Oxford: Oxford University Press.

Bartels, N. (ed.) (2005a). *Applied linguistics and language teacher education*. New York: Springer.

(2005b). Applied linguistics and language teacher education: What we know. In N. Bartels (ed.), *Applied linguistics and language teacher education* (pp. 405–24). New York: Springer.

Basturkmen, H., Loewen, S. and Ellis, R. (2004). Teachers' stated beliefs about incidental focus on form and their classroom practices. *Applied Linguistics*, 25(2), 243–72.

Benke, E. and Medgyes, P. (2005). Differences in teaching behaviour between native and non-native speaker teachers: As seen by the learners. In E. Llurda (ed.), *Non-native language teachers: Perceptions, challenges and contributions to the profession* (pp. 195–215). New York: Springer.

Benner, P., Tanner, C. and Chesla, C. (1996). *Expertise in nursing practice: Caring, clinical judgment and ethics*. New York: Springer.

Beretta, A. and Davies, A. (1985). Evaluation of the Bangalore Project. *ELT Journal*, 39(2), 121–7.

Berliner, D. (1994). Expertise: The wonder of exemplary performances. In J. Mangieri and C. Block (eds.), *Creating powerful thinking in teachers and students* (pp. 161–86). Fort Worth, TX: Harcourt Brace College.

(2001). Learning about and learning from expert teachers. *International Journal of Educational Research*, 35(5), 463–82.

Berry, R. (1997). Teachers' awareness of learners' knowledge: The case of metalinguistic terminology. *Language Awareness*, 10(2/3), 136–46.

Bhatt, R. M. (1995). Prescriptivism, creativity and world Englishes. *World Englishes*, 14(2), 247–59.

Biber, D., Johansson, S., Leech, G., Conrad, S. and Finegan, E. (1999). *The Longman grammar of spoken and written English*. Harlow: Longman.

Bloomfield, L. (1933). *Language*. New York: Holt, Rinehart and Winston.

Bloor, T. (1986). What do language students know about gammar? *British Journal of Language Teaching*, 24(3), 157–60.

Bolitho, R. and Tomlinson, B. (1980). *Discover English* (1st edn). London: George Allen and Unwin.

(1995). *Discover English* (2nd edn). Oxford: Heinemann.

Bolitho, R., Carter, R., Hughes, R., Ivanič, R., Masuhara, H. and Tomlinson, B. (2003). Ten questions about language awareness. *ELT Journal*, 57(3), 251–9.

Borg, S. (1998). Teachers' pedagogical systems and grammar teaching: A qualitative study. *TESOL Quarterly*, 32(1), 9–37.

(1999a). The use of grammatical terminology in the second language classroom: A qualitative study of teachers' practices and cognitions. *Applied Linguistics*, 20(1), 95–126.

(1999b). Studying teacher cognition in second language grammar teaching. *System*, 27, 19–31.

(1999c). Teachers' theories in grammar teaching. *ELT Journal*, 53(3), 157–67.

(2003a). Teacher cognition in grammar teaching: A literature review. *Language Awareness*, 12(2), 96–108.

(2003b). Teacher cognition in language teaching: A review of research on what language teachers think, know, believe, and do. *Language Teaching*, 36, 81–109.

(2005). Experience, knowledge about language and classroom practice in teaching grammar. In N. Bartels (ed.), *Applied linguistics and language teacher education* (pp. 325–40). New York: Springer.

(2006). *Teacher cognition and language education*. London: Continuum.

Braine, G. (ed.) (1999). *Non-native educators in English language teaching*. Mahwah, NJ: Lawrence Erlbaum.

Braine, G. (2005). A critical review of the research on non-native speaker English teachers. In C. Gnutzmann and F. Intemann (eds.), *The globalisation of English and the English language classroom* (pp. 275–84). Tübingen: Gunther Narr.

Bransford, J., Darling-Hammond, L. and LePage, P. (2005a). Introduction. In L. Darling-Hammond and J. Bransford (eds.), *Preparing teachers for a changing world: What teachers should learn and be able to do* (pp. 1–39). San Francisco: Jossey-Bass.

Bransford, J., Derry, S., Berliner, D., Hammerness, K. and Beckett, K. L. (2005b). Theories of learning and their roles in teaching. In L. Darling-Hammond and J. Bransford (eds.), *Preparing teachers for a changing world: What teachers should learn and be able to do* (pp. 40–87). San Francisco: Jossey-Bass.

Breen, M. P., Hird, B., Milton, M., Oliver, R. and Thwaite, A. (2001). Making sense of language teaching: Teachers' principles and classroom practices. *Applied Linguistics*, 22, 470–501.

Brooks, N. (1964). *Language and language learning* (2nd edn). New York: Harcourt, Brace and World.

Brophy, J. (ed.) (1991). *Advances in research on teaching* (Vol. II). Greenwich, CT: JAI Press.

Brumfit, C. J. (1978). 'Communicative' language teaching: An assessment. In P. Strevens (ed.), *In honour of A. S. Hornby* (pp. 33–44). Oxford: Oxford University Press.

(1984). *Communicative methodology in language teaching: The roles of fluency and accuracy*. Cambridge: Cambridge University Press.

(1988). *Language in teacher education*. London: NCLE.

Brumfit, C. J. and Mitchell, R. (1995). *Trainee teachers' knowledge about language*. Occasional Papers, 33. University of Southampton.

Brumfit, C. J., Mitchell, R. and Hooper, J. (1996). 'Grammar', 'language' and classroom practice. In M. Hughes (ed.), *Teaching and learning in changing times* (pp. 70–87). Oxford: Blackwell.

Calderhead, J. (ed.) (1987). *Exploring teachers' thinking*. London: Cassell.

Canagarajah, A. S. (1999). Interrogating the 'native speaker' fallacy: Non-linguistic roots, non-pedagogical results. In G. Braine (ed.), *Non-native educators in English language teaching* (pp. 77–92). Mahwah, NJ: Lawrence Erlbaum.

Candelier, M. (1992). Language awareness and language policy in the European context. *Language Awareness*, 1(1), 27–32.

Carter, K. (1990). Teachers' knowledge and learning to teach. In W. R. Houston (ed.), *Handbook of research on teacher education* (pp. 291–310). New York: Macmillan.

Carter, K., Cushing, K., Sabers, D., Stein, P. and Berliner, D. C. (1988). Expert–novice differences in perceiving and processing visual classroom information. *Journal of Teacher Education*, 39(3), 25–31.

Carter, R. (1994). How aware should language aware teachers and learners be? Paper presented at the International Language in Education Conference, Hong Kong, 14–16 December 1994.

Carter, R. (2003). What are the relationships between Language Awareness and existing theories of language? (p. 253) In R. Bolitho, R. Carter, R. Hughes, R. Ivanič, H. Masuhara and B. Tomlinson (2003). Ten questions about language awareness. *ELT Journal*, 57(3), 251–9.

(ed.) (1990). Knowledge about language and the curriculum: The LINC reader. London: Hodder Stoughton.

Carter, R. and McCarthy, M. (1997). *Exploring spoken English*. Cambridge: Cambridge University Press.

(2006). *Cambridge grammar of English*. Cambridge: Cambridge University Press.

Celce-Murcia, M. (2002). Why it makes sense to teach grammar in context and through discourse. In E. Hinkel and S. Fotos (eds.), *New perspectives on grammar teaching in second language classrooms* (pp. 119–34). Mahwah, NJ: Lawrence Erlbaum.

Celce-Murcia, M., Dörnyei, Z. and Thurrell, S. (1997). Direct approaches in L2 instruction: A turning point in communicative language teaching? *TESOL Quarterly*, 31(1), 141–52.

(1998). On directness in communicative language teaching. *TESOL Quarterly*, 32(1), 116–19.

Chamberlain, J. and O'Neill, E. F. (1994). *New effective English 4: Paper 3*. Hong Kong: Witman.

Chandler, P., Robinson, W. P. and Noyes, P. (1988). The level of linguistic knowledge and awareness among students training to be primary teachers. *Language and Education*, 2(3), 161–73.

Chastain, K. (1971). *The development of modern language skills: Theory to practice*. Philadelphia: Center for Curriculum Development.

Chomsky, N. (1965). *Aspects of the theory of syntax*. Cambridge, MA: MIT Press.

(1968). *Language and mind*. New York: Harcourt, Brace and World.

Clandinin, D. J. (1992). Narrative and story in teacher education. In T. Russell and H. Munby (eds.), *Teachers and teaching: From classroom to reflection* (pp. 124–37). Sussex: Falmer Press.

Clark, C. M. and Peterson, P. L. (1986). Teachers' thought processes. In M. C. Wittrock (ed.), *Handbook of research on teaching* (pp. 255–96). New York: Macmillan.

Coniam, D. and Falvey, P. (2002). Selecting models and setting standards for teachers of English in Hong Kong. *Journal of Asian Pacific Communication,* 12(1), 13–38.

Connelly, F. M. and Clandinin, D. J. (1985). Personal practical knowledge and the modes of knowing. In E. Eisner (ed.), *Learning and teaching the ways of knowing (84th yearbook of the national society for the study of education)* (Vol. II, pp. 174–98). Chicago: University of Chicago Press.

Cook, V. (2005). Basing teaching on the L2 user. In E. Llurda (ed.), *Non-native language teachers: Perceptions, challenges and contributions to the profession* (pp. 47–62). New York: Springer.

Corder, S. P. (1976). The study of interlanguage. Paper presented at the Fourth International Conference of Applied Linguistics, Munich, Hochschulverlag.

Curriculum Development Committee (1983). *Syllabuses for secondary schools: Syllabus for English* (Forms I–V). Hong Kong: Government Printer.

Curriculum Development Council (1999). *Syllabuses for secondary schools: English Language* (Secondary 1–5). Hong Kong: Education Department.

Darling-Hammond, L. (2000). *Teacher quality and student achievement: A review of state policy evidence.* Education Policy Analysis Archives 8,1. Downloaded 10 January 2006 from http://epaa.asu.edu/epaa/v8n1/.

Darling-Hammond, L. and Sykes, G. (eds.) (1999). *Teaching as the learning profession: Handbook of policy and practice.* San Francisco: Jossey-Bass.

Davies, A. (1996a). Proficiency or the native speaker: What are we trying to achieve in ELT? In G. Cook and B. Seidlhofer (eds.), *Principles and practice in applied linguistics* (pp. 145–57). Oxford: Oxford University Press.

(1996b). Review article: Ironising the myth of linguicism. *Journal of Multilingual and Multicultural Development,* 17(6), 485–96.

(2001). Review of Bex, T. and Watts, R. J. Standard English: The widening debate. *Applied Linguistics,* 22(2), 272–82.

DeKeyser, R. (1998). Beyond focus on form: Cognitive perspectives on learning and practising second language grammar. In C. Doughty and J. Williams (eds.), *Focus on form in classroom second language acquisition* (pp. 42–63). Cambridge: Cambridge University Press.

Donmall, G. (ed.) (1985). *Language awareness NCLE Reports and Papers 6.* London: Centre for Information on Language Teaching and Research.

Doughty, C. (1991). Second language instruction does make a difference. *Studies in Second Language Acquisition,* 13, 431–69.

Doughty, C. and Williams, J. (eds.) (1998). *Focus on form in classroom second language acquisition.* New York: Cambridge University Press.

Dreyfus, H. L. and Dreyfus, S. E. (1986). *Mind over machine.* New York: Free Press.

Duff, T. (ed.) (1988). *Explorations in teacher training: Problems and issues.* Harlow: Longman.

Dulay, H. and Burt, M. (1973). Should we teach children syntax? *Language Learning,* 23, 245–58.

Edge, J. (1988). Applying linguistics in English language teacher training for speakers of other languages. *ELT Journal,* 42(1), 9–13.

References

Education Commission (1995). *Education Commission report No.6: Enhancing language proficiency: A comprehensive strategy.* Hong Kong: Government Printer.

Elbaz, F. (1983). *Teacher thinking: A study of practical knowledge.* London: Croom Helm.

Ellis, R. (1989). Are classroom and naturalistic acquisition the same? A study of the classroom acquisition of German word order rules. *Studies in Second Language Acquisition,* 11, 305–28.

(1990). *Instructed second language acquisition.* Oxford: Blackwell.

(1992). *Second language acquisition and language pedagogy.* Clevedon: Multilingual Matters.

Ellis, R. (1994). *The study of second language acquisition.* Oxford: Oxford University Press.

(2002a). Methodological options in grammar teaching materials. In E. Hinkel and S. Fotos (eds.), *New perspectives on grammar teaching in second language classrooms* (pp. 155–79). Mahwah, NJ: Lawrence Erlbaum.

(2002b). The place of grammar instruction in the second/foreign language curriculum. In E. Hinkel and S. Fotos (eds.), *New perspectives on grammar teaching in second language classrooms* (pp. 17–34). Mahwah, NJ: Lawrence Erlbaum.

(2003). *Task-based language learning and teaching.* Oxford: Oxford University Press.

(2004). The definition and measurement of explicit knowledge. *Language Learning,* 54(2), 281–318.

(2005). Principles of instructed language learning. *System,* 33, 209–24.

Evans, S. (1996). The context of English language education: The case of Hong Kong. *RELC Journal,* 27(2), 30–55.

Fairclough, N. (ed.) (1992). *Critical language awareness.* London: Longman.

Fang, Z. (1996). A review of research on teacher beliefs and practices. *Educational Research,* 38, 47–65.

Fenstermacher, G. D. (1979). A philosophical consideration of recent research on teacher effectiveness. In L. S. Shulman (ed.), *Review of research in education* (Vol. VI, pp. 157–85). Itasca, IL: Peacock.

Ferguson, R. F. (1991). Paying for public education: New evidence on how and why money matters. *Harvard Journal on Legislation,* 28(2), 465–98.

Fillmore, L. W. and Snow, C. E. (2002). What teachers need to know about language. In C. Adger, C. Snow and C. Christian (eds.), *What teachers need to know about language.* Washington, DC and McHenry, IL: Center for Applied Linguistics and Delta Systems Co. Inc.

Forestier, K. (2005). Globalisation puts English on agenda. *South China Morning Post,* 10 December 2005.

Fotos, S. (2002). Structure-based interactive tasks for the EFL grammar learner. In E. Hinkel and S. Fotos (eds.), *New perspectives on grammar teaching in second language classrooms* (pp. 135–55). Mahwah, NJ: Lawrence Erlbaum.

(2005). Traditional and grammar translation methods for second language teaching. In E. Hinkel (ed.), *Handbook of research in second language teaching and learning* (pp. 653–70). Mahwah, NJ: Lawrence Erlbaum.

Freeman, D. (2002). The hidden side of the work: Teacher knowledge and learning to teach. *Language Teaching*, 35, 1–13.

Garvey, E. and Murray, D. (2004). The multilingual teacher: Issues for teacher education. *Prospect*, 19(2), 3–24.

Gess-Newsome, J. (1999). Pedagogical content knowledge: An introduction and orientation. In J. Gess-Newsome and N. G. Lederman (eds.), *Examining pedagogical content* (pp. 3–17). Dordrecht: Kluwer.

Gess-Newsome, J. and Lederman, N. G. (eds.) (1999). *Examining pedagogical content knowledge*. Dordrecht: Kluwer.

Gnutzmann, C. (1992). Reflexion über 'Fehler'. Zur Förderung des Sprachbewusstseins im Fremdsprachenunterricht. *Der Fremdsprachliche Unterricht Englisch*, 8, 16–21.

(1997). Language Awareness: Progress in language learning and language education, or reformulation of old ideas? *Language Awareness*, 6(2/3), 65–74.

Golombek, P. (1998). A study of language teachers' personal practical knowledge. *TESOL Quarterly*, 37(2), 447–64.

Gombert, J. E. (1992). *Metalingustic development*. New York: Harvester Wheatsheaf.

Goodman, Y. (1990). The development of initial literacy. In R. Carter (ed.), *Knowledge about language and the curriculum: The LINC reader* (pp. 135–44). London: Hodder and Stoughton.

Gower, R. and Walters, S. (1983). *Teaching practice handbook*. London: Heinemann.

Grossman, P. and Schoenfeld, A., with Lee, C. (2005). Teaching subject matter. In L. Darling-Hammond and J. Bransford (eds.), *Preparing teachers for a changing world: What teachers should learn and be able to do* (pp. 201–31). San Francisco: Jossey-Bass.

Hales, T. (1997). Exploring data-driven language awareness. *ELT Journal*, 51(2), 217–23.

Halliday, M. A. K. (1971). Introduction. In P. Doughty, J. Pearce and G. Thornton (eds.), *Language in use (Schools Council programme in linguistics and English teaching)*. London: Edward Arnold.

(1985). *An introduction to functional grammar* (1st edn). London: Edward Arnold.

(2004). Lexicology. In M. A. K. Halliday, W. Teubert, C. Yallop and A. Cermakova (eds.), *Lexicology and corpus linguistics* (pp. 1–22). London: Continuum.

Hammerness, K., Darling-Hammond, L., Bransford, J., with Berliner, D., Cochran-Smith, M., McDonald, M. and Zeichner, K. (2005). How teachers learn and develop. In L. Darling-Hammond and J. Bransford (eds.), *Preparing teachers for a changing world: What teachers should learn and be able to do* (pp. 358–89). San Francisco: Jossey-Bass.

Harmer, J. (2003). Do your students notice anything? *Modern English Teacher*, 12(4), 5–14.

Hatano, G. and Inagaki, K. (1986). Two courses of expertise. In Stevenson, H., Azuma, H. and Hakuta, K. (eds.), *Child development and education in Japan* (pp. 262–72). New York: Freeman.

Hatano, G. and Oura, Y. (2003). Commentary: Reconceptualising school learning using insight from expertise research. *Educational Researcher*, 32(8), 26–9.

Hawkins, E. W. (1984). *Awareness of language: An introduction*. Cambridge: Cambridge University Press.

(1992). Awareness of language / knowledge about language in the curriculum in England and Wales: An historical note on twenty years of curricular debate. *Language Awareness*, 1(1), 5–18.

(1994). Percept before precept. In L. King and P. Boaks (eds.), *Grammar! A conference report* (pp. 109–23). London: Centre for Information on Language Teaching and Research.

(1999). Foreign language study and language awareness. *Language Awareness*, 8(3/4), 124–42.

Haycraft, J. (1988). The first International House Preparatory Course: An historical overview. In T. Duff (ed.), *Explorations in teacher training: Problems and issues* (pp. 1–9). Harlow: Longman.

Hinkel, E. and Fotos, S. (2002). From theory to practice: A teacher's view. In E. Hinkel and S. Fotos (eds.), *New perspectives on grammar teaching in second language classrooms* (pp. 1–12). Mahwah, NJ: Lawrence Erlbaum.

Hornby, A. S. (1950). The situational approach in language teaching. *English Language Teaching*, 4(4–6).

House, J. (1999). Misunderstanding in intercultural communication: Interactions in English as a Lingua Franca and the myth of mutual intelligibility. In C. Gnutzmann (ed.), *Teaching and learning English as a global language* (pp. 73–89). Tübingen: Stauffenberg.

Howatt, A. P. R. (1984). *A history of English language teaching*. Oxford: Oxford University Press.

Huberman, M. (1993). *The lives of teachers*. London: Cassell.

James, C. (1992). Awareness, consciousness and language contrast. In C. Mair and M. Markus (eds.), *New departures in contrastive linguistics* (Vol. II, pp. 183–98). Innsbruck: Innsbrucker Beiträge zur Kulturwissenschaft.

(1996). Review of 'Language teaching and skill learning' by Keith Johnson. *Language Awareness*, 5(3/4), 222–4.

James, C. and Garrett, P. (eds.) (1991a). *Language awareness in the classroom*. Harlow: Longman.

James, C. and Garrett, P. (1991b). The scope of language awareness. In C. James and P. Garrett (eds.), *Language awareness in the classroom* (pp. 3–20). Harlow: Longman.

Jenkins, J. (1998). Which pronunciation norms and models for English as an international language? *ELT Journal*, 52(2), 119–26.

(2000). *The phonology of English as an international language: New models, new norms, new goals*. Oxford: Oxford University Press.

(2006). Current perspectives on teaching World Englishes and English as a Lingua Franca. *TESOL Quarterly*, 40(1), 157–81.

Johnson, K. (1980). The 'deep-end' strategy in communicative language teaching. In K. Johnson (ed.), *Communicative syllabus design and methodology* (pp. 176–82). Oxford: Pergamon.

(1996). *Language teaching and skill learning*. Oxford: Blackwell.

(2001). *An introduction to foreign language learning and teaching*. Harlow: Longman.

Johnson, K. and Johnson, H. (eds.) (1998). *Encyclopedic dictionary of applied linguistics*. Oxford: Blackwell.

Johnson, K. E. (1994). The emerging beliefs and instructional practices of pre-service English as a second language teachers. *Teaching and Teacher Education*, 10, 439–52.

Johnston, B. and Goettsch, K. (2000). In search of the knowledge base of language teaching: Explanations by experienced teachers. *Canadian Modern Language Review*, 56(3), 437–68.

Kachru, B. B. (1985). Standards, codification and sociolinguistic realism: The English language in the outer circle. In R. Quirk and H. G. Widdowson (eds.), *English in the world: Teaching and learning the language and literatures* (pp. 11–30). Cambridge: Cambridge University Press.

(1990). World Englishes and applied linguistics. *World Englishes*, 9(1), 3–20.

(1991). Liberation linguistics and the Quirk concern. *English Today*, 7(1), 3–13.

(1997). English as an Asian language. In M. L. S. Bautista (ed.), *English is an Asian language: The Philippine context* (pp. 1–23). Sydney: Macquarie Library Pty.

Kagan, D. M. (1992). Implications of research on teacher belief. *Educational Psychologist*, 27, 65–90.

Kamhi-Stein, L. (ed.) (2004). *Learning and teaching from experience: Perspectives on nonnative English speaking professionals*. Ann Arbor, MI: University of Michigan Press.

Kelly, L. G. (1969). *25 centuries of language teaching*. Rowley, MA: Newbury House.

Kerr, P. (1993). Language training on pre-service courses for native speakers. *Modern English Teacher*, 2(4), 40–3.

(1998). Language Awareness: Practices and progress? *English Language Teacher Education and Development*, 4(1), 1–7.

Kirkpatrick, A. (2007). *World Englishes: Implications for international communication and for English language teaching*. Cambridge: Cambridge University Press.

Kolb, D. A. (1984). *Experiential learning: Experience as a source of learning and development*. Englewood Cliffs, NJ: Prentice-Hall.

Kramsch, C. (1999). Response to Carmen Chaves Tesser and Eugene Eoyang. *ADFL Bulletin*, 31(1), 33–5.

Krashen, S. (1981). *Second language acquisition and second language learning*. Oxford: Pergamon.

(1982). *Principles and practice in second language acquisition*. Oxford: Pergamon.

(1985). *The input hypothesis: Issues and implications*. London: Longman.

Krashen, S. and Terrell, T. (1983). *The Natural Approach: Language acquisition in the classroom*. Oxford: Pergamon.

Kuo, I. C. (2006). Addressing the issue of teaching English as a Lingua Franca. *ELT Journal*, 60(3), 213–21.

Lantolf, J. (ed.) (2000). *Sociocultural theory and second language learning.* Oxford: Oxford University Press.

Larsen-Freeman, D. (2002). The grammar of choice. In E. Hinkel and S. Fotos (eds.), *New perspectives on grammar teaching in second language class-rooms* (pp. 103–18). Mahwah, NJ: Lawrence Erlbaum.

(2003). *Teaching language: From grammar to grammaring.* Boston: Heinle and Heinle.

Leech, G. (1994). Students' grammar – teachers' grammar – learners' grammar. In M. Bygate, A. Tonkyn and E. Williams (eds.), *Grammar and the language teacher* (pp. 17–30). Hemel Hempstead: Prentice Hall.

(2000). Grammars of spoken English: New outcomes of corpus-oriented research. *Language Learning*, 50(4), 675–724.

Leech, G. and Svartvik, J. (1975). *A communicative grammar of English.* Harlow: Longman.

Leinhardt, G. (1989). A contrast of novice and expert competence in mathe-matics lessons. In J. Lowyck and C. M. Clark (eds.), *Teacher thinking and professional action* (pp. 75–98). Louvain: Louvain University Press.

Leung, C., Harris, R. and Rampton, B. (1997). The idealised native speaker, reified ethnicities, and classroom realities. *TESOL Quarterly*, 31(3), 543–60.

Levelt, W., Sinclair, A. and Jarvella, R. (1978). Causes and functions of language awareness in language acquisition. In A. Sinclair, R. Jarvella and W. Levelt (eds.), *The child's conception of language* (pp. 1–14). Berlin and New York: Springer.

Lewis, M. (1993). *The lexical approach.* Hove: Language Teaching Publications.

Lightbown, P. and Spada, N. (1990). Focus-on-form and corrective feedback in communicative language teaching: Effects on second language learning. *Studies in Second Language Acquisition*, 12, 429–48.

Little, D. (1997). Language awareness and the autonomous language learner. *Language Awareness*, 6(2/3), 93–104.

Littlewood, W. (1981). *Communicative language teaching: An introduction.* Cambridge: Cambridge University Press.

Livingston, C. and Borko, H. (1989). Expert–novice differences in teaching: A cognitive analysis and implications for teacher education. *Journal of Teacher Education*, 40(4), 36–42.

Llurda, E. (2004). Non-native-speaker teachers and English as an International Language. *International Journal of Applied Linguistics*, 14(3), 314–23.

(ed.) (2005a). *Non-native language teachers: Perceptions, challenges and con-tributions to the profession.* New York: Springer.

(2005b). Non-native TESOL students as seen by practicum supervisors. In E. Llurda (ed.), *Non-native language teachers: Perceptions, challenges and contributions to the profession* (pp. 131–54). New York: Springer.

Long, M. (1983). Does second language instruction make a difference? A review of the research. *TESOL Quarterly*, 17(3), 359–82.

(1991). Focus on form: A design feature in language teaching methodology. In K. De Bot, R. Ginsberg and C. Kramsch (eds.), *Foreign language research in cross-cultural perspective* (pp. 39–52). Amsterdam: John Benjamins.

Long, M. and Robinson, P. (1998). Focus on form: Theory, research, and practice. In C. Doughty and J. Williams (eds.), *Focus on form in classroom second language acquisition* (pp. 15–41). Cambridge: Cambridge University Press.

Lortie, D. C. (1975). *Schoolteacher: A sociological study*. Chicago: University of Chicago Press.

Lowyck, J. and Clark, C. M. (eds.) (1989). *Teacher thinking and professional action*. Louvain: Louvain University Press.

McCarthy, M. (1991). *Discourse analysis for language teachers*. Cambridge: Cambridge University Press.

McCarthy, M. and Carter, R. (1994). *Language as discourse: Perspectives for language teaching*. Harlow: Longman.

McNeill, A. (1999). Teachers' awareness of lexical difficulty in ESL reading texts. Unpublished PhD thesis, University of Wales.

(2005). Non-native speaker teachers and awareness of lexical difficulty in pedagogical texts. In E. Llurda (ed.), *Non-native language teachers: Perceptions, challenges and contributions to the profession* (pp. 107–28). New York: Springer.

Marton, F. (1994). On the structure of teachers' awareness. In I. Carlgren, G. Handal and S. Vaage (eds.), *Teachers' minds and actions: Research on teachers' thinking* (pp. 28–42). London: Falmer Press.

Medgyes, P. (1994). *The non-native teacher*. London: Macmillan.

Mitchell, R. and Hooper, J. (1991). Teachers' views of language knowledge. In C. James and P. Garrett (eds.), *Language awareness in the classroom* (pp. 40–50). London: Longman.

Mitchell, R. and Myles, F. (1998). *Second language learning theories*. London: Arnold.

Mitchell, R., Hooper, J. and Brumfit, C. J. (1994). *Final report: 'Knowledge about language', language learning and the national curriculum*. Occasional Papers, 19. University of Southampton.

Morris, L. (2002). Age and uptake in TESL training: Differing responses to declaratively- and procedurally-oriented grammar instruction. *Language Awareness*, 11(3), 192–207.

(2003). Linguistic knowledge, metalinguistic knowledge and academic success in a language teacher education programme. *Language Awareness*, 12(2), 109–23.

Murray, H. (1998). The development of professional discourse and language awareness in EFL teacher training. *IATEFL Teacher Trainers SIG Newsletter*, 21, 3–7.

Nassaji, H. and Swain, M. (2000). A Vygotskyan perspective on corrective feedback in L2: The effect of random versus negotiated help on the learning of English articles. *Language Awareness*, 9(1), 34–51.

Nattinger, J. and DeCarrico, J. (1992). *Lexical phrases and language teaching*. Oxford: Oxford University Press.

Nelson, C. (1995). Intelligibility and world Englishes in the classroom. *World Englishes*, 14(2), 273–9.

Newmark, L. (1966). How not to interfere in language learning. Reprinted in Brumfit, C. and Johnson, K. (eds.), *The communicative approach to language teaching* (pp. 160–6). Oxford: Oxford University Press.

Norris, J. and Ortega, L. (2001). Does type of instruction make a difference? Substantive findings from a meta-analytic review. *Language Learning*, 51(S1), 157–201.

Nunan, D. (1992). The teacher as decision-maker. In J. Flowerdew, M. Brock and S. Hsia (eds.), *Perspectives on second language teacher education* (pp. 135–65). Hong Kong: City Polytechnic of Hong Kong.

(1996). An organic approach to the teaching of grammar. *Hong Kong Journal of Applied Linguistics*, 1(1), 65–86.

(1999). *Second language teaching and learning*. Boston: Heinle and Heinle.

(2004). *Task-based language teaching*. Cambridge: Cambridge University Press.

Oxford English Dictionary Online. Downloaded on 15 October 2004 from http://www.oed.com/.

Pajares, M. F. (1992). Teachers' beliefs and educational research: Cleaning up a messy construct. *Review of Educational Research*, 62, 307–32.

Palfreyman, D. (1993). How I got it in my head: Conceptual models of language and learning in native and non-native trainee EFL teachers. *Language Awareness*, 2(4), 209–23.

Palmer, H. E. (1917). *The scientific study and teaching of languages*. London: Harrap.

Pawley, A. and Syder, F. (1983). Two puzzles for linguistic theory: Native-like selection and native-like fluency. In J. Richards and R. Schmidt (eds.), *Language and communication* (pp. 191–226). Harlow: Longman.

Phillipson, R. (1992). *Linguistic imperialism*. Oxford: Oxford University Press.

Pica, T. (1983). Adult acquisition of English as a second language under different conditions of exposure. *Language Learning*, 33, 465–97.

Pienemann, M. (1984). Psychological constraints on the teachability of languages. *Studies in Second Language Acquisition*, 6(2), 186–214.

(1985). Learnability and syllabus construction. In K. Hyltenstam and M. Pienemann (eds.), *Modelling and assessing second language acquisition* (pp. 23–75). Clevedon: Multilingual Matters.

Prabhu, N. S. (1987). *Second language pedagogy*. Oxford: Oxford University Press.

Quirk, R. (1985). The English language in a global context. In R. Quirk, H. G. Widdowson and Yolande Cantù (eds.), *English in the world: Teaching and learning the language and literatures* (pp. 1–6). Cambridge: Cambridge University Press.

(1990). Language varieties and standard language. *English Today*, 21, 3–10.

Quirk, R., Greenbaum, S., Leech, G. and Svartvik, J. (1985). *A comprehensive grammar of the English Language*. London: Longman.

Rajagopalan, K. (1997). Linguistics and the myth of nativity: Comments on the controversy over new/non-native Englishes. *Journal of Pragmatics*, 27(2), 225–31.

(1999). Of EFL teachers, conscience, and cowardice. *ELT Journal*, 53, 200–6.

(2005). Non-native speaker teachers of English and their anxieties: Ingredients for an experiment in action research. In E. Llurda (ed.), *Non-native language teachers: Perceptions, challenges and contributions to the profession* (pp. 283–303). New York: Springer.

Rampton, M. B. H. (1990). Displacing the 'native-speaker': Expertise, affiliation, and inheritance. *ELT Journal*, 44, 338–43.

Richards, J. and Farrell, T. (2005). *Professional development for language teachers: Strategies for teacher learning*. Cambridge: Cambridge University Press.

Richards, J. C. (1996). Teachers' maxims in language teaching. *TESOL Quarterly*, 30(2), 281–96.

(2002). Accuracy and fluency revisited. In E. Hinkel and S. Fotos (eds.), *New perspectives on grammar teaching in second language classrooms* (pp. 35–50). Mahwah, NJ: Lawrence Erlbaum.

Richards, J. C. and Rodgers, T. S. (2001). *Approaches and methods in language teaching* (2nd edn). Cambridge: Cambridge University Press.

Roberts, J. T. (1998). Grammar teaching. In K. Johnson and H. Johnson (eds.), *Encyclopedic dictionary of applied linguistics* (pp. 146–53). Oxford: Blackwell.

Robinson, P. (1997). Individual differences and the fundamental similarity of implicit and explicit adult second language learning. *Language Learning*, 47(1), 45–99.

Rutherford, W. (1987). *Second language grammar: Learning and teaching*. London: Longman.

Rutherford, W. and Sharwood Smith, M. (1985). Consciousness-raising and universal grammar. *Applied Linguistics*, 6(3), 274–81.

(eds.) (1988). *Grammar and second language teaching*. Rowley, MA: Newbury House.

Sampson, N. (1994). *English 2000 Book 3*. Hong Kong: Macmillan.

Schmidt, R. (1990). The role of consciousness in second language learning. *Applied Linguistics*, 11, 129–58.

(1993). Awareness and second language acquisition. *Annual Review of Applied Linguistics*, 13, 206–26.

(1994). Deconstructing consciousness in search of useful definitions for applied linguistics. *AILA Review*, 11, 11–26.

(2001). Attention. In P. Robinson (ed.), *Cognition and second language instruction* (pp. 3–32). Cambridge: Cambridge University Press.

Schon, D. A. (1983). *The reflective practitioner: How professionals think in action*. New York: Basic Books.

SCOLAR (2003). *Summary of recommendations*. Downloaded on 8 October 2004 from http://cd1.emb.hkedcity.net/cd/scolar/html/ilangedreview_e n.htm.

Seidlhofer, B. (1999). Double standards: Teacher education in the expanding circle. *World Englishes*, 18(2), 233–45.

(2002). Habeas corpus and divide et impera: 'Global English' and applied linguistics. In K. S. Miller and P. Thompson (eds.), *University and diversity in language use* (pp. 198–217). London: Continuum.

(2004). Research perspectives on teaching English as a Lingua Franca. *Annual Review of Applied Linguistics*, 24, 209–39.

219

Seliger, H. (1979). On the nature and function of language rules in language teaching. *TESOL Quarterly*, 13, 359–69.

Sharwood Smith, M. (1981). Consciousness-raising and the second language learner. *Applied Linguistics*, 2(2), 159–69.

(1991). Speaking to many minds: On the relevance of different types of language information for the L2 learner. *Second Language Research*, 7(2), 118–32.

Shavelson, R. J. and Stern, P. (1981). Research on teachers' pedagogical thoughts, judgments, decisions, and behavior. *Review of Educational Research*, 51(4), 455–98.

Shulman, L. S. (1986a). Paradigms and research programs in the study of teaching: A contemporary perspective. In M. C. Wittrock (ed.), *Handbook of research on teaching* (3rd edn) (pp. 3–36). New York: Macmillan.

(1986b). Those who understand: Knowledge growth in teaching. *Educational Researcher*, 15(2), 4–14.

(1987). Knowledge and teaching: Foundations of the new reform. *Harvard Educational Review*, 57(1), 1–22.

(1999). Foreword. In L. Darling-Hammond and G. Sykes (eds.), *Teaching as the learning profession: Handbook of policy and practice* (pp. xi–xiv). San Francisco: Jossey-Bass.

Shulman, L. S. and Shulman, J. H. (2004). How and what teachers learn: A shifting perspective. *Journal of Curriculum Studies*, 36(2), 257–71.

Sinclair, J. M. (1985). Language awareness in six easy lessons. In G. Donmall (ed.), *Language awareness NCLE Reports and Papers 6* (pp. 33–7). London: Centre for Information on Language Teaching and Research.

Skehan, P. (1996). Second language acquisition research and task-based instruction. In J. Willis and D. Willis (eds.), *Challenge and change in language teaching* (pp. 17–30). Oxford: Heinemann.

(2003). Task-based instruction. *Language Teaching*, 36, 1–14.

Soars, L. and Soars, J. (2006). *New Headway*. Oxford: Oxford University Press.

South China Morning Post (8 December 2005). Reason for teacher bias.

(12 December 2005). Unqualified teachers.

Spada, N. (1986). The interaction between types of content and type of instruction: Some effects on the L2 proficiency of adult learners. *Studies in Second Language Acquisition*, 8, 181–99.

Squire, L. (1992). Declarative and non-declarative memory: Multiple brain systems supporting learning and memory. *Journal of Cognitive Neuroscience*, 4, 232–43.

Stern, H. H. (1983). *Fundamental concepts of language teaching*. Oxford: Oxford University Press.

Stevick, E. W. (1980). *Teaching languages: A way and ways*. Rowley, MA: Newbury House.

Strauss, R. and Sawyer, E. (1986). Some new evidence on teacher and student competencies. *Economics of Education Review*, 5(1), 41–8.

Swain, M. (1985). Large-scale communicative language testing: A case study. In Y. P. Lee, A. C. Y. Y. Fok, R. Lord and G. Low (eds.), *New directions in language testing* (pp. 35–46). Oxford: Pergamon.

Swan, M. (1994). Design criteria for pedagogic language rules. In M. Bygate,

A. Tonkyn and E. Williams (eds.), *Grammar and the language teacher* (pp. 45–55). Hemel Hempstead: Prentice Hall.

(2001). Review of Thornbury (1999) and Parrott (2000). *ELT Journal*, 55(2), 203–8.

Thornbury, S. (1997). *About language*. Cambridge: Cambridge University Press.

(1998). Comments on Marianne Celce-Murcia, Zoltán Dörnyei, and Sarah Thurrell's 'Direct approaches in L2 instruction: A turning-point in communicative language teaching?' A reader reacts. *TESOL Quarterly*, 32(1), 109–16.

(1999). *How to teach grammar*. Harlow: Longman

(2001a). *Uncovering grammar*. Oxford: Macmillan Heinemann.

(2001b). The unbearable lightness of EFL. *ELT Journal*, 55(4), 391–6.

(2006). *An A–Z of ELT*. Oxford: Macmillan Education.

Timmis, I. (2002). Native-speaker norms and international English: A classroom view. *ELT Journal*, 56(3), 240–9.

Tonkyn, A. (1994). Introduction: Grammar and the language teacher. In M. Bygate, A. Tonkyn and E. Williams (eds.), *Grammar and the language teacher* (pp. 1–14). Hemel Hempstead: Prentice Hall.

Trappes-Lomax, H. and Ferguson, G. (eds.) (2002). *Language in language teacher education*. London: John Benjamins.

Tsui, A. B. M. (2003). *Understanding expertise in teaching: Case studies of second language teachers*. Cambridge: Cambridge University Press.

Tsui, A. B. M., Coniam, D., Sengupta, S. and Wu, K. Y. (1994). Computer-mediated communication and teacher education: The case of TELENEX. In N. Bird, P. Falvey, A. B. M. Tsui, D. M. Allison and A. McNeill (eds.), *Language and learning* (pp. 352–69). Hong Kong: Institute of Language in Education.

Tsui, A. B. M., Tong, A. K. K., Andrews, S., Harfitt, G., Lam, R. Y. H., Lo, M. M., Ng, M. M. Y., Tavares, N. and Wong, A. T. Y. (2005). *Study of good practices in secondary schools: Enhancing students' English language proficiency*. Education and Manpower Bureau, Hong Kong Government Consultancy Study.

Turner-Bisset, R. (1999). The knowledge bases of the expert teacher. *British Educational Research Journal*, 25(1), 39–55.

(2001). *Expert teaching*. London: David Fulton.

UCLES (1996). *CELTA: Pilot syllabus and assessment guidelines*. Cambridge: University of Cambridge Local Examinations Syndicate.

(1998). *DELTA: Pilot syllabus guidelines for course tutors and assessors* and *DELTA: Pilot assessment guidelines for course tutors and assessors*. Cambridge: University of Cambridge Local Examinations Syndicate.

Ur, P. (1988). *Grammar practice activities*. Cambridge: Cambridge University Press.

van Essen, A. (1992). Language awareness in the Netherlands. *Language Awareness*, 1(1), 19–26.

van Lier, L. (1995). *Introducing language awareness*. London: Penguin.

(1996). *Interaction in the language curriculum: Awareness, autonomy and authenticity*. London: Longman.

Vygotsky, L. S. (1978). *Mind in society: The development of higher psychological processes*. Cambridge, MA: Harvard University Press.

Walsh, S. (2001). Characterising teacher talk in the second language classroom: A process model of reflective practice. Unpublished PhD thesis, Queen's University, Belfast.

Webbe, J. (1622). *An appeal to truth, in the controversies between art, and use; about the best, and most expedient course in languages. To be read fasting.* London: H. L. for George Latham (Scolar Press 42, 1967).

Wenger, E. (2004). *Communities of practice: A brief introduction.* Downloaded on 15 January 2006 from http://www.ewenger.com/theory/index.htm.

Westerman, D. (1991). Expert and novice teacher decision making. *Journal of Teacher Education*, 42(4), 292–305.

Widdowson, H. G. (1990). *Aspects of language teaching.* Oxford: Oxford University Press.

(1991). The description and prescription of language. In J. E. Alatis (ed.), *Georgetown University round table on languages and linguistics, 1991* (pp. 11–24). Washington, DC: Georgetown University Press.

(1998). Linguistic foundation for language teaching. *EFL Gazette*: June.

(2004). A perspective on recent trends. In A. P. R. Howatt and H. G. Widdowson, *A history of English language teaching* (2nd edn) (pp. 353–72). Oxford: Oxford University Press.

Wideen, M., Mayer-Smith, M. and Moon, B. (1998). A critical analysis of the research on learning to teach: Making a case for an ecological perspective on inquiry. *Review of Educational Research*, 68(2), 130–78.

Wilkins, D. A. (1976). *Notional syllabuses: A taxonomy and its relevance to foreign language curriculum development.* Oxford: Oxford University Press.

Williams, J. (2005). Learning without awareness. *Studies in Second Language Acquisition*, 27(2), 269–304.

Williamson, J. and Hardman, F. (1995). Time for refilling the bath?: A study of primary student-teachers' grammatical knowledge. *Language and Education*, 9(2), 117–34.

Willingham, D. B., Nissen, M. J. and Bullemer, P. (1989). On the development of procedural knowledge. *Journal of Experimental Psychology: Learning, Memory and Cognition*, 15, 1047–60.

Wilson, S. M., Floden, R. E. and Ferrini-Mundy, J. (2001). *Teacher preparation research: Current knowledge, gaps, and recommendations: A research report prepared for the US Department of Education.* Seattle, WA: Center for the Study of Teaching and Policy.

Woods, D. (1996). *Teacher cognition in language teaching.* Cambridge: Cambridge University Press.

Wray, D. (1993). Student-teachers' knowledge and beliefs about language. In N. Bennett and C. Carre (eds.), *Learning to teach* (pp. 51–72). London: Routledge.

Wright, T. (1991). Language awareness in teacher education programmes for non-native speakers. In C. James and P. Garrett (eds.), *Language awareness in the classroom* (pp. 62–77). Harlow: Longman.

(1994). *Investigating English.* London: Edward Arnold.

(2002). Doing language awareness: Issues for language study in language teacher education. In H. Trappes-Lomax and G. Ferguson (eds.), *Language in language teacher education* (pp. 113–30). Philadelphia: John Benjamins.

Wright, T. and Bolitho, R. (1993). Language awareness: A missing link in language teacher education? *ELT Journal*, 47, 292–304.

(1997). Language awareness in in-service programmes. In L. van Lier and D. Corson (eds.), *Encyclopedia of language and education*, Vol. VI: *Knowledge about Language* (pp. 173–81). Dordrecht: Kluwer.

Zhu, X. Y. (2004). *The development of pedagogical content knowledge in novice secondary school teachers of English.* Nanjing: Nanjing Normal University Press.

Index

Index

IH *see* International House
Immersion Education 55, 56
implicit knowledge 13–16, 48, 53–4, 58
implicit learning 16
Inagaki, K. 140
inflections 61
innateness hypothesis 53–4
input
  definition 16n
  in Natural Approach 54
  role of TLA 37–9, 39*f*
input enhancement 17, 65, 130–1
input hypothesis 34
intake: definition 16n
interface position 15, 78–9
interlanguage 2, 16n, 28, 29, 56, 65, 178
International House (IH) 151, 182, 184

James, C. 10–11, 17–18
Jenkins, J. 162, 163
Johnson, H. 82
Johnson, K. 15, 55, 60, 82
Johnson, K. E. 71

Kachru, B. B. 146, 150
Kagan, D. M. 71
Kamhi-Stein, L. 147
Kelly, L. G. 49–50
Kerr, P. 184
Kirkpatrick, A. 150
Knowledge About Language (KAL) 31
  history of and LA 10–13
  terminology 10
  and TLA 21
Kolb, D. A. 186
Kramsch, C. 145–6
Krashen, S. 15, 34, 50–1, 54–5, 56
Kuo, I. C. 163

L2 curriculum and grammar
  parallel/modular approach 59–60
  integrated approach 59–60
L2 education 18–21
  and content-based approaches 54
  and grammar 19, 20–1, 51
  and Language Awareness 12–13, 20,
    182–3
  and Teacher Language Awareness 20–1
  and teacher training 19–20, 19n, 151–2,
    182
  and teacher's role 19
  see also Communicative Language
    Teaching; teacher learning: LA courses
language acquisition 15, 16, 54
language affiliation 147
Language Awareness (journal) 10, 13, 20
Language Awareness (LA) 9–22

and 'consciousness-raising' 17–18, 65
and declarative/procedural knowledge
  14–15, 31
  definitions 11, 12, 18
and explicit/implicit knowledge 13–16,
  48
and Knowledge About Language 10–13
and L2 education 12–13, 20, 182–3
and levels of awareness 16
and Teacher Language Awareness 20–1
  terminology 10
Language Awareness 'movement' 9–10, 11
language behaviour: deficit model 11
language competence 27
language inheritance 147
language proficiency 27, 28, 31*f*, 40, 153–5
Lantolf, J. P. 177
Larsen-Freeman, D. 64, 66
Latin 49
learner perspective 4, 5, 27, 29
learning 15, 16
  see also content of learning; student
    learning and TLA; teacher learning: LA
    courses
Leech, G. 36, 63, 64
Leinhardt, G. 118
lesson preparation 41–3, 42–3*t*
Leung, C. et al. 149
Levelt, W. et al. 18
Lewis, M. 63
lexis 62–3
Lightbown, P. 59
linguistic imperialism 145–6, 150
linguistics 53, 151, 202
Little, D. 14
Littlewood, W. 52
Livingston, C. 118
Llurda, E. 145–6, 153, 159
Long, M. 32–3, 57, 58
Lortie, D. C. 188
Lowyck, J. 71

McCarthy, M. 61, 62, 63, 64
McNeill, A. 123, 125, 160–1, 175–6
Marton, F. 74, 84
Medgyes, P. 150, 152, 153–4, 155, 157,
  159
message and code 59
metacognitions 27, 28–9, 188
metalanguage 13–14
Mitchell, R. M. 16
Mitchell, R. M. et al. 10, 12, 21
modality 4
modular approach 59–60
Monitor Model 51
morphology 61
Morris, L. 21

226

Index

Publisher's acknowledgements

The authors and publishers acknowledge the following sources of copyright material and are grateful for the permissions granted. While every effort has been made, it has not always been possible to identify the sources of all the material used, or to trace all copyright holders. If any omissions are brought to our notice, we will be happy to include the appropriate acknowledgements on reprinting.

Pearson Education Ltd for the following extracts from *Grammar and the language teacher,* ed. M. Bygate, A. Tonkyn and E. Williams © Copyright 1994: on p. 4 from M. Swan, 'Design criteria for pedagogic language rules'; on p. 35 from S. Andrews, 'The grammatical knowledge/awareness of native speaker EFL teachers: what the trainer says'; on p. 36 from G. Leech, 'Student's grammar – teacher's grammar – learner's grammar'. Used by permission of Pearson Education Ltd.

Extract on p. 7 from Earl W. Stevick, *Teaching languages: A way and ways* © 1980.

Professor Ronald Carter for the extract on p. 12, from 'How aware should language aware teachers and learners be?', a paper presented at the International Language in Education Conference, 1994. Used by kind permission of Ronald Carter.

Extract on p. 29 from 'Knowledge and teaching: foundations of the New Reform', *Harvard Educational Review*, 57(1) (February 1987), p. 15 © 1987 by the President and Fellows of Harvard College. All rights reserved. Reprinted with permission.

Cambridge University Press for the following extracts: on p. 35 from Scott Thornbury, *About language* © 1997; on p. 52 from Peter Skehan, 'Second language acquisition research and task-based instruction', in *Challenge and change in language teaching*, ed. J. Willis and D. Willis © 1996; on p. 54 from Jack Richards and Theodore S. Rodgers, *Approaches and methods in language teaching,* 2nd edition © 2001; on p. 150 from Randolph Quirk, 'The English language in a global context', in *English in the World: Teaching and learning the language and literatures*, ed. Randolph Quirk, H. G. Widdowson and Yolande Cantù © 1985. Used by permission of Cambridge University Press.

Blackwell Publishing Ltd for the following extracts: on p. 63 from Geoffrey Leech, 'Grammars of spoken English: New outcomes of corpus-oriented research', *Language Learning* 50(4), 2000; on p. 155 and p. 159 from Barbara Seidlhofer, 'Double standards: teacher education in the expanding circle', *World Englishes* 18(2), 1999; on p. 177 from Ali Aljaafreh and James P. Lantolf, 'Negative feedback as regulation and second language learning in the zone of proximal development', *Modern Language Journal* 17(4), 1994.

Georgetown University Press for the extract on p. 66 from Henry Widdowson, 'Description and prescription of language', in *Georgetown University Round Table on Languages and Linguistics,* ed. James E Alatis © 1991 by Georgetown University Press. Reprinted by permission. www.press.georgetown.edu;

Thomson Learning for the extract on p. 72 from D. Jane Clandinin, 'Narrative and story in teacher education', in *Teachers and Teaching: From classroom to reflection,* ed. T. Russell and H. Munby © 1992. Used by permission of Thomson Learning.

TESOL for the following extracts: on p. 72 from Jack Richards, 'Teachers' maxims in language teaching', *TESOL Quarterly*, 1996; on p. 163 from Jennifer Jenkins, 'Current perspectives on teaching World Englishes and English as a Lingua Franca', *TESOL Quarterly*, 2006. © TESOL Teachers of English to Speakers of other languages Inc.

Taylor & Francis for the text on pp. 75–84 from Stephen Andrews, 'Just like instant noodles. L2 Teachers and their beliefs about grammar pedagogy'. This is an electronic version of an article published in the *Teachers and Teaching Theory and Practice* © 2003 Taylor & Francis; Teachers and Teaching Theory and Practice is available online at www://journalsonline.tandf.co.uk/.

Witman Publishing for the extract on p. 110 from J. Chamberlain and E. F. O'Neill, 'Formal writing', in *New Effective English 4: Paper III* © 1994. Used by permission of Witman Publishing (Hong Kong) Ltd.

Springer Science and Arthur McNeill for the text on pp. 124-31 from A. McNeill and S. Andrews, 'Knowledge about Language and "good" language teachers', in *Applied linguistics and language teacher education* (pp. 159-78), ed. N. Bartels © 2005. Used with kind permission of Springer Science and Media Business and Arthur McNeill.

John Wiley & Sons for the following extracts from *Preparing teachers for a changing world: What teachers should learn and are able to do*, ed. Darling-Hammond and Bransford © 2005: on p. 140 from J. Bransford, S. Derry, D. Berliner, K. Hammerness and K. Beckett, 'Theories of learning and their roles in teaching'; on p. 169 from J. Bransford, L. Darling-Hammond and LePage, 'Introduction'; on p. 191 from K. Hammerness, L. Darling-Hammond, J. Bransford, D. Berliner, M. Cochran-Smith, M. McDonald and K. Zeichner, 'How teachers learn and develop'; also for the extract on p. 201 from L. Shulman, 'Foreword', in *Teaching as the*

Publisher's acknowledgments

learning profession: Handbook of policy and practice, ed. L. Darling-Hammond and G. Sykes. Reprinted with permission of John Wiley & Sons, Inc

The two letters on pp. 144-5 from 'Reason for teacher bias' and 'Unqualified teachers', *South China Morning Post*, 8 December 2005 and 12 December 2005 (name and address supplied).

Springer Science and Professor Kanavillil Rajagopalan for the extract on p. 154 from Kanavillil Rajagopalan, 'Non-native speaker teachers on English and their anxieties: ingredients for an experiment in action research', in *Non-native language teachers: Perceptions, challenges and contributions to the profession*, ed. E Llurda. © 2005. With kind permission of Springer Science and Media Business and Professor K Rajagopalan.

The extracts on p. 155 and p. 159 from Peter Medgyes, *The non-native teacher* © 1994.

Springer Science and Vivian Cook for the extract on p. 160 from Vivian Cook, 'Basing teaching on the L2 user', in *Non-native language teachers: Perceptions, challenges and contributions to the profession*, ed. E Llurda © 2005. With kind permission of Springer Science and Media Business and Vivian Cook.

Oxford University Press for the following extracts: on pp. 163-4 from H. G. Widdowson, 'A perspective on recent trends', in *A History of English Language Teaching*, ed. A. P. R. Howatt and H. G. Widdowson, 2nd edition © 2004; on p. 202 for the quotation by H. Widdowson, cited by Scott Thornbury, 'The unbearable lightness of EFL', *ELT Journal* 55(4), 2001. Used by permission of Oxford University Press.